North American Border Conflicts
Race, Politics, and Ethics

North American Border Conflicts

Race, Politics, and Ethics

Laurence Armand French
Magdaleno Manzanarez

CRC Press
Taylor & Francis Group
Boca Raton London New York

CRC Press is an imprint of the
Taylor & Francis Group, an **informa** business

CRC Press
Taylor & Francis Group
6000 Broken Sound Parkway NW, Suite 300
Boca Raton, FL 33487-2742

© 2017 by Taylor & Francis Group, LLC
CRC Press is an imprint of Taylor & Francis Group, an Informa business

No claim to original U.S. Government works

Printed on acid-free paper
Version Date: 20161116

International Standard Book Number-13: 978-1-4987-8034-6 (Hardback)

This book contains information obtained from authentic and highly regarded sources. Reasonable efforts have been made to publish reliable data and information, but the author and publisher cannot assume responsibility for the validity of all materials or the consequences of their use. The authors and publishers have attempted to trace the copyright holders of all material reproduced in this publication and apologize to copyright holders if permission to publish in this form has not been obtained. If any copyright material has not been acknowledged please write and let us know so we may rectify in any future reprint.

Except as permitted under U.S. Copyright Law, no part of this book may be reprinted, reproduced, transmitted, or utilized in any form by any electronic, mechanical, or other means, now known or hereafter invented, including photocopying, microfilming, and recording, or in any information storage or retrieval system, without written permission from the publishers.

For permission to photocopy or use material electronically from this work, please access www.copyright.com (http://www.copyright.com/) or contact the Copyright Clearance Center, Inc. (CCC), 222 Rosewood Drive, Danvers, MA 01923, 978-750-8400. CCC is a not-for-profit organization that provides licenses and registration for a variety of users. For organizations that have been granted a photocopy license by the CCC, a separate system of payment has been arranged.

Trademark Notice: Product or corporate names may be trademarks or registered trademarks, and are used only for identification and explanation without intent to infringe.

Visit the Taylor & Francis Web site at
http://www.taylorandfrancis.com

and the CRC Press Web site at
http://www.crcpress.com

Contents

Foreword ix

1 Introduction: Contravening Worldviews of People Competing for Boundaries and Resources 1

Aboriginal Harmony Ethos and Restorative Justice 6
The Protestant Ethic and New World Conflicts: Protestants, Aboriginals, Catholics 8

2 Colonial Intrusion and Border Battles 17

Aboriginals and Their Pre-Columbian Boundaries 17
Colonial Encroachment and Conflict 19
The Acadian Expulsion: The Roots of Manifest Destiny, Ethnic Cleansing, and Cultural Genocide 24
Changing Spanish America 28
   Introduction 28
   New Spain's Adaptations to the New World 33
Adaptations to Colonial Intrusions 34

3 The Emerging United States and Its Expansionist Mandate 39

Manifest Destiny and White Protestant Supremacy: Boundary Maintenance 1776–1865 39
   Indian Removal: The U.S. Experiment with Ethnic Cleansing 41
   Intrusions into Canada 45
   The New Frontier: Acquiring Spanish/Mexican Territory 47
      The Adams-Onís Treaty of 1819 47
      The Empresario Land Grants 48
      The Mexican Constitution and the Slavery Issue 51
      The Emerging Texas Republic 53
      Slavery and the Texas Constitution 54
     Prelude to the U.S. Civil War: Annexation of Texas 56
      Polk's War and a Divided Nation 57
      The Unresolved Slavery Issue 61

The Road to Political Disorganization Following the Mexican War: Whigs Exit, Republicans Emerge	63
The Ostend Manifesto and Gadsden Purchase	65
The Monroe Doctrine and Imperial Designs: 1865–1917	70
Canadian Challenges during the Monroe Doctrine Era	71
The Fenian Challenge	73
Dominion of Canada	75
Louis Riel and the Indian/Métis Rebellions	76
Turbulence in Mexico: The Road to Revolution	79
The Reign of Porfirio Díaz: America's Favorite Despot	79
The Porfiriato Setting the Stage for the Mexican Revolution	79
Seeds of Mexican Discontent	83
The Texas Rangers's Reign of Terror: Prelude to Pancho Villa's U.S. Raid	84
Pancho Villa's Raid on the United States	86
Harsh Treatment of the Villista Prisoners	87
Policing American Indians: Boundary Maintenance through Laws and Force	88
Introduction	88
U.S. Army and the Indian Wars of 1865–1891	89
Indian Police and Policing Indian Country: Military versus Civilian Jurisdictions	92

4 North America and the Neocolonial Conflicts of the 20th Century — 101

Introduction	101
The United States and Its "Indian Problem": Changing Boundaries and Identities	101
Allotment: Dismantling Indian Country	101
Reorganization	103
Termination/Relocation	104
Indian Self-Determination and the New Federalism for Indian Country	109
Indian Religious Freedom	113
New Federalism and Indian Child Welfare	114
Extending the Monroe Doctrine in the 20th Century: Hemispheric Exploitation and Cold War Fears	117
Justice Issues: The Role of De Facto Discrimination	121
Canada Comes of Age and the Perils of Quebec Separatism	129
Influence of French Leaders in Canada	129
Quebec Separatism and the "Quiet Revolution"	132

Contents   vii

      Mexico in the 20th Century: Growth, Corruption,
      and U.S. Interventions   139
         Implementing the New Constitution of 1917
         with Interference from the United States   139
         Revolutionary Changes Finally Enacted   140
         U.S. Cold War Interventions   141
         Oppression and Change: Transitioning to Globalization   142

5   From NAFTA to the 21st Century   145

      Introduction   145
      Border Perspective Since 9/11   146
      Impact of the Militarization of the U.S. Borders   147
      Border Security's Impact on North American Indians   150
         Status of Canada's Indigenous People   151
         Post–9/11 Border Requirements and Their Impact
         on Border Tribes   152
      Mexico's Daunting Role as a Filter for Drug and Human
      Trafficking   154
         Central America and the Cold War   155
         Mexican War on Drugs   157
            U.S. Drug, Security, and Immigration Concerns   158

Appendix I: Chronology of Major Events   167

Appendix II: Maps   177

Endnotes   191
      Chapter 1   191
      Chapter 2   192
      Chapter 3   193
      Chapter 4   197
      Chapter 5   200

Index   203

Foreword

This book, *North American Border Politics*, represents 20 years of collaborative research in the areas of international relations, social justice, and minority issues with particular focus on indigenous Indian groups. Both authors come from working-class ethnic families. Magdaleno Manzanarez was born in Mexico and is of Mestizo heritage, and Laurence French's grandparents (paternal grandmother and maternal grandfather) were born in French Canada. Both their individual and joint research endeavors reflect a strong ethnomethodologic component. They have presented their research both nationally and internationally, including in the following conference venues:

- 5th Biennial Conference: International Perspectives on Crime, Justice and Public Order, Bologna, Italy, 2000
- American Society of Criminology (ASC), Toronto, Canada, 1999; San Francisco, CA, 2000; Atlanta, GA, 2001; Nashville, TN, 2004; Toronto, Canada, 2005; San Francisco, CA, 2010; Chicago, IL, 2011; San Francisco, CA, 2014
- American Association of Behavioral & Social Sciences (AABSS), 1997–2015, Las Vegas, NV
- VIII International Conference on Social Justice & Social Exclusion, Rishon LeZiion, Israel, 2000
- Society of Applied Anthropology, Merida, Yucatan, Mexico, March/April, 2001
- Western Social Science Association (WSSA) Annual Conference, Reno, NV, 2001; Albuquerque, NM, 2002; 2014; Portland, OR, 2015; Reno, NV, 2016
- International Police Executive Symposium (IPES) Annual Meeting, Szezytno, Poland, 2001; Czech Republic, 2005; Ohrid, Macedonia, 2009; Sofia, Bulgaria, 2014
- IX International Social Justice Conference, University of Skovde, Sweden, 2002
- Addictions 2002, Eindhoven, the Netherlands, 2002
- 6th Biennial Conference on International Perspectives on Crime, Justice and Order, London, England, 2002

- Academy of Criminal Justice Sciences (ACJS), Boston, MA, 2003; Las Vegas, NV, 2004; Boston, MA, 2009; San Diego, CA, 2010; Toronto, Canada, 2011; Philadelphia, PA, 2014
- XIII World Congress of Criminology, Rio de Janeiro, Brazil, 2003
- International Vernacular Colloquium, Puebla, Mexico, 2003; 2005
- 1st Key Issues Conference, Societies of Criminology, Paris, France, 2004
- Annual Conference of the European Society of Criminology, Amsterdam, the Netherlands, 2004; Bologna, Italy, 2007; Vilnius, Lithuania, 2011
- 8th International Investigative Psychology Conference, London, England, 2005
- 26th International Congress of Applied Psychology, Athens, Greece, 2006
- Biennial International Criminal Justice Conference, Ljubljana, Slovenia, 2002; 2006
- Canadian Psychology Annual Convention, Ottawa, Canada, 2007; Montreal, 2009; Winnipeg, 2010
- XXXI Inter-American Congress of Psychology, Caracas, Venezuela, 1999; Mexico City, 2007; Guatemala City, Guatemala, 2009; Lima, Peru, 2015
- American Psychological Association (APA) Annual Convention, San Francisco, CA, 1998; Boston, MA, 1999; Honolulu, HI, 2004; Toronto, Canada, 2009; San Diego, CA, 2010; Washington, DC, 2014
- Law & Society Association Joint Annual Meeting, Montreal, Canada, 2008
- European Congress of Psychiatry, Munich, Germany, 2010; Nice, France, 2013; Madrid, Spain, 2016
- Raoul Dandurant Border Conference, Montreal, Canada, 2011; 2013; 2016
- 21st World Congress of Social Psychiatry, Lisbon, Portugal, 2013
- Association of Borderland Studies (ABS)—1st World Conference, Joensuu, Finland, 2014
- XV Congreso Internacional sobre Intgracion Regional, Fronters y Globaliacion en el Continents Americano & IV Congreso Internacional de Ciudades Fronterizas, Juárez, Mexico, 2015

Their early research resulted in the publication of their first book, *NAFTA & Neocolonialism: Comparative Criminal, Human & Social Justice* (2004, University Press of America). The current book is a compilation of subsequent research, much of it vetted by input at conference presentations, and/or publications.

1

Introduction: Contravening Worldviews of People Competing for Boundaries and Resources

The 21st century is witnessing a reawakening of boundary disputes, most of them secondary to war and related social unrest. Many of these conflicts are residuals of the long-term Euro–American colonial wars that provided two world wars during the 20th century in addition to numerous "lesser" conflicts, such as Korea, Vietnam, the Balkan Wars (former Yugoslavia), and the Gulf Wars (Iraq, Kuwait, Afghanistan). Added to this list are conflicts in Africa, again among former European colonies, and continued disputes among members of the former Soviet Union. These conflicts are being addressed by the emerging Association of Border Studies, which provides research and insights from a number of academic disciplines, including geography, political sciences, anthropology, sociology, philosophy, and psychology. These studies generally address fixed borders, another Euro–American conceptualization stemming from the colonial era. Our work goes beyond fixed boundaries to include precolonial aboriginal or tribal societies as well as the psychology of geopolitical boundaries. Often ignored is the concept of sociocultural superiority imposed upon the colonized peoples and the intergenerational impact this has had. It is necessary to address contravening psychocultural differences among North America's peoples, both historically and today, in order to better understand the "ethics" of border politics. This analysis also addresses race, ethnic, or sectarian divides as well.

North American border politics is closely linked not only to geography, but to population demographics as well. Pre-Columbian Americans were illiterate for the most part. The best written documentation follows the advent of Europeans bent on colonizing these lands. As best as can be determined, the pre-Columbian natives of North, Central, and South America and the Caribbean represented a diversity of cultures and societies from hunting and gathering tribes to horticultural groups and even sophisticated city-states, such as those developed by the Aztec, Inca, and Mayan empires of Mexico and Central and South America. The population of pre-Columbian America is estimated to have been between 15 and 80 million at the time of white contact.

Indigenous Indian groups north of central Mexico and extending through Canada were not as developed as their southern Mesoamerican counterparts. In the southeastern United States, archeological evidence traces these groups to hunter societies during the isolated Paleo-Indian era (10,000–8500 BC). More archaeological evidence dating to the Woodland Phase (700 BC–AD 600) indicates band-level horticultural settlements among the Eastern Woodland tribes while hunting and gathering activities still predominated in the mountainous regions. Archaeological evidence indicates that the eastern Indian groups made the transition from hunting and gathering to horticultural settlements during the Late Archaic Phase (3000–1000 BC).

In a similar fashion, Preston Holder describes the aboriginal lifestyle of the Plains Indians in his book *The Hoe and the Horse on the Plains*. In it, he defines the Plains as the area from North Dakota to the Gulf Coast of Texas with the Rocky Mountains marking the western boundary and the 96th and 100th meridians establishing the eastern boundary. The pre-Columbian Indian groups in this region lived a more primitive existence mainly as nomadic hunting and gathering societies with some marginal horticultural traits. European influence affected all native groups with these changes and adaptations forcing many tribes westward as whites encroached on their traditional lands and lifestyles. The horticultural tribes mainly lived along waterways, divided into small temporary or seasonal settlements made up of families and clans. These settlements were scattered along the rivers and often separated by substantial spaces between villages, allowing for adequate hunting, fishing, gardening, and gathering. Home villages united the scattered clans with seasonal ceremonial rites held in the mother clan's village. The introduction of the horse, along with the increased threat of outside raids and European encroachment, led these outlying groups to consolidate into larger villages if only for mutual protection. This consolidation of Indian groups began in the southwest in the 16th century and encompassed the entire region by the middle of the 18th century. Even then, certain Indian groups remained nomadic, greatly expanding their hunting territory via the use of the horse. Holder notes that this interaction process resulted in rapid cultural adaptation not only among Indian groups but among whites as well. Indeed, this merging of cultures was most prevalent among the French trappers:

> The French developed a system which utilized lower-class members who had much to gain and little to lose in changing cultures. Working as individuals, these men formed the avant-garde of French colonial ambitions. Taking the native peoples as their model and becoming somewhat more than half native themselves; they sketched in the lines of communication and supply which were later expanded in an organized fashion… In changing culture these men may well have found more status among the indigenous people than they had in their own society.[1]

Introduction

The noted Smithsonian ethnographer, James Mooney, estimated the U.S. pre-Columbian aboriginal population to be about 1,200,000.[2] Douglas H. Ubelaker felt that this was a low estimate in that Mooney most likely did not factor in deaths brought about by epidemics of European and African diseases, such as smallpox, measles, and plague. More recent data puts the pre-Columbian aboriginal population at about five million.[3] By 1800, the American Indian population in the United States was estimated to be only 600,000. And according to the 1910 U.S. census, following the end of the Indian Wars, the official count was 266,000, less than 10% of what it was in the 16th century.[4]

While the indigenous Indian population was being greatly reduced by disease, slaughter, slavery, wars, and cultural genocide (removal, concentration camps, militarized boarding schools, etc.), some 15 million African slaves were brought to the Americas between the 16th and 19th centuries. Nearly half (seven million) arrived during the 1700s. Although some North American Indian tribes kept captured enemies as individual slaves prior to white contact, this practice paled in comparison with the enslavement of the Tlaxcalan Indians by the Aztec Indian empires of central Mexico. Thus, although Indian slavery did exist in the Americas prior to European conquests and the arrival of African slaves, the colonial powers expanded this practice considerably among the tribes north of central Mexico. Indeed, Indian and black slavery played a significant role in both the colonial trade and the extermination of most of the southeastern tribes in the United States. The Indian slave trade involved all the horrors associated with the worst practices of this institution, including beatings, killings, and tribal and family separation. And the British were not alone in this practice. The Spanish had Indian slaves in their western American colonies, where they were used to build and maintain the Catholic missions staggered along the Pacific Coast. Enslaved Indians in British colonies were often forced to fight against other colonial powers, notably the French and Spanish. Indian and African slaves were often forced by their European masters to quell each group's uprisings bringing these two groups together, resulting in inter-race miscegenation, leading to another form of Mestizo—the *Black Indian*. This interracial contact between Indian and black slaves led to alliances of escaped slaves hiding mainly in the swamplands of Florida. The Indian slave trade continued for more than a century. Indian slaves are credited with having built Charleston, South Carolina. In 1708, the Carolina settlement census registered 5,300 whites, 2,900 black slaves, and 1,400 Indian slaves.[5]

Fernandez-Armesto notes that slaves, notably African slaves, were needed especially in the tropical and subtropical plantations that emerged in colonial America from South America to the southern United States. Tobacco, sugar, cotton, and rice were all labor-intense crops that needed tending by slaves. Given the subhuman status assigned to both Indians and

African blacks, European colonists were not inclined to attempt to assimilate their captured workforce. Accordingly, black slaves, from Brazil to the U.S. south, were left to transport elements of their African cultures to the Americas, practicing their own religions, speaking their own language, maintaining their own household patterns, and preparing their own food. From this emerged African slave subcultures that, over time, differed either from that of their colonial masters or their own indigenous African tribal cultures.[6] Common to both the aboriginal Indian customs and those of displaced African slaves was a shared economic worldview based on cooperation in contrast to the Eurocentric concept of economic competition. Both African slaves and North American Indians subscribed to some variation of a "harmony ethos"—one that viewed their existence as being in balance with nature, for example, Mother Earth and Father Sky. Post-Columbus slave communities were determined by the plantation system.

At the time of U.S. independence, African slaves were disproportionately represented in Brazil, Jamaica, Cuba, and Puerto Rico compared with Mexico or the U.S. south. Fernandez-Armesto notes that by the mid-1800s only six of the fifteen slave states had a substantial black population, and in most of the other slave states, the population was less than a quarter of the total population. By the same token, intermarriage between whites and blacks was more predominant in those countries where the black population represented the majority, accounting for the substantial Afro–Anglo mix throughout the Caribbean and Atlantic South America. In Latin-American societies, African native religions blended with Catholicism, leading to unique religious practices, notably some version of voodoo (hoodoo in the United States) and Santeria, providing the cultural foundation of their slave cultures that extended into their post-slave cultures. In the United States, on the other hand, the concept of white supremacy was more pronounced, creating a virtual caste system.[7]

Slavery in the United States was unique even for North America with both Mexico and Canada banning the practice. Slavery represented an interdependency, a symbiotic relationship between the manufacturing north and the plantation south, and from this dependency emerged a common negative stereotype assigned to blacks. The U.S. Civil War (the War between the States) was fought mainly to preserve the Union and not specifically in order to emancipate black slaves. There was no commanding order that slaves were to be freed. Indeed, it was the decision of local Union commanders to either allow or discontinue slavery in territories they occupied in the South. It was this piecemeal, unplanned process and not any unified, manifested directive that contributed to the end of slavery and President Lincoln's Emancipation Proclamation leading to the Thirteenth Amendment to the U.S. Constitution in 1865. Because of the inconsistencies of Reconstruction policies under the administration of Lincoln's vice president and successor, Andrew Johnson (born in North Carolina), racism became the norm, replacing the slave stigma of freedmen, a process reinforced by segregation (Jim Crow) laws that the U.S. Government failed to adequately address until the 1960s.

Equally compelling is the aboriginal worldview of North America's indigenous peoples. Intergroup wars and intragroup conflicts abounded throughout aboriginal North America as they always have among human groups. Each major linguistic group identified themselves as *the people* while, at the same time, identifying neighboring competing tribes by some derogatory terms, names that Europeans later used to identify these various tribal groups. Aboriginal life in the Americas was challenging due to the lack of rapid mobility with no evidence that any of these tribes made use of the wheel prior to white contact. Mobility was also greatly restricted because the advent of the horse as a form of transportation and a beast of burden was not present until these items, along with iron and steel weapons, came with European explorers. Once introduced into their culture, American Indians rose out of their semi-Stone Age existence making great advances as horsemen as well as adapting to steel implements, such as agricultural implements, knives, and firearms.[8]

Although most of these tribal societies subscribed to a harmonious worldview, conflict and competition were part of their cycle of maintaining both intra- and intergroup balance or harmony. These were societies in which tradition was passed on orally with major events documented with some form of graphic presentation. It is estimated that there were some 350 different native languages spoken by indigenous groups in what is now the United States and Canada, including Eskimos and Aleuts, and another 1,500 languages spoken in Mexico and Central and South America. Tribal groups generally formed larger allegiances based on shared language; no tribal group is known to have had a written language during aboriginal times. Clan folkways provided the basic control mechanism and psychocultural identity for the group sharing a common language and geographical region. Indeed, linguistic groupings and clan membership predated the contemporary *tribal* classification adopted by Euro-Americans in identifying aboriginal groups. At the same time, Euro-American ethnocentrism relegated indigenous peoples as biologically and racially inferior with some colonists actually labeling them as subhumans and identifying them as they would animals: bucks, does, fawns. These Eurocentric views prevailed despite the awareness of the great Aztec pyramid of Cholula in Mexico and similar aboriginal achievements. On the other hand, these endeavors also pointed to the use of slaves in pre-Columbian America. The Aztecs regularly raided their neighbors, the Tlaxcalan Indians, for the purpose of both slave labor and sacrificial victims. This long history of victimization of the Tlaxcalan Indians resulted in their aiding the Spanish in their conquest of the Aztec empire; with Spain making the Tlaxcalan tribal lands an autonomous tribal community resulting in the current Mexican State of Tlaxcala.[9]

Aboriginal Harmony Ethos and Restorative Justice

Prior to European contact, North American Indians were a varied lot composed of hundreds of separate social units further divided into a number of linguistic groups. Yet, they shared a common metaphysical belief system, one based upon harmony with their natural environment. Although these myths of origin vary from group to group, they all share a similar theme: a cooperative harmonious ethos, especially among their own people. Indeed, most aboriginals referred to themselves as "the people" or "the principal people," labels that signify strong in-group ethnocentrism. Although they felt strongly about their own group, most North American aboriginals had a rather humble self-perception especially in relation to their natural environment. They had considerable respect not only for powerful natural phenomenon, but for other living organisms sharing their ecosystem as well. They referred to their tangible natural environment as "Mother Earth" and view extraterrestrial elements, those interacting with Mother Earth, as "Father Sky." Harmonious relationships, according to this logic, reflect fertile interactions between Mother Earth and Father Sky. By the same token, chaos and conflict illustrate unfavorable relationships between these two metaphysical entities that could be resolved within the harmonious perspective. However, white contact introduced a new era, one of constant chaos and increased brutality in the form of both physical and cultural genocide.

Within the harmony ethos, order and control were dictated by folkways, mores, and customs without the aid of formal institutions such as those evident within Western-style societies. Nonetheless, traditional aboriginal cultures involved a complex system of oral education, one that involved all aspects of their existence from birth to death, including the afterlife. In this sense, many of the values of the harmony ethos differed dramatically from those of Western societies, which subscribed to the Protestant ethic, hence pitting the North American Indian's cooperative lifestyle against that of the competitive European groups that came to colonize the Americas. During aboriginal times, the clan provided the basic group structure. Clan folkways provided the basic control mechanism and psychocultural identity for the group sharing a common language and geographical region. Indeed, linguistic grouping and clan membership predate the contemporary *tribal* classification format. European ethnocentrism regarded American Indians as illiterate, subhumans living a Stone Age existence, being both biologically and racially inferior to whites. This view prevailed despite the fact that the great Aztec pyramid of Cholula in the Mexican State of Puebla is the largest ancient pyramid monument in the world. Granted, American Indian groups north of central Mexico, extending through Canada, were not as developed as their southern Mesoamerican counterparts. Nonetheless, the North American Indian groups shared strong elements of the harmony ethos.

Despite competition among clans within a linguistic group and seasonal conflict between tribes, a balance was maintained on the basis of the harmony ethos, values derived from the natural relationship existing between Mother Earth and Father Sky. The particular values fostered by the harmony ethos rest with the group's creation myths but have a common core.

1. The avoidance of overt hostilities regarding interpersonal matters and an emphasis on nonaggression in intrafamilial, clan, or tribal interactions.
2. The use of a neutral third person, or intermediary, for resolving personal altercations within the tribal community (avoidance of direct intragroup confrontations).
3. A high value placed on independence (personal freedom to act as long as these actions conform to traditional folkways and do not violate sacred taboos).
4. A resentment of imposed authority (leaders command respect as opposed to demanding subordination by forced authority).
5. A general hesitancy to command others.
6. Caution in interactions with others, especially strangers.
7. A reluctance to refuse favors and an emphasis on generosity within the clan or tribe (the basis for "giveaways").
8. Reluctance to voice individual opinions publicly (because the person's identity is tied to the larger clan persona).
9. Avoidance of eye and body contact when interacting with others, especially those outside the family or clan structure.
10. Emphasis placed on group cooperation and not on individual competition.
11. Deference to elders (old equals good and honor).
12. Challenging life in the raw (exploring life firsthand for the sake of the experience itself: counting coup, dog soldiering).

Restorative justice within the aboriginal harmony ethos differed markedly from the Western-based adversarial punitive model in that the concept of individual victims and offenders only had relevance within the clan structure. The clan, and not the individual who perpetrated the offending act, was held accountable for injustices, and justice was only restored through clan negotiations. Once an interclan agreement was forged, then the matter was resolved and forgotten. Absent are the lingering labels of individual *victims* and *offenders* as exists within Euro–American jurisprudence.[10]

The Protestant Ethic and New World Conflicts: Protestants, Aboriginals, Catholics

Max Weber, the noted social philosopher of the early 20th century, probably best articulated the relationship between Protestantism and capitalism. According to Weber, in his work *The Protestant Ethic and the Spirit of Capitalism*, this change of worldview from that of cooperative peasant or feudal societies was associated with the introduction of new Christian perspectives on *predestination*, notably Calvinism, Pietism, Methodism, and the Baptist Sects. Briefly stated, Catholicism, especially the doctrine practiced during the Middle Ages, posited that humans were predisposed with *original sin* and that life itself was a trial of good versus evil challenges with a preponderance of one over the other, along with the appropriate sacraments, determining one's place in the hereafter.

With the Reformation, especially the work of Calvin and his brand of Protestantism—Calvinism—a new worldview perspective emerged based on moral predestined superiority, a process that would become evident during one's lifetime by earthly successes. In its religious conception, the Protestant ethic, a predestined individual would be identified by certain virtues: elevated social status, private wealth, and asceticism. The element of social status and private wealth provided the seeds for capitalism, according to Weber. Eventually the sacred element of asceticism was greatly diminished, paving the way for a secular mode of capitalism along with its new virtues of material wealth, social privilege, and conspicuous consumption. High social status also took on a secular flavor along with the connotation of social superiority.[11]

Although it could be argued that initially there were few differences between the religious doctrines of the Church of England and those of the Roman Catholic Church, this was not the case in the New World colonial milieu. French and Spanish colonies remained Roman Catholic, treating the indigenous peoples as human beings, and English Protestant colonies saw the indigenous peoples as subhumans. The Catholic perspective on the New World populace stemmed from Pope Julius II's decree in 1512 declaring that American Indians were descended from Adam and Eve, like their white counterparts. This status was not afforded American Indians residing in the United States until 1879 when a U.S. federal court officially declared indigenous peoples as being "persons" and not some subset of the animal world.[12] In England, Catholicism was modified under King Henry VIII with the emergence of the Anglican Church, which did not recognize the Roman Catholic Pope as head of their church. Nonetheless, King Henry VIII reaffirmed his commitment to the practices of Catholicism with passage of the Six Articles Act in 1539. Although attempts were made by Henry's son and successor, Edward VI, to institute the more conservative Calvinist Protestantism in England, his short tenure obviated this movement. His sister, Queen Mary (Bloody Mary), went to the other extreme of reinstating Catholic doctrine within the Church of England. It was, however, her sister, Elizabeth I, who repealed Mary's Catholic doctrines, creating a compromise between Catholicism and the foundations of Protestantism. Thus, by the late 1500s, the foundations of the Church of England were laid and have survived to the present despite Oliver Cromwell's Calvinist conservative Protestant Revolt, which was inspired largely by the works of John Cotton, the Puritan leader of the Massachusetts Bay Colony during his reign in the mid-17th century.[13]

As the British Empire expanded, so did the acceptance of cultural and religious differences allowing for the forging of the complex nature of the British Commonwealth that exists today. The Church of England also transformed into the Anglican Communion with two closely related branches, the Anglican Church of England and Canada and the Episcopal Church in the United States and other commonwealth nations. The more conservative Puritans, in turn, split into two branches as well: the Congregationalists (conservative Puritans) and the more liberal Presbyterians (notably Scotch–Irish congregations). These latter were the predominant denominations in the Canadian and New England English colonies reconciled by the Cambridge Synod of 1648. Other conservative branches of Calvinism in the British North American colonies included the Methodists and Baptists. These denominations emerged mainly in the southern colonies of what is now the United States of America. Conservative Calvinistic Protestantism and its belief in predestined moral superiority existed from the beginning in the New World colonies in both New England and Canada. Max Weber noted that American capitalism, as espoused by Benjamin Franklin, went beyond secular capitalism by attaching a moral ethos as justification for its expansionistic designs. This sense of religious and ethnic superiority, supported by the colonists' self-proclaimed *Covenant of Divine Providence (Manifest Destiny)* paved the way for the moral justification of expansionism and *ethnic cleansing*.

A myth often used in justification of U.S. intervention and territorial expansionism was that of seeking religious tolerance, including the justification cited as the impetus for British Empire settlements in the New World. The emerging United States of America had its auspicious beginning as a business capitalist endeavor contracted with the British government. The Massachusetts Bay Colony was chartered as a business corporation with legal authority to exercise law and order among its inhabitants. Charters were managed by a governor, deputy governor, and a board of 18 stockholders, also known as "freemen." The latter constituted the "general court" that met four times a year to admit new members, elect officers, and make regulations. This governmental model was carried over into the New Republic, especially in the northern states. A similar process was in effect when Anglos settled portions of New Spain (Mexico).

What was lacking in the Massachusetts Bay Colony was religious freedom. Indeed, the Puritan leaders held an elitist view of Protestantism in which only male church members were enfranchised, and membership was strictly limited so that most colonists were not part of the ruling elite. Until 1630, church membership required a minister's endorsement, creating a strict social stratification even among free whites. Indentured whites and people of color (blacks and Indians) suffered even more within this restricted social milieu. Kai Erikson articulated this theocratic philosophy in his work, *Wayward Puritans*:

> God has chosen an elite to represent Him on earth and to join Him in Heaven. People who belonged to this elite learned of their appointment through the agency of a deep conversion experience, giving them a special responsibility and a special competence to control the destinies of others.[14]

Intolerance against fellow Anglos occurred as they became more isolated from their home base in England. Cromwell's Puritan forces not only defeated the King of England, it also split his followers into two general groups: the Scottish Presbyterian moderates and the Congregational Independents. The latter eventually represented the New England colonies, becoming the recognized *church of state*.

The asceticism of the Puritans, in general, and the Congregationalists, in particular, fueled not only ethnocentric elitism, but a ferocious hatred of anything that they saw as being based in superstition, such as the aboriginal beliefs and practices of the indigenous American Indians whose land they were stealing. With blatant disregard for native occupants, the Congregationalists established their own communities (congregations), making each one a separately constituted unit, supposedly free from a central church authority. To illustrate, New Hampshire was a very conservative Congregationalist colony and later state in which each town came to represent a congregation along with its own church. The higher authority came from the colonial and, later, the state legislatures. Hence, New Hampshire was among the most conservative and intolerant of the New England colonies and, later, the New Republic. It effectively removed all aboriginals from the state, mostly by physical genocide, setting an example for other states.

Within this setting came the bloodletting against challenges to the New England Puritan theocracy, notably the Quaker persecutions of 1656–1665. Essentially, the anti-Quaker law carried the death penalty for anyone professing to be a Quaker within the Puritan colonies. Other forms of religious intolerance occurred in New England following their Declaration of Independence from Great Britain. The legislation of morality was a common practice in the colonies. These restrictions on public and private behaviors, most notably on the Christian Sabbath (Sunday), were commonly known as "blue laws." Although the source of this term is obscured by history, some sources attribute the name to the color of the paper on which the laws were written or to the cover of the statutes. These laws clearly established the New England colonies as Puritan theocracies. This same theocracy advocated for the extermination of the indigenous Indian population. This effort was so effective that with the exception of a spillover of Canadian Algonquian tribes along the northeastern border of the United States (New York and Maine), the American Indian population was virtually exterminated (physical and cultural genocide) in the New England colonies.

New Spain (Mexico), on the other hand, had a long colonial history extending to the early 1500s. The Spanish, more so than their British and French colonial counterparts, had a highly structured stratification based on laws of the Indies. And like the fledging United States, the newly independent Mexico patterned its legal, social, and economic structure on that of its colonial parent, Spain. One major difference was that the Spanish colonial system (Spanish America) was highly centralized with the top echelon constituting the military, Catholic Church, and civil service system staffed by Spanish-born officials. In the British colonies, on the other hand, the congregational structure of the quasi-official churches (Congregationalists in the northern colonies and English Episcopal in the South) allowed for local independence and responsibility with many governmental positions held by locally born men.

Accordingly, the basic rationale for independence from European colonialism differed significantly between the United States and Mexico, a schism that played a major role later in the Texas Revolution. The 13 English colonies fought for control from the elite of Great Britain, and the 1810 Mexican Revolution was one for freedom from the Spanish feudal system. Here, the colonial experience in New Spain was one of strict stratification, a virtual caste system with the Spanish-born elite, the peninsulares, occupying the most important positions in government, the Church, and the military. History shows that only three Criollos (Mexicans born of Spanish parents) held the coveted position of Viceroy of Mexico during the three centuries of Spanish rule. During the same period, only 18 out of 754 high civil and military positions in all of Spanish America were held by locally born Criollos (also known as Creoles).[15]

The feudal system of New Spain evolved from the *encomiendas* system in which large land holdings, including indigenous settlements, were given by the Spanish crown to the early Spanish explorers (*conquistadors*). This system included a provision to educate and convert the American Indian population to Catholicism. American Indians, in turn, served as vassals to their Spanish lords. The *encomiendas* system lasted from 1521 until 1550 when it was replaced with the *repartimento* system in response to the aging population of the original conquistador peninsulars. Again, Spanish-born peninsulars held large tracks of land on which American Indians, Mestizos (those of mixed Indian and white or black heritage), and rural *indomestizos* served as indentured sharecroppers. This feudal system then evolved into the *hacienda* system of large estates in which the lower strata of society was dependent on the large landholders for subsistence. It was a variation of the hacienda system that attracted slaveholding émigrés from the United States to New Spain just prior to the Mexican War for independence from Spain.

New settlers to New Spain (later Mexico) were provided with substantial land grants—termed *empresarios*, a type of hacienda. The *empresario* was essentially a land agent who would provide settlers for his land grant. Spain, seeking to protect its northeastern territory, known then as Coahuila and Tejas, from intrusions from the United States and other European colonial forces, attempted first to entice people from the interior to move to this region but with little success. DeLeon, in his 1993 book *Mexican Americans in Texas*, details the early settlement picture. He noted that Mexico City sent troops to what is now east Texas in 1716 in response to French activity in the area. The expedition force established the San Antonio settlement, home to the Alamo fortification. In 1731, immigrants from the Canary Islands arrived in San Antonio, and more settlements were established along the Rio Grande in the 1740s and 1750s, including Laredo. A census in 1777 showed more than 3,000 *pobladores* (settlers) residing in the area, most in San Antonio. Voluntary migration from the interior to the northeastern frontier was thwarted mainly by resistance on the part of hacienda owners fearing a labor shortage if sufficient numbers of rural Mexicans migrated north.[16]

French colonies in the Americas were the most native-friendly in that they did not come so much to inhabit the land but to exploit it for its resources. Toward this end, most of the colonists were men. And many cohabited with Native women, creating a substantial *Métis* population. Catholic priests, like their Spanish counterparts, were sent to convert the indigenous groups as well as regulate the various trading outposts scattered throughout what is now eastern Canada, the Maritimes, and extending along the North American major waterways from the St. Lawrence to the Mississippi all the way to New Orleans. The fate of French colonization in North America was closely linked to wars with other major European countries, notably England, wars that had a strong sectarian element that played a role in the New World colonies.

France also experienced turbulence with religious civil wars between the traditional Catholic population and the emerging Protestant Huguenots, the French version of Calvinism. When Henry VIII of England was refused the Catholic title of Emperor of the Holy Roman Empire, he hired French Huguenots in his retaliation against the Pope in Rome, using them to attack Catholic Church possessions. In France, Henry's counterpart, King Francis I

Introduction

(1515–1574) initially put forth measures protecting the Huguenots from the growing animus of the majority Catholics, then changed his policies in 1534 leading to open civil war between Roman Catholics and Protestant Huguenots. Adhering to the tenets of Calvinist predestination and its capitalist manifestation, more and more French nobles and city merchant families joined the Huguenot ranks. The Edict of Saint-Germain in 1562 led to the official recognition and rights of Huguenots in France. Even then, bloodshed continued between French Catholics and Protestants with the St. Bartholomew's Day massacre in 1572, resulting in tens of thousands of deaths on both sides. A general amnesty was granted in 1573, pardoning all those involved in these atrocities.

In 1598, King Henry IV issued the Edict of Nantes, establishing Catholicism as the state religion of France with continued protection for the Huguenots under the existing Edict of Saint-Germain. But in 1685, King Louis XIV, under the Edict of Fontainebleau, revoked the Edict of Nantes, subsequently declaring Protestantism illegal in France. Many Huguenots then left France, immigrating to Protestant-friendly countries, including British North America. Many of the early Calvinist Huguenots who came to North America became wealthy traders and shipowners, and other settlements in South Carolina and north Florida failed due to the strong Spanish Catholic influence in these areas at that time. Huguenot emigrants to North America usually assimilated with existing English or Dutch/German Protestant churches.[17]

Paul Revere (Rivoire), of American Revolution fame, was a Huguenot, but otherwise it was not the French who played a significant role in that conflict. It was Louis XVI's 100-million-dollar funding of Washington's Continental Army and the assistance of Gilbert du Motier (the Marquis de Lafayette) that turned the tide for the colonial rebels. And it was French Admiral de Grasse, and not General Washington, who masterminded the defeat of the British at Yorktown in October 1781 with a combined Yankee and French force. France later played a significant role in both sectarian and geopolitical issues worldwide. The United States doubled in size due to Napoleon Bonaparte's selling of the Louisiana Territory in 1803 while, at the same time, establishing the Napoleonic Civil Code in French Canada, a system still in effect in Quebec Provence. It was under Napoleon Bonaparte that Haiti gained its independence following a bloody slave revolt. During the Napoleonic Wars (1804–1815), he was credited with providing Jews religious rights freeing them from their ghettoes as well as guaranteeing religious rights for both Protestants and Catholics in areas where they were the minority as well as diminishing the role of the Catholic Pope, setting the stage for a secular France.[18]

Clearly, Catholicism, Protestantism (notably its Puritan strains), and aboriginal belief systems clashed in colonial North America pitting Anglos against both the French and Hispanics—all vying for coveted land and resources. Intergroup conflicts intensify when sectarian divides enter into the equation. The belief in racial superiority is also a potent factor. When combined, they are often quite deadly. Boundary maintenance, especially physical boundaries defining communities and nations, provoke intense feelings whenever these boundaries are challenged. Accompanying these external threats is the psychological threat of having one's identity challenged. Geog Simmel articulated this process in his theory governing group dynamics: *out-group hostility increases in-group cohesion*. Regarding group divisions, Simmel put forth a functional analysis of social conflict in the early 20th century stating that hostilities tend to preserve group boundaries and positing that conflicts serve to establish and maintain the identity and boundaries of societies and groups: patterned enmities and reciprocal antagonisms tend to conserve social divisions and systems of stratification. Here, *realistic conflict*, like the current fight over ideology (Islam versus Christianity, democracy versus autocratic rule) and resources (oil), is when war is used as a deliberate means toward desired ends. He also stated that wars help society overcome its internal divisions, marginality, anomie, and alienation by providing an external source to target while, at the same time, increasing the internal cohesion of the group.

Ambiguous situations, such as wars and other forms of conflict, which Emile Durkheim calls "anomie" and Erik Fromm termed "alienation," often fuel intense hostilities, even hatred for the perceived out-group members. Intense intergroup conflicts often result in atrocities, even genocide. Even after the conflict ends, group hatred continues to fester, manifesting itself in discrimination. Rational judgment is often replaced by a collective form of *attribution bias*. Human behavior is such that we often tend to perceive the actions of in-group members differently than those of out-group members. If someone within the in group succeeds at a task, we tend to attribute his or her success to inherent factors; on the other hand, if someone in the out group succeeds along similar lines, we tend to attribute this to external factors, including luck or unfair advantage. And if someone in the in group fails or is caught doing something illegal, we tend to look for external factors and influences to explain this fluke of behavior. On the other hand, if someone in the out group fails, members of the in group commonly attribute this behavior exclusively to the individual's inferior status, excluding any mitigating circumstances. This perception, individually and collectively, provides the foundation of racism and discrimination. It is an important element in our discussion of border politics.[19]

The race or sectarian factor is critical when looking at North American border politics. Anglo colonists viewed black slaves as livestock, property to be used and abused as they saw fit. At the same time, they placed indigenous Indians in the same category as wild animals, and as such, they could be hunted and killed like any other nuisance beast. Following the stratification model of Europe at this time, Caucasians themselves were stratified into "superior" and "lesser white" categories. The conservative Puritan ethos assigned French and Spanish Catholics into the "inferior" white category. The phenomenon was articulated by Kenneth Davis in his "God and Country" article in the October 2010 issue of the *Smithsonian*:

> Throughout the colonial era, Anglo-American antipathy toward Catholics—especially French and Spanish Catholics—was pronounced and often reflected in the sermons of such famous clerics as Cotton Mather and in statutes that discriminated against Catholics in matters of property and voting. Anti-Catholic feelings even contributed to the revolutionary mood in America after King George III extended an olive branch to French Catholics in Canada with the Quebec Act of 1774, which recognized their religion.[20]

Colonial Intrusion and Border Battles

2

Aboriginals and Their Pre-Columbian Boundaries

North American aboriginals existed for thousands of years without the benefit of the wheel, horse, forged metal tools or weapons, or domestic animals with the exception of dogs that were related to the wolf. Yet trade routes, using mainly waterways, extended from South and Central America deep into North America. To illustrate, tobacco from the eastern coastal tribes in what is now the southeastern United States was traded with the Plains Indians for pipestone.

These walking or running trails and waterways were used by European colonists as they extended their hold on these former tribal lands. Canada had both American Indians and Inuit, each with their own defined territory shared collectively among linguistic groups. Often this territory extended into what is now the United States. Along the eastern provinces of the Atlantic were the Beothuk, Maliseet, Innu, Abenaki, and Mi'kmaq or Micmac. Further in, on the Canadian side of the Great Lakes, were the Anishinaabe, Algonquin, Iroquois, and Wyandot; and in the northern woodlands were the Cree and Chipewyan. On the plains that extended into the United States were the Blackfoot, Kainai, Sarcee, and Northern Peigan. Along the Pacific Coast resided the Haida, Salish, Kwakiutl, Nuu-chah-nulth, Nisga'a, and Gitxsan; and in the northwest were the Athapaskan-speaking people, the Dine, and the Tutchone-speaking people and Tlingit, the same groups that inhabited what is now Alaska.

In what is now the United States of America, tribes inhabited the New England area that also resided in that portion of Canada with the same for the Great Lakes Region and the Great Plains. A major difference was the Pueblo tribes that populated the Rio Grande River basin in what is now New Mexico, extending their territory into northern Mexico. The southeastern United States also had unique tribes related historically to the *mound builders* (Choctaw, Creek, Chickasaw) and several Iroquoian linguistic groups: the Cherokee and Catawba. The Northern Plains Indians (Omaha, Dakota, Ponca) shared their territory with their Siouan neighbors residing in Canada as did the Cheyenne and Crow, and the Comanche, Kiowa, Arapaho, and others populated this region. The southwestern region of the United States had two major Athapaskan groups: the Apache and the Navajo (Dine) as well as Pueblo tribes and other groups that also resided in northern Mexico, such as Pima, Mohave, Yavapai, Havasupai, Yaqui, and Papago (Tohono O'odham). Texas was another indigenous borderland with tribes that transcended Spanish and English colonial holdings. These tribes included the Apache, Bidai, Coahuiltecan and Carrizo, Caddo, Comanche, Karankawa, Kiowa, Kitsai, Tawakoni, Tonkawa, and Wichita tribes and the Jumano, Suma, and Piro pueblos. Those tribes forced into Spanish Texas by white settlers in the 13 colonies included the Alabama, Cherokee, Coushatta, and Kickapoo tribes as well as the Tigua Pueblo Indians.

Mexico had a more dense indigenous population than its North American counterparts during the colonial period and today has the largest Indian population, estimated to be over 25 million people. The vast majority of the rest of the Mexican population also share an Indian heritage with Mestizo and Indians constituting 90% of the current Mexican population. Indeed, there are 68 native linguistic groups in Mexico today. Indigenous groups of over 100,000 population currently residing in Mexico include the Nahuati, Maya, Zapotec, Mixtec, Otomi, Totonac, Tzotzil, Mazahua, Mazatec, Huastec, Ch'ol, Chinantec, Purepecha, Mixe, Tiapanec, and Tarahumara. In northern Mexico's mountains reside the Tarahumara, and the majority of Mexico's aboriginal peoples share the culture of others residing in Mesoamerica living in city-states and building monuments (pyramids) used to worship their gods. This included the Olmeca and Maya of central Mexico. The Maya resided then, as they do now, in both the mountains and the rain forests of Mexico, Guatemala, and Belize, including the Yucatan. Chaco Canyon, in what is now New Mexico in the United States, provided archeological evidence of the reach and influence of Mesoamerican groups into what is now the United States, linking the more developed and populated aboriginal peoples with the rest of North America.

Aboriginal tribes of North America occupied territory but did not perceive ownership of these lands. This was a Euro–American concept that led to treaty corruption and exploitation of the indigenous peoples during both the colonial era and the United States expansionistic era under its God-given mandate: *Manifest Destiny*. European influences included the introduction of the horse and domestic sheep, metal tools and weapons, and the wheel among other implements that altered their aboriginal ways considerably. Christianity was another significant factor in the rapid adaptation by North American Indians from their aboriginal pre-Columbian lifestyle and beliefs to their current pan-Indian status.[1]

Colonial Encroachment and Conflict

As stated earlier, the first European settlements in North America were established by capitalist enterprises with the purpose of exploiting the virtually untapped resources long protected by the native inhabitants. The existence of these early settlements was contingent upon the hospitality of the indigenous group that occupied the land. Once established, white settlers often became greedy, leading to conflict with their original host tribes. The Jamestown settlement illustrates the process of Indian exploitation. Jamestown, in what is now Virginia, began as an English joint-stock company whose initial survival was dependent upon the Algonquian tribe residing in the area for both food and shelter. This dependency on the Powhatan was nurtured for 15 years (1607–1622) until the settlers had sufficient membership to encroach on the tribal lands and resources. With sufficient numbers, the colonists forcefully took over the Indian cornfields, which accounted for thousands of acres. With this seizure of lands came aggression against the tribes that initially had befriended them.

On March 22, 1622, a member of the Powhatan Confederacy of the Algonquian tribes, Opechancanough, led an attack on the white settlements, killing 347. By reacting, the London capitalist leaders of the colonial enterprises forged the basis of the British North American Indian policy: extermination by removal to reservations, enslavement, or hunting them down with horses and hounds and killing them. In order to justify this policy, the American Indian was defined as a rude, barbarous, savage, naked people, who deserved to be hunted down and torn apart by hounds for sport. This policy was so successful that by the time of the American Revolution the Powhatan Confederacy was reduced to fewer than a thousand members.[2]

Another major event occurred in what is now the western United States, involving the North American Spanish colonies in New Spain. American Indian historians noted that Indian missions, run by Catholic priests and monks, in the northern territories were authoritarian, coercive, totalitarian institutions in which the Indian wards were treated as slaves. An account of mission slavery was depicted by Tony Pinto, tribal chairman of the Cuyapaipe Reservation:

> They fed them actually as little as possible. They beat them and killed them if they were sick, or couldn't work, or didn't agree to do certain work. They forced them to become Catholics. They specially whipped and killed the older people. That way they couldn't complain about the lack of food… We feel that the missions did not do us any good. They did us a lot harm instead.[3]

Rape of enslaved Indian women by soldiers was another problem endemic to the Spanish mission, a situation that the Catholic priests could have stopped but did not because it made the military more compliant to the missions' mandate of controlling, converting, and exploiting the native population. Although the mission system began to break down following the Mexican Revolution (1822–1848), it was not until the Treaty of Guadalupe Hidalgo (signed in 1848, ratified by the U.S. Congress in 1850) and California statehood that mission slavery was officially abolished.[4]

The Spanish had other difficulties in the West outside of California, notably among the Pueblo Indians. In 1680, the Pueblo and Hopi, with the exception of the Piros tribe far to the south of New Mexico, drove the Spanish from what is now New Mexico and Arizona. It was one of the most successful Indian campaigns in North America. Fifty years in the planning, its success lasted only a dozen years. This coordinated attack extended hundreds of miles along the Rio Grande River where the Pueblos were located. When the coordinated attack took place, the only major resistance was in Santa Fe, New Mexico, the capital of the northern Spanish frontier. Surrounded by Indians and with their water and food supplies cut off, Otermin, the besieged territorial governor, finally fled south.

The fighting continued with Spanish attacks on the rebellious Pueblo tribes, and in retaliation, the Indians destroyed Catholic churches and missions. In 1689, the Spanish attempted a new technique, issuing land grants to the Pueblo villages in exchange for the Spanish return to their former colonial territory. A severe drought plus continued raids by neighboring Ute and Apache tribes convinced some Pueblo leaders to acquiesce, and in 1692, a contingent of leaders from the Jemez, Zia, Santa Ana, San Felipe, Pecos, and Tanos Pueblos went to Guadalupe del Paso, Mexico, and invited the Spanish to return, if only for their mutual protection from other tribes. Nonetheless, the Hopi continued to resist the Spanish return, becoming a safe haven for other Pueblo Indians seeking refuge from colonial influences.

Spanish General de Vargas embarked on a 4-month expedition beginning in August 1692, eventually restoring Spanish colonial rule to 23 Pueblos entering the territorial capital, Santa Fe, on September and returning to Guadalupe del Paso on December 20, 1692. Spanish colonists began to return north in 1693, making up the current white Hispanic population of New Mexico and Arizona, a group that adamantly distinguishes themselves from the mixed Indian–Spanish population (many the results of rape by Spanish soldiers) known as Mestizos. The Pueblo tribes eventually accepted their Spanish land grants with 19 Pueblos located in New Mexico and the Hopi in their traditional mesas currently located within the larger Navajo Nation.[5]

In the British and French North American colonies, the European colonial wars of the 17th and 18th centuries impacted the colonies in the

Colonial Intrusion and Border Battles

Americas, notably New England, New France, and Spanish Florida. Caught up in these fights over control of North America were the indigenous peoples whose lands and resources were being claimed by Europeans. Most histories of the colonial Indian Wars usually begin with the conflicts involving the major European powers and their fights over their colonial claims in North America beginning with King William's War in 1687. However, another conflict predated this event: King Philip's War of 1675–1676. This Indian War is often overlooked because King Philip was not a European monarch. He was Metacom, also known as King Philip, a Wampanoag chief who led an alliance of tribes in fighting the Puritans of the Plymouth colony. With his death at the hands of the colonists in 1676, the eradication of the rest of the Indians continued until all major tribes were driven from what is now known as the New England states with Maine being the exception due to the fact that the state's border with New Brunswick, Canada, was not settled until 1842. New Hampshire played a role in the 1677 retribution toward those tribes involved in the King Philip War when the local militia leader, Major Waldron, a wealthy shipbuilder in Dover, devised a way to trick and capture unsuspecting Indians. The trick was to invite tribes to a day of sporting events being held in Dover, resulting in 400 Indians accepting the invitation. The Puritan settlers then turned their guns on the tribes with hundreds captured. The chiefs were taken to Boston and hanged, and more than 200 other captured Indians were sent to England and sold as slaves.[6]

The European French and Indian Wars (1689–1763) illustrated by the conflicts between the British and French over control of North America were unique in that each side recruited local tribes as allies. These conflicts began with King William's War (1689–1697), also known as the War of the Grand Alliance or the War of the League of Augsburg. It was during this conflict that New France allied itself with the Algonquin tribes of the northeast, which together comprised the Wabanaki Confederacy, and the New England colonies allied themselves with the Iroquois Confederation (Iroquoian linguistic tribes of the northeast). Both sides used their Indian confederates on raids on enemy settlements. Abenaki and Pennacook Indians raided Dover, New Hampshire, in 1689 with captives taken to New France (Quebec), and Benjamin Church, a major in the New England militia, made raids into French Acadia, including New France's claims in present-day Maine. The New England raids on Port Royal (now Nova Scotia) forced the French governor of Acadia to move the provincial capital inland to Fredericton (now New Brunswick). Although the battles in Quebec and Port Royal represented the major battles during King William's War, the constant fear of Indian raids on white settlements throughout the region in both New France and New England indicated that the native inhabitants were not pleased with the European expansion into their traditional homelands. The Treaty of Ryswick in 1697 settled this round of the French and Indian Wars with little gained by either side although the French were successful in signing a peace accord with the Iroquois. This peace would only last 5 years.[7]

In the northeast, the English again fought the French and Wabanaki (Algonquin) Confederacy, and the Iroquois remained neutral. Colonist Major Benjamin Church again mounted raids on Fort Royal under the authority of Massachusetts Governor Joseph Dudley, resulting in its capture in 1710. An armistice was declared in 1712 followed by the Treaty of Utrecht in 1713, resulting in Great Britain having control of Acadia (Nova Scotia) and sovereignty over Newfoundland and the Hudson Bay area and the Caribbean Island of St. Kitts. France, on the other hand, continued to maintain control over Cape Breton Island as well as all other islands in the Gulf of Saint Lawrence in addition to fishing rights in Newfoundland. The 1713 Treaty of Utrecht not only ended this portion of the French and Indian Wars but also sowed the seeds of discontent among the British colonies in New England with France's insistence that the French inhabitants who chose to remain in Canada retain the free exercise of their religion—Catholicism. This privilege did not exist among Catholics in Great Britain at the time. Residents of the ceded portions of New France to Great Britain were also given a year to exercise the option to leave. Most stayed. The only condition for staying as French Catholics and British citizens was the signing of an *oath of allegiance* to Britain with the provision that they would not be required to fight against the French in Canada or elsewhere but would be required to fight against Indians who were considered to be hostile to British settlers. The French in Acadia and Newfoundland were also allowed to continue to maintain their feudal community system of seigneurs and habitants, much to the consternation of the Puritans of New England who coveted this land for themselves.[8]

Conflicts between colonial settlers and indigenous tribes continued as the British settlers continued to encroach on Indian lands. Nonetheless, the European wars, notably those involving Britain, France, and Spain, continued to play out in the Americas. In Europe, chaos again erupted with the death of Charles VI, Emperor of Austria, in 1740 and the decision of Frederick the Great of Prussia to invade Austria. The resulting battles engulfed most of Europe, and a segment involved the North American colonies. Here, it was known as King George's War (1744–1748) and involved the British colonial forces from the provinces of Massachusetts, New Hampshire, New York, and Nova Scotia pitched against the French and Indians in both the Maritimes (Acadia) and the province of Quebec.[9]

The conflict in North America intensified in 1745 when French and Indian forces destroyed Saratoga, New York, and the British colonial forces captured the French fortress Louisburg. Governor Shirley's efforts to capture Louisburg were supported by New England merchants who wanted both the Acadian market and its rich fisheries. G. G. Campbell, a Canadian historian, notes that Shirley's war against the French in Acadia occurred during

Colonial Intrusion and Border Battles

a time of intensified anti-Catholic sentiment in the New England colonies, raising the furor to the level of a holy war. When the Massachusetts legislature initially turned down Shirley's plan to invade Acadia, a petition, signed by Boston merchants, was then presented to the legislature causing them to change their mind. William Pepperell, a Boston merchant, was selected by his capitalist backers to lead this endeavor. The Puritan clergy also gave strong support for this crusade led by merchants. Campbell notes, "Nothing could better illustrate the peculiar New England talent for finding good religious reasons to endorse what was sound business policy."[10] The merchant's crusade included 3,000 men from Massachusetts (including Maine) and another 1,000 each from New Hampshire and Connecticut. However, the capture of Louisburg was at considerable cost to Governor William Shirley and his Puritan militia, whose losses took a heavy toll especially on the male population of the colonial forces of Massachusetts and Maine (which was part of Massachusetts). Making matters worse was the Treaty of Aix-la-Chapelle that not only ended the war, but resulted in Louisburg being returned to France by the British in exchange for the city of Madras (a major outpost of the British East India Company) in India from the French. This did not endear the Puritan colonists to their European homeland. Instead, it was one of the seeds that eventually led to the United States first civil war: the Revolutionary War.[11]

The conflict termed the French and Indian War (1756–1763), also known as the Seven Year War, is significant in that it reflects the final North American colonial conflict prior to the American Revolution while, at the same time, establishing its military aristocracy—those who would play a significant role in the American Revolution. This conflict actually began in 1754 in North America, predating the Diplomatic Revolution in Europe (the Seven Year War) that began in 1756. The most notable of these individuals was George Washington, who distinguished himself in this phase of the French and Indian Wars as an officer with the Virginia militia. In 1753, a wealthy Virginia aristocrat, a young George Washington (age 21), then a major in the Virginia militia, was placed in charge of a force that challenged the French over western territory that both colonial powers claimed.

Governor Robert Dinwiddie and Washington's family were shareholders in a company that would benefit from British colonial expansion into the Ohio valley long claimed by New France. The following year, Washington was promoted to the rank of colonel in the Virginia militia leading a force against the French at Fort Duquesne (Pittsburgh, Pennsylvania) making him a hero in both England and the British colonies. Due to his heroism in these battles, fighting alongside British General Edward Braddock (who was killed in battle), Washington was made commander of all Virginia troops at age 23. Following General Braddock's death, Governor William Shirley of Massachusetts assumed command of all British troops in North America.

In 1758, Washington's forces were part of a larger British force that finally defeated the French and captured Fort Duquesne. Washington, disenchanted with the lack of support for the war as well as his failure to obtain a real commission in the British military, resigned his militia commission and returned home to serve in the Virginia House of Burgesses.[12]

The final French and Indian War also saw action in New England and Canada with the capture of Louisburg again a priority. The fighting in North America ended in 1760, for the most part, but the conflict raged on in the European theatre with all fighting ending in early 1763. The Treaty of Paris, ending the North American component, was signed on February 10, 1763, followed by the Treaty of Hubertusburg (February 15), ending the conflict in Europe. The Treaty of Paris gave Britain control of all New France claims in North America except the islands of Saint Pierre and Miquelon and fishing rights in the Gulf of St. Lawrence. This included some 80,000 Catholic French Canadians. France, on the other hand, gave Spain Louisiana in compensation for its support in the conflict, which was later traded back to France and sold to the United States in 1803. The residents of Quebec were provided the same conditions offered their Acadian cousins in the 1713 Treaty of Utrecht that ceded Nova Scotia (Acadia) to the British. The colonial governors of both Massachusetts and Nova Scotia used this French and Indian War as an excuse for embarking on a campaign of *ethnic cleansing*. The French and Indian War of 1754–1763 also provided the Puritan-based colonies of Massachusetts Bay (including Maine, which did not become a separate state until 1820) and New Hampshire an opportunity to finally purge their territory of the indigenous Algonquin tribes, pushing them into French Canada where they were better tolerated.[13]

The Acadian Expulsion: The Roots of Manifest Destiny, Ethnic Cleansing, and Cultural Genocide

The roots of Manifest Destiny extend to the colonial era with the Puritan concept of their God-given predestined supremacy over all others. This social philosophy played a crucial role in the Puritans' plan to exterminate Indian groups as well as excluding other whites of different denominational affiliations. The principle of *predestination* that drove policies of discrimination and genocide were introduced into Nova Scotia in the Canadian Maritimes once control over the indigenous Mi'kmaq (Micmac) and French settlers was transferred to the British Colonial governors. The Acadian Expulsion began 100 years after the Quaker persecutions of the mid-1600s when anti-Quaker laws sanctioned the death penalty for anyone professing to be a Quaker within the Puritan colonies.

Colonial Intrusion and Border Battles

In the mid-1700s, the Mi'kmaq's original population was decimated by diseases inadvertently introduced through European contact, reducing the tribe to several thousand Indians, a mere 10% of its pre-Columbian total. The Acadian French, on the other hand, were unique because these male fishermen and coastal farmers lived among the Mi'kmaq, adopting elements of their lifestyle and forming common law families with indigenous women, creating the first substantial *Métis* population in Canada (mixed European and Indian heritage). Thus, the Acadian French differed from most other white colonial settlers in the part of North America that is Canada and the United States in that they integrated into the Mi'kmaq (Micmac) culture, forging a harmonious community of mixed Indian and white people as well as enduring the wrath of the Puritans. The fact that England allowed for French self-governance in Quebec further angered the Yankee Puritans, increasing their angst toward French Catholics, especially those who tolerated the indigenous population.

The expulsion scheme was devised by the British colonial governors of Nova Scotia and Massachusetts (including what is now Maine) who in 1755 authorized the forceful removal of the Acadian French, citing their friendliness with the local Indians as a pretext for this exercise in ethnic cleansing. Yale University history professor John Mack Faragher cites a September 4, 1755, article in the *Pennsylvania Gazette* that justified the expulsion order:

> We are now upon a great and noble Scheme of sending the neutral French out of this Province, who have always been secret enemies, and have encouraged our Savages to cut our Throats. If we effect their Expulsion, it will be one of the greatest Things that ever the English in America; for by all Accounts, that Part of the Country they possess, is as good Land as any in the World: In case therefore we could get some of good English farmers in their Room, this Province would abound with all Kinds of Provisions.[sic][14]

Consequently, some 7,000 French-speaking, Catholic Acadians were forcefully removed from the rich lands and waterways along the shores of the Bay of Fundy so that English colonists could occupy them. This action also gave the British-American colonists an excuse to displace and disperse the Mi'kmaq Indians.

Acadia was the name the French gave to the region comprising Nova Scotia, New Brunswick, Prince Edward Island, Quebec's Gaspe Peninsula, and portions of northern Maine bordering on the Gaspe and New Brunswick. This entire region, except Prince Edward Island and the Cape Breton section of Nova Scotia, was claimed by Great Britain following the Treaty of Utrecht in 1713. The plan to forcefully remove the French, Métis, and Mi'kmaq Indians from this region was orchestrated by William Shirley, governor of Massachusetts Bay in New England, and Charles Lawrence, governor of the

Canadian Maritimes headquartered in Halifax, Nova Scotia.[15] Both colonial leaders, Shirley and Lawrence, ignored the pleas of Major General Paul Mascarene (French Huguenot decent), who was the British military commander of the region prior to the expulsion order. General Mascarene also noted that the Acadian French, Métis, and Mi'kmaq were not a threat and were not involved in any of the French and Indian raids on British colonies in America. But a stronger voice from the past prevailed among the British colonies, that of Cotton Mather (1663–1728), who provided the incendiary anti-French, Indian, and Catholic rhetoric decades earlier. Faragher notes Mather's feelings about this group: "The natives and the French blurred into a common enemy, one Cotton Mather stigmatized as 'Half Indianized French and Half Frenchified Indian'" with the French being the chief source of New England miseries. Clearly, the New England colonial leaders already were setting the stage for their self-interest and not for England. G. G. Campbell, in his history of Nova Scotia notes, "Lawrence had been correct in thinking that the authorities in England, while they had not authorized the expulsion, would be willing to accept the accomplished fact."[15] During the expulsion, Acadian families were rounded up and placed in stockades, and their communities were burned, animals killed, and food supplies destroyed. Harry Bruce, in his history of Nova Scotia notes, "The troops compelled to do the dirty work during 'le grand derangement' were mostly blue-coated American soldiers like (John) Winslow New England Protestants were at last expelling Acadian Catholics. …This was the expulsion: they forced everyone at bayonet point to embark on boats in the midst of confusion, without any concern as to whether they put on the same boat members of the same family…" Bruce also notes,

> The Acadian people were effectively scattered. They were set ashore in the English colonies, along two thousand miles of the American coast. Hundreds were taken to France, many by way of prisons in England. The West Indies received large numbers, and others ended their wanderings in Quebec and in the French possessions along the Mississippi. The sea took heavy toll of them, through sickness and shipwreck. Along the trails and in the fastnesses of the forest many perished of hunger and exposure. …The expulsion did more than drive a people from its land. It disrupted the Acadian community with its traditions and distinctive ways of life, and left it scattered and stranded amidst alien and unsympathetic peoples.[16]

Robert Leblanc, a cultural geographer, notes that this ethnic cleansing exercise lasted from 1755, through the French and Indian War, until the Louisiana Purchase in 1803 at a cost of thousands of French, Métis, and Mi'kmaq lives. More than 10,000 residents were displaced, many sent as slaves or prisoners of war to southern colonies, the Caribbean, and other colonies in the Americas and Europe. They provided an infusion of French into the Louisiana region leading to its unique Acadian–Cajun population. Henry Wadsworth Longfellow depicted this tragedy with his tale, *Evangeline*. Most significant, the Acadian expulsion set the stage for the new U.S. Republic's policy of expulsion, the forceful removal of Indian tribes from coveted lands, making them available for white settlers. LeBlanc noted that Governor Lawrence's plans were clearly to get rid of the French Acadians and open up their lands to New England Yankee Protestants. He lists four migration periods: 1755–1757, 1758–1762, 1763–1767, and 1768–1785 with scattered migrations until 1803. Some of these migrations were initiated by France, Spain, and places in the United States that wanted to remove the Acadians for various reasons. The most successful of these migrants were those who were able to get back to Eastern Canada (notably New Brunswick) and those who were expelled to Louisiana. In Louisiana, a new French Cajun subculture emerged. The displaced Acadians who slipped into Quebec became part of the mill migration to the United States during the 1870 to 1910 era.[17]

The subsequent expulsions by Governor Lawrence were designed to round up stragglers who hid out in New Brunswick at Miramichi, Richibucto, and Buctouche among the Maliseet Indians during the 1755–1756 expulsion. The Maliseet Indians, Algonquin cousins of the Mi'kmaq, resided along the major rivers in what is now New Brunswick. By the end of July 1761, the militia had rounded up more than 1,000 Acadians who were held under military guard in Halifax. They were loaded onto military transport ships in Halifax Harbor in August 1762 and set sail to Boston. However, the Massachusetts general assembly refused to allow them to disembark even temporarily so they could be dispatched to other places like the first wave. The death of Governor Lawrence in late 1760 coupled with the cessation of active combat among French and British troops tended to deflate the anti-Acadian furor. The signing of the Treaty of Paris in 1763 not only eliminated the fear of France's influence in Canada, it also extended the citizenship conditions afforded the Quebec French to the Acadian French, resulting in the return of Acadian refugees within the New England colonies. Many migrated to Quebec Province settling in L'Achigan, Saint-Gregoire, Nicolet, Bécancour, St. Jacques-l'Achigan, St. Philippe, and La Prairie. A determined group of about 900 Acadian exiles in the Boston area set forth on a hazardous 4-month trek in 1766 to New Brunswick Province in an attempt to resettle in their homeland. Later, they would be competing with the Loyalists, among them former Blue Coats forced out of the emerging United States by the rebels.[18]

The ulterior motive for the Acadian expulsion is clouded by the fact that the French, Métis, and Mi'kmaq all clearly stated their neutrality during the ongoing French and British conflicts, refusing to take sides and not participating in the raids cited as justification by Shirley and Lawrence for their removal. The purpose for the Acadian expulsion soon became clear. It was to rid the region of what the Puritans considered to be Indian-loving Catholic

Frenchmen and to provide this fertile land to Protestant Yankee families from Massachusetts (including Maine and parts of New Hampshire), Rhode Island, and Connecticut. Thousands of New Englanders migrated to Nova Scotia during the resettlement period of 1760 to 1765. This included farmers and fishermen who established townships that laid the foundation for the English-speaking communities of Nova Scotia today.

When Nova Scotia, the British name for all that once was French Acadia, became the newest and youngest North American British colony, it anguished over the composition of its assembly. The Puritan settlers wanted an assembly like that of Massachusetts (and New Hampshire) with a weak executive branch, but this was rejected by the other groups as being too radical with disproportionate authority vested in the legislature, which could then be easily manipulated by the majority representation. They chose instead an assembly modeled on that of Virginia, which had a more balanced distribution of government between the executive and legislative branches. The new assembly met in 1758. The government of Nova Scotia consisted of an executive branch comprised of the governor and a council of 12, all appointed by the crown, and the governor and a 12-member legislative council along with the assembly composed the legislative branch. The chief justice was part of the governor's council.

Catholics could neither vote nor be a member of the government. The dynamics of Nova Scotia's government changed markedly following the U.S. Revolutionary War and the influx of Loyalists into Canada. Indeed, when General Gage, George Washington's colleague in the French and Indian Wars, returned to the American colonies in May 1774 as both the military commander of the 13 colonies and royal governor of the Massachusetts Bay Colony, he attempted to establish a stronger executive authority. This did not go well with the assembly, resulting in the declaration of martial law later that year. This, along with his failed attempt at having Samuel Adams and John Hancock arrested, fueled the discontent among the rebels, leading to the so-called Battle of Bunker Hill. Britain recalled Gage, forcing him into retirement, replacing him with General Howe in the 13 colonies and Sir Guy Carleton in British Canada. The change in the 13 colonies was too late given that the seeds of revolution had already been sown, pitting the Loyalists against the rebels.

Changing Spanish America

Introduction

Mexico is a land of contrasts. On the one hand, it embraces globalization, and on the other, it resists change. The country's history traces its current 68 living native languages to the people who have lived for 42,000 years in what is now the Mexican republic. In its quest to be part of the global community, this Mestizo land accelerated its insertion into the global community at the dawn of the 20th century, only to be stopped in its tracks by the very people on whose national identity it built a nation.

In the 1920s, as the Mexican Revolution's most violent stage came to an end and reconstruction began, there was a new impetus coming from the new government to reach back in history and rescue the nation's indigenous past. Vast national projects were started, supporting public education in all its manifestations, including a strong support for the arts. In school textbooks, the figure of the noble, courageous, and wise Indian was elevated to the national consciousness, and in public buildings, a corresponding campaign made use of the most illustrious Mexican muralists to celebrate the grandeur of the nation's pre-Columbian past through their art. The masses were then exposed to the historical roots of the Mexican nation in an ever-present lesson as depicted by these fabulous murals.

Education policy, however, contemplated the immersion of indigenous people into the Mestizo culture. Consequently, it provided for the learning of Spanish with its corollary expectations through which the indigenous population would forsake its identity for that of the Mexican nation, that is, Mestizo. To this day, as in the decades following the consolidation of the regime that emerged from the Mexican Revolution, the country's indigenous past is venerated. However, the contemporary Mexican Indian is seen as backward and is consistently portrayed as cunning or dimwitted on television and in movies.

The story of the Mexican Indian is interwoven by moments of individual achievement laced with a long history of exploitation and attempted cultural genocide. Chicano historian Ramón Eduardo Ruíz in *Triumphs and Tragedy: A History of the Mexican People* writes convincingly about how such iconic figures as Zapotec Indian Benito Juárez, who had an illustrious career in his native Oaxaca state, as a member of the Mexican Supreme Court, and eventually as the country's president, became one of the nation's most admired heroes; but nearly a century and a half after his death, Zapotecs and other native people of the region still live in abject poverty. Even though Mexican history is peppered with examples of individuals who have achieved great success (one of the wealthiest men on earth is Mexican Carlos Slim), the bulk of the population has lived and is living in desperate economic conditions: the individual *triumphs* of the relatively few and the *tragedy* of the many. In this scheme, the indigenous people fare even worse than the general population.

The history of the vanquished has yet to penetrate the consciousness of the Mexican people, not as a poem to declaim the exploits of deceased native heroes, but in the form of unequivocal public policies aimed at improving their lot. The tragedy of what Ruiz writes about is the consistent poor state of affairs under which Mexican people—and, by extension, the native population—have lived for more than 500 years. The exploitation of the Indian population and its descendants has been vastly recorded from many perspectives. The early chronicles of the conquest paint the daily lives of the autochthonous people and their views of the new reality under the Spaniards. The work of Fray Bernardino de Sahagún, for example, depicts in great detail the multiple facets of the lives of central Mexico's inhabitants in terms of overall interaction with each other, their rulers, and their gods. The *General History of the Things of New Spain*, written by Sahagún in the third quarter of the 16th century, anthropologically compiles, from the works and words of the natives, profiles of their belief system. Originally authored in 12 tomes, this history demonstrates the complexity of the socioeconomic, political, and cultural underpinnings of life in much of the Mexica/Aztec land.

The violent encounter of the two worlds and what the future held in store for the native population was already noticeable in the accounts of the stories of the conquest. From the conqueror's perspective, the images left in the pages of *The History of the Conquest of New Spain* describe the meaning of the conquest: search for wealth (gold) and the conversion of souls (religion). In this search, the fierce wars for acquisition of wealth and souls, through the sword and the cross, left the native Mexican population reduced to unimaginable numbers after a century of European presence from nearly 25 million in 1519 to less than one million in 1620. The scars of the conquest and the subsequent subjugation of most indigenous people found in the vast Mexican Territory left an indelible mark on the national consciousness.

A passage in the book *Visión de los vencidos: Relaciones indígenas de la Conquista* illustrates the agony of defeat upon the fall of Tenochtitlan, the center of Mexica/Aztec life, now Mexico City. "…[F]riends, cry and understand that with the results of these events we have lost the Mexican nation."[19] For myriad circumstances, chief among them the stigma of being looked at and treated as the conquered and therefore lesser people, Mexicans have tried to shed their indigenous past, resulting in the ever-present paradox of denying equality to the living Indians while elevating the dead ones. In a country in which the indigenous DNA runs deep, only a handful accepts and welcomes the Indian as part of his own individual self. The contemporary Indians are the *other*: the backward, the poor, and the Mexican who has trouble speaking Spanish fluently.

It can reasonably be assumed that conditions over the last 500 years have impacted the collective psyche of the Mexican nation. In the early part of the 20th century, philosopher Samuel Ramos wrestled with the tendencies, as he saw it, of Mexicans to adopt foreign ideas and practices to resolve internal challenges. At the end of the 19th century, the adoption of positivism, put into practice by the long regime of General Porfirio Diaz, did bring peace to the country, but the price was paid by the indigenous people and the peasants—Mexico was mostly an agrarian society at the time. Eventually, the Mexican Revolution exploded in 1910. Ramos's criticism of Mexican intellectuals, educators, and politicians was their practice of always looking outside instead of inside to explain and meet the challenges facing the nation. Octavio Paz talked about "masks" the Mexican wears to deflect and conceal, at the same time, a reality about himself and about the country: Here is a buried Mexico that is still alive. This concept embraces more than the indigenous reality, but by definition, it includes it, too. A common theme in the writings of these two towering figures of 20th-century Mexico is their attempts to explain the cultural underpinnings of the nation. In doing so, they touched on the deep, yet denied, presence of the past and present Indian influence in contemporary Mexican culture.

The long road to denial started on August 13, 1521, the day when Mexico/Tenochtitlan was taken by the conquerors. It marks the beginning of the Mexico that was built on the ashes—almost literally—of great civilizations. The creation of their world and the development of their people are weaved in a tapestry of history and myth. The grandeur of the Olmecs, Teotihuacans, Toltecs, and others also suffered a defeat once the Mexica/Aztecs fell to the conquering Spaniards. The pre-Hispanic world had ceased to exist because of the encounter between the Europeans and the autochthonous people of what became the Americas. The rapid depopulation of the area due to diseases—many of which were brought by the Europeans—and extreme working conditions created the circumstances for the export of African slaves.

The New Laws of 1542 abolished Indian slavery; in that year, there were nearly 200,000 in such condition, but legal restraints did not stop the practice of labor exploitation for the next 400 years—that is, in the sense that those practices were pretty much consistent during the whole colonial period (1521–1821) and the first 100 years of independent Mexico. From the start of the colonial period with the granting of *encomiendas*—a practice that assured the conquerors large numbers of Indian labor—the autochthonous inhabitants of central Mexico were given by royal decree to the Spaniards. For instance, Hernán Córtez officially received in *encomienda* 20,000 Indians although some historians contend he got 50,000. The *encomienda* system called for the conquerors to offer education to and overall good care of the conquered; in reality, the only intermittent type of education they received was a religious one to convert the native population to Catholicism. In exchange for "taking care" of them, the *encomendado* Indian was expected to supply free labor to the Spaniard for short periods of time. This labor requirement was not to take place during the *encomendado*'s time during which he was tending his own fields. Needless to say, this rarely ever happened.

The abuses to which the indigenous population was exposed contributed to what a contemporary lexicon would call genocide. By the time the Indian population reached its lowest number between 1620 and 1650, there were already 120,000 African slaves in New Spain. Most of them were employed on sugar plantations and in mining activities. That number was kept almost constant throughout the colonial period. It is no small wonder that in many regions of Mexico there is still a very palpable Afro-Mexican influence. This has been accomplished despite myriad sociopolitical and economic forces that have conspired to erase Afro-Mexican history.

Although New Spain's authorities has kept count of free and slave African descendants since the early days of the colonial period through Mexican independence in 1821, the ensuing decades legally erased blacks from the census counts. Upon gaining independence, Mexico abolished slavery and the caste system that has been part and parcel of colonial administration. In this human typology, Indians and blacks as well as the offspring of their mixed marriages and partnerships were also viewed as inferior. The classification of races and ethnicities, with some variations during the 300 years of colonial rule, had the *peninsulares*, the immigrants from Spain, at the top of the caste system. They were followed by the *Criollos*, the children of Spaniards born in the Americas. The *Mestizo*, an offspring of either a *peninsular* or *Criollo* and an Indian—normally a woman—enjoyed the benefit of the doubt as far as acceptability. If a Mestizo resembled a European more than an Indian, then he or she had a better chance of passing as *Criollo*. Below the Mestizo were blacks, mulattos, and sambos.

Once the caste system was abolished, no record of any other race or ethnicity was kept because the aim was to build an egalitarian nation free of the abhorrent classification that had existed before. Consequently, Afro-Mexicans did not appear in official demographic counts; legally they were nonexistent. It has been only recently that Afro-Mexican history and traditions are beginning to be studied. The groundbreaking study conducted by Gonzalo Aguirre Beltrán in 1946 unearthed for the rest of Mexico a piece of hidden history and culture. The three centuries of the caste system lived—and perhaps still lives—in the Mexican collective consciousness as most Mexicans tend to reject both the Indian and, in many cases, the African in him. It is common for Mexicans to consider a person of light skin as "more" beautiful than a "moreno" (dark-skinned one). From 1521, European, inclusive of American, influences have played a key role in perpetuating a Mexican view of what is considered "beautiful." How do these historical and sociopolitical elements play out in the context of the United States–Mexico border? That is partly what occupies this work. This question becomes even more relevant when one considers that after more than 500 years the denial of indigenous and Afro-Mexican culture and rights is real.[20]

New Spain's Adaptations to the New World

Felipe Fernandez-Armesto reminds us that the Spanish–American colonial experience was earlier and far superior to that of the British, French, and Dutch settlements in North America. This process began with Columbus's second expedition and the development on Hispaniola. The Spanish colonies in the Caribbean and Central and South America were more populous and developed at the time of their arrival and, hence, more easily exploitable. They had the Aztec and Inca empires to exploit as well as a sizeable slave workforce. Fernandez-Armesto notes,

> By the end of the sixteenth century—before the French or English had established a single enduring colony anywhere in the hemisphere, the Spanish monarchy in the New World effectively included all the biggest and most productive islands of the Caribbean and a continuous swath of territory from the edge of the Colorado plateau to the north of the River Bio-Bio in southern Chile; it extended from sea to shining sea across the narrow reaches of the hemisphere ... Spain had preempted potential rivals, except on the Brazilian coast, where, by agreement with Spain, Portugal had a series of sugar-producing colonies.[21]

In northern New Spain, the deplorable conditions of the indigenous and rural populations in Mexico have existed since Spain transformed ancient Mexico into a new political entity. Since 1521, the non-European side of Mexico, the great majority of Mexicans, have been on the defensive. Mexico went through 300 years of formal colonial experience. This period is said to be worse for the Indian population. In other times and with other, different, perpetrators, this human catastrophe might have been called genocide. In central Mexico, there were more than 25 million Indians in 1519, the year the conquerors arrived; 100 years later, there were fewer than one million Indians in this part of the country. Slavery was perpetrated through the *encomienda* and *repartimiento* systems. The *encomienda* system was introduced by the Spanish crown as a means of rewarding the conquerors. To illustrate, Hernan Cortes, the conqueror of Mexico, received 20 towns with a population of 23,000 Indians as his reward from the Spanish crown. Cortes was also made the Marquee of the Valley of Oaxaca. The idea of the *encomienda* was to ensure that the conquerors remained loyal to the crown. The Spanish use of Indians for slave labor differed from that of the British colonies in that those receiving land grants from the crown were also responsible for educating, albeit resocializing, the Indian population residing within their specific *encomienda*.

By the 1550s, the crown abolished the *encomienda* system, and this was met with an outcry from the *Criollos*, Mexican-born Spanish. So in its place, the Spanish crown created a system designed to maintain control over the Indians and secure loyalty to their white overlords. Under this new system, the *repartimiento*, free labor from the Indians remained part of this arrangement. In this Indian sharecropper arrangement, indigenous laborers were supposed to work no more than 45 days a year in a period of not longer than a week at a time for the honor of being allowed to live on their traditional lands. And only adults were supposed to engage in this type of labor with free time to spend on their own crops. Instead, Indians were often forced to work during their own harvest times and for periods longer than those prescribed by law and to live under horrid conditions, leading to a rapid decline in their population.

The *repartimiento* system was eventually outlawed and replaced by the *hacienda* system. Under it, Indians and peasants were treated as indentured servants. Again, as in the previous systems of labor, the hacienda had little positive effect on the peasants, who were, for the most part, Indians and Mestizos. Some of these large estates consisted of hundreds of thousands of acres with one, the Sanchez Navarro hacienda, extending more than 11 million acres by the early 1600s. The conditions under which the laborers lived continued unabated until the Mexican Revolution of 1910 destroyed this system of indentured slavery and trickery. Although some of the haciendas were purchased directly from the crown before Mexico's independence, other lands were taken, much like those in the American colonies, by deceit and trickery usually by fraud or coercion. Eventually, many of the Indian communal lands were restored to the tribes by the royal government during the later colonial era, a process followed by the Mexican government following its independence in 1821. Even then, this system continued in many areas of Mexico, providing a model for the United States *Jim Crow* system in the South following the War Between the States (the second U.S. Civil War). Workers living on hacienda land were required to buy the meager things they needed for their existence from the *tienda de raya*—the "company store." This system was specifically designed to keep the Indians and other peasants in perpetual debt, and even following death, the workers' children inherited their debts. The Indians and other peasants lived under these conditions for 300 years.[22]

Adaptations to Colonial Intrusions

Indian tribes in Canada and the United States started to form confederations, consolidating their forces against white intrusions and resulting only in delaying the inevitable. This provided the foundation of Pan-Indianism that exists today in both counties although to a far lesser extent in Mexico. The common "traditional" cultures associated with numerous tribes are actually adaptations made during the colonial era: Sheep, wool, looms, and rugs among the Navajo and hunting buffalo on horseback by the Plains Indians, among others, are adaptations introduced to the New World by the Europeans. Distilled alcohol was introduced to the American Indians by the European colonists. Steel tools allowed for more sophisticated jewelry making as well as mining the stones.

New variations of Christianity emerged both among the black slaves and American Indians. Along with the trappers and traders, conquistadors, and plantation owners came an onslaught of missionaries of Roman Catholic and various Protestant denominations, and each sect attempted to either convert or control the indigenous population. Within this process emerged a mixing of traditional African and/or Indian rituals into the Christian liturgy, especially given that the introduction of "Christianity" was not for the purpose of equal assimilation, but rather for the purpose of forcing the new converts to realize their inferior status vis-à-vis white Christians. These Christian variants occurred mainly because these sects insisted on segregated churches and congregations. Some religions, such as the Puritans and its offshoots, did not attempt to convert either black slaves or American Indians, closing their sects to what they considered heathens or animals. Some tribes radically changed their aboriginal lifestyle to conform to the European model with the hopes of being able to remain on their traditional lands in the southeastern colonies. These were known as the "Five Civilized Tribes" (Cherokee, Choctaw, Chickasaw, Creek, and Seminole) with the Cherokees being the largest of the groups. In order to become "civilized" the Cherokee had to abandon their aboriginal practice of universal suffrage under which all adults, men and women, had one vote, which they cast in the clan townhouses regarding all community matters. They had to disenfranchise women so as to satisfy their Euro–American counterparts. Another condition for these southern tribes was the need to acquire black slaves to work their plantations. They adopted a form of governance based on that of their respective colonies with laws, police, and courts as well as allowing for Christian missionaries and churches—all in the hope of being able to continue to live in their traditional villages as they had for thousands of years.

The so-called civilized Europeans also taught the indigenous peoples how to scalp, a practice falsely linked to the aboriginal "savage." Georg Friederici, in a 1906 article in the *Annual Report of the Smithsonian Institution* notes,

> Scalping in its commonly known form and greatest extent was largely the result of the influence of white people, who introduced firearms, which increased the fatalities in a conflict, brought the steel knife, facilitating the taking of the scalp, and finally offered scalp premiums.[23]

The practice of pitting tribes against each other during the colonial era did much to educate the American Indians in the ways of modern warfare as practiced by the Europeans at the time.

Queen Anne's War (1702–1713), also known as the Spanish Succession, was a more complex conflict involving the English against the French and Spanish, subsequently resulting in battles being fought on three fronts: a renewal of the conflict involving Quebec and Acadia and battles in Spanish Florida and the Carolina colonies as well as battles over Newfoundland and the Hudson Bay region. The fight in the Carolinas and Spanish Florida was primarily for control over the Mississippi River trade routes, a needed ingredient for future inland expansion within the British colonies. This portion of the war led to the virtual destruction of the indigenous tribes within Spanish Florida as well as the creation of new Indian alliances and, subsequently, intertribal conflicts in the Carolinas. These battles involved military resources from the Caribbean as well. Removing the Spanish from this territory led to the creation of the 13th British province—that of Georgia in 1732. In the northeast, the English again fought the French and Wabanaki (Algonquin) Confederacy, and the Iroquois remained neutral.[24]

Cultural adaptation also occurred among ethnic whites as in the case of the French Canadians following the 1713 Treaty of Utrecht allowing the substantial French population, the majority in all of Canada, to retain both their religion and culture. This arrangement left French Canadians in a time warp, maintaining the same lifestyle for the next 200 years, existing in a virtual vacuum, resisting British influences while being denied an infusion of interference from France. What set the French Canadian culture apart from the United States and other British North American colonies was the "seigneurial" system. J. M. S. Careless, in his book *Canada: Story of Challenge*, articulated the essence of the seigneurial system and how it differed from the British and American system.[25]

The major difference here was that New France was based on an authoritarian hierarchy with power concentrated with the Catholic clergy: "Power was concentrated at the top of society, and the mass of the colonists were used to obeying authority, not to governing their own lives."[25] But he goes on to say that this did not necessarily mean that they fostered an attitude of dependence and meek docility—only that they did not challenge matters of religion, government, and class relations. Hence, unlike the British North American colonies, notably those that broke away to form the United States of America, there was little demand for religious independence, self-government, or social equality among the populace of New France apart from the rebellion of the late 1830s. Even then, the Patriote and ultramontane nationalists saw the rural, agrarian French Canadian lifestyle as being the ideal model for maintaining the French culture. This was especially true for the French residing along the St. Lawrence River agricultural basin.

Colonial Intrusion and Border Battles

The parish priest (*cure*) worked with the male-dominated extended family (*famille souche*) in regulating the rural lifestyle of their agricultural society. The land grants made to the seigneurs by the French crown were mainly along the St. Lawrence River and were long and narrow, often only 100 to 200 feet wide and miles in length with the wood lot furthest from the river and the fields closest to the water source. Habitants leased farm plots from the seigneurs. These collections of closely situated farmsteads formed small communities called *rangs*, which together former the larger parish.[26]

New France brought to America its own feudal system, one that had ended in England in the 17th century but continued on in British-controlled Ireland. In Canada, the seigneurial system provided a unit of local government and defense as well as a means for settling the land. The seigneuries in Canada were mostly given to the Catholic church by the French whereby the common folks, the habitants, then leased farms from the land owners. Both the seigneurs and habitants comprised the parish membership. The system in New France differed considerably from that in France in that social distance between the seigneurs and the habitants was not that great given that mutual cooperation was needed to survive in the wilderness of the New World. The habitant owed a few days work per year, *corvees*, on the seigneur's own farm and had to pay a small annual rent (*cens et rentes*), which could be paid with agricultural products. Given this relationship between the seigneurs and habitants, the latter differed greatly from his counterpart in France in that he was no downtrodden peasant but rather a self-sufficient, self-respected farmer. The parish priest (*cure*) played the most important role mediating relations between the seigneurs and the habitants.

And although Huguenots were also present in Canada, they played an insignificant role in Lower Canada, which became Quebec Province. Quebec Province was dominated by the Jesuits and Bishop Laval, the Catholic head of New France, who made French Canada an ultramontane citadel. The ultramontanism began in France in the 17th century in reaction to the king's interference in matters of the Catholic Church. As stated earlier, ultramontanism essentially posits submission to papal authority and the supremacy of the Catholic Church over the state. Toward this end, the Catholic Church exercised its power through its control over the educational institutions in New France, a phenomenon that continued even following British control in 1760.

The history of the French Canadian community resided with the cures. Parish priests kept all records, and all decisions awaited their approval. Religion and education were inseparable institutions in French Canada even following British control. The French Catholic Church defined the French Canadians within their social, cultural, and normative systems. However, the patriarchal family provided the real basis of rural life in the parish. Large families were encouraged by the church so as to maintain a sizeable population to challenge the influx of immigrants from Great Britain, Ireland, and Europe.

Daily prayers and compulsory church attendance helped weld the family into a sacred unit. Mores and folkways provided effective, informal modes of control both within the family and the larger parish community. The Catholic Church exerted considerable control over the family both morally and economically as the parish or community's ultimate father. Social mobility was not encouraged among the working class (habitants). Sons took on the occupations of their fathers, such as farming, logging, trapping, or fishing and later mill and factory work. The women and children held subservient positions in the family scheme. In this hierarchy, both the community and family were controlled by men with the parish priest holding the highest status, followed by the family patriarch and his married sons by age seniority, and the women and children ranked last, playing submissive, subordinate roles. The Catholic Church itself provided the highest aspirations for the French Canadians and nearly every extended family had at least one member in the church as a priest, brother, or nun. Like many religious orders of the day, women were subservient to their male counterparts within the Catholic Church. Nuns (sisters) either performed servitude roles for the priests and brothers or taught in the parish parochial schools. Brothers, or friars, taught higher education within the Catholic parochial system. This system was adequate until the fertile farmlands, notably those along the St. Lawrence River, became overused with fewer subdivisions available for married sons.[27]

The Emerging United States and Its Expansionist Mandate 3

Manifest Destiny and White Protestant Supremacy: Boundary Maintenance 1776–1865

The newly independent United States Republic expanded rapidly from its original 13 British colonies with intrusions into both British and Spanish (later Mexican) territories while, at the same time, exterminating and/or consolidating the indigenous tribes onto squalid reservations. Clearly, the longest conflict in the United States was its Indian Wars. The Puritan Yankees' experimentation with Indian removal and extermination in New Hampshire and other parts of the northeast coupled with the successful expulsion of the Acadian French from most of the Maritime provinces only embolden their resolve to continue on with these policies once the New Republic was established following the Revolutionary War. Colin Calloway, in his book *The American Revolution in Indian Country*, posited that the real war for independence from an oppressive intruder was that waged by American Indians in an effort to save their traditional homelands. He stated that the Indians' "War of Independence" was well under way before 1775 and was waged on many fronts—economic, cultural, political, and military—and continued long after 1783.[1]

All of Indian Country east of the Mississippi River was engulfed in the ravages of the Revolutionary War, forcing Indian refugees into western French-held territory and south into Spanish-held territory. No one treated American Indians as badly as did the Americans. In the end, American Indians were excluded from the republic. It soon became clear that the American revolutionaries wanted to replace the British, French, and Spanish as colonial powers so that they alone could dominate the continent. The emerging New Republic was committed to expansionism from the start with a vision of a new society—one based on white supremacy and free from interference from Native Americans or those who supported them, such as the French Canadians.

One of the first actions of the New Republic was to refine what constitutes an American Indian (later Alaska Native). This was a necessary step if any legal protection was to be afforded this ethnic group. In this regard, the United States chose to restrict the legal status of American Indians as it did for African slaves, instead relegating both groups as "lesser humans." Accordingly, this process consolidated American Indians into political units that did not necessarily exist prior to U.S. independence, raising questions as to who was a federally recognized Indian. It is these statutory definitions, subjected to judicial review, that have regulated Indian policy from the late 18th century to the present. It was difficult to gain sympathy from the first leaders of the United States because most were slaveholders, including Washington and Jefferson. Indeed, of the first 18 U.S. Presidents, from Washington to U.S. Grant's term (1869–1877), all but three were slaveholders. The exceptions were the second and sixth presidents, John Adams and John Quincy Adams, and Abraham Lincoln although the White House during the Lincoln administration was staffed by black slaves.[2]

George Washington set the stage in September 1783 with his policy statement on "Indian and Land Policy" in which he referred to Indians as being less than human and equating them with wolves and other predatory animals. By referring to American Indians as simple-minded savages, President Washington set the stage for the *trickery by treaty* government policy that was to dominate U.S.–Indian relations during the treaty era from 1783 until 1947. This was in response to the fact that white settlers were encroaching on Indian lands and establishing unauthorized settlements from the beginning of the republic. The Indian land grab soon came under the exclusive authority of the U.S. Congress, which began the farce of treaty negotiations with those they selected as Indian leaders. These treaties were written in English, a language not common to all Indian groups at the time, and often after the Indians were sufficiently lubricated with alcohol. Thus, under President Washington's advisement, the treaty process of deception officially began October 15, 1783. And in anticipation of its long war with Indians, the War Department was established by the first Congress under the new Constitution on August 7, 1789.

President Thomas Jefferson, prior to the acquisition of lands west of the Mississippi River following the Louisiana Purchase in 1803, offered a false hope to Indian groups still residing east of the former boundaries of the United States. The Jefferson policy was that these tribes could remain on their traditional homeland if they changed their cultural ways to those of the Anglo-Protestant model. Those groups that followed this advice became known as the "civilized tribes." However, with the Louisiana Purchase, President Jefferson now felt that he had another solution to what he described as the "Indian problem"—that of creating new homelands for Indian groups in the territory west of the Mississippi River, thus sowing the seeds for the U.S. formal policy of Indian expulsion, or ethnic cleansing, known officially as the "Removal Policy." President Jefferson initiated the Lewis and Clark Expedition led by Meriwether Lewis and William Clark in May 1804 to explore the newly acquired Louisiana Purchase mainly as a scouting expedition in order to gain a better knowledge of the Indian tribes residing in this new addition to the United States and how they might hinder opening up the territory to white settlers. The 18-month expedition mapped out the territory and made famous the Shoshone woman, Sacajawea, who assisted in this process. Indeed, today (2000–2008) she adorns the collectable, gold-colored U.S. dollar coin. What is often omitted is her French Canadian husband, Toussaint Charbonneau, an interpreter with the expedition and the father of her Métis child also depicted on the coin.[3]

The Louisiana Purchase doubled the size of the United States with lands extending west of the Mississippi River, north to the Canadian border, and east of the Missouri River, setting the stage for the War of 1812, the War with Mexico in 1846, and the U.S. Civil War (second Civil War) as well as the bloody Indian Wars of the 19th century. The moral justification for Manifest Destiny is articulated by the words of the sixth U.S. President, John Quincy Adams, a staunch New England Puritan, in a letter to his father, John Adams, the second U.S. President:

> The whole continent of North America appears to be destined by Divine Providence to be peopled by one nation, speaking one language, professing one general system of religion and political principles, and accustomed to one general tenor of social usages and customs.[4]

Clearly, Adams linked the destiny of the United States to the Old Testament's divine providence. From this perspective, providence had provided the North American continent for the United States to conquer, occupy, and convert. Here, the "finger of God" directed the Puritans to America for its domination. White supremacy under the dictates of Manifest Destiny coupled with the newly purchased Louisiana Purchase emboldened states, notably those in the south, to forcefully remove American Indian tribes west of the Mississippi into an area designated Indian Territory (later the State of Oklahoma).[5]

Indian Removal: The U.S. Experiment with Ethnic Cleansing

Indian sovereignty posed a major obstacle to Indian removal. The first of a series of judicial reviews was *Johnson v. McIntosh* in 1823. Here, Chief Justice John Marshall of the U.S. Supreme Court reinforced the authority of the federal government as major arbitrator with Indian groups, overthrowing the purchase of tribal lands by private individuals prior to the establishment of the Trade and Intercourse Act established on July 22, 1790. In his decision, Justice Marshall made reference to the European colonial tenet guaranteeing Indian tribes collective occupancy of their traditional lands even when colonial ownership changed, thus establishing the legal rights of Indian tribes to occupy their traditional lands under the concept of "aboriginal title" or "Indian title." In this ruling, the High Court protected Indian lands from being taken by individuals, corporations, or political entities other than the U.S. Government and then only through purchase or conquest.

Solutions to the Indian Problem changed dramatically under the presidency of Andrew Jackson (1829–1837). Jackson's anti-Indian sentiments were well known, fostering strong support for the forceful removal of the major southern tribes, including the Five Civilized Tribes, west of the Mississippi River into Jefferson's Indian Territory. Toward this end, President Jackson was instrumental in getting the Indian Removal Act passed by a bitterly divided Congress.

> An Act to provide for an exchange of lands with the Indians residing in any of the states or territories, and for their removal west of the Mississippi.
> Be it enacted … that it shall and may be lawful for the President of the United States to cause so much of any territory belonging to the United States, west of the river Mississippi, … to be divided into a suitable number of districts, for the reception of such tribes or nations of Indians…[6]

The Removal Act set the stage for the State of Georgia to lay claim to parts of the Cherokee Nation lying within its boundaries. Ironically, although Jefferson's earlier concerns were with his state's (Virginia's) westward expansion, he inadvertently set the stage for Georgia's challenge to federal exclusive jurisdiction over Indian Country leading to two more U.S. Supreme Court decisions. Following Jackson's ascendency to the Presidency, Georgia attempted to extinguish Indian title within its state boundaries, essentially invalidating the laws of the Cherokee Nation. The catalyst for this sudden change was white prospectors finding gold within the Cherokee Nation boundaries and a massive invasion of whites, a malady that continue to subvert future treaty conditions. This event led to the 1831 U.S. Supreme Court case, *Cherokee Nation v. the State of Georgia*:

> This bill is brought by the Cherokee nation, praying an injunction to restrain the state of Georgia from the execution of certain laws of that state, which, as is alleged, go directly to annihilate the Cherokees as a political society, and to seize, for the use of Georgia, the lands of the nation which have been assured to them by the United States in solemn treaties repeatedly made and still in force. …Though the Indians are acknowledged to have an unquestionable, and, heretofore, unquestioned right to the lands they occupy, until that right shall be extinguished by a voluntary cession to our government; yet it may well be doubted whether those tribes which reside within the acknowledged boundaries of the United States can, with strict accuracy, be denominated foreign nations. They may, more correctly be denominated *domestic dependent*

nations. They occupy a territory which we assert a title independent of their will, which must take effect in point of possession when their right of possession ceases. Meanwhile, they are in a state of pupilage. Their relation to the United States resembles that of a ward to his guardian. ...The Court has bestowed its best attention on this question, and, after mature deliberation, the majority is of opinion that an Indian tribe or nation within the United States is not a foreign state in the sense of the Constitution, and cannot maintain an action in the Courts of the United States. ...The Motion for an injunction is denied.[7]

The U.S. Supreme Court heard yet another challenge in the following session, this one involving the arrest of white missionaries serving the Cherokee Nation. This case involved Samuel A. Worcester, a missionary who refused to abide by the Georgia law forbidding whites to reside within the Cherokee Nation without first swearing an oath of allegiance to the State of Georgia and obtaining an official permit:

The plaintiff is a citizen of the state of Vermont, condemned to hard labor for four years in the penitentiary of Georgia; under colour of an act which he alleges to be repugnant to the Constitution and laws of the United States, the rights, if they have any, the political existence of a once numerous and powerful people, the personal liberty of a citizen, are all involved in the subject now to be considered. ...The Cherokee Nation, then, is a distinct community occupying its own territory, with boundaries accurately described, in which the laws of Georgia can have no force, and which the citizens of Georgia have no right to enter, but with the assent of the Cherokees themselves, or in conformity with treaties, and with the acts of Congress. The whole intercourse between the United States and this nation, is, by our Constitution and laws, vested in the government of the United States. ...It is the opinion of this Court that the judgment of the Superior Court for the county of Gwinnett, in the state of Georgia, condemning Samuel A. Worcester to hard labor in the penitentiary of the state of Georgia, for four years, was pronounced by that Court under colour of a law which is void, as being repugnant to the Constitution, treaties, and laws of the United States, and ought, therefore, to be reversed and annulled.[8]

These early decisions of the U.S. Supreme Court laid the foundation for policies relevant to federally recognized Indian tribes and what was to be termed "Indian Country." Chief Justice John Marshall, in the 1831 *Cherokee Nation v. Georgia* decision, established that Indian tribes were "domestic dependent nations," essentially protected wards of the U.S. Government. The 1832 *Worcester v. Georgia* decision further articulated what constitutes Indian Country by noting that tribes were distinct political entities with territorial boundaries (established by the U.S. Government) and land held in common, protected by the federal government. This decision consolidated the federal government's authority over Indian Country, superseding that of the states, with the exception of those states that had prior recognition and protective treaties with their tribes (which were eventually transferred to federal protection status). Initially, Indian Country reflected the boundaries assigned to tribes, including those removed to Indian Territory west of the Mississippi River where tribes were allowed to administer their own affairs as long as they conformed to the moral standards of the missionaries and Indian Agents assigned to them as representatives of the U.S. Government. That said, the era of removal began with the U.S. Army acting as the enforcing agent. Although the Indian removal became official U.S. policy with passage of the Indian Removal Act of 1830, Gloria Jahoda traces the removal era to 1813 to the Creek War under General Andrew Jackson. Later it was President Andrew Jackson who initiated the physical removal of American Indians under the guns and bayonets of the U.S. Army.[9]

Jackson, an unabashed white supremacist, subscribed to the *trickery by treaty* format established during the Washington administration. Here, tribes were often duped or coerced into signing treaties resulting in their removal to Indian Territory. Indian removal clearly indicated that the United States had no intention of accepting nonwhites into the larger American society, one that openly welcomed Europeans to help populate the emerging nation. And the fact that the U.S. Government would completely ignore the marked changes that the Five Civilized Tribes made in radically changing their societies in order to conform to the Euro–American format showed the prevailing racist attitudes that supported either physical and/or cultural genocide. Moreover, a common government ploy was to cause divisions within Indian groups, pitting one faction against another. This "divide-and-conquer" technique was contrary to the long-held consensus model stemming from the aboriginal harmony ethos. One of the most dramatic illustrations of the policy was the Cherokee removal, known as the Trail of Tears.

Tribes were often duped or coerced into signing treaties resulting in their removal to Indian Territory. The Cherokee removal is an early example of this process. The forceful removal of the majority of the Cherokees in 1838, also reflects the duplicity of federal policy in its clandestine attempts to cause dissention within tribes by often legitimizing certain groups that they felt they could better influence. The 1830 Indian Removal Act compelled all southeastern tribes to relocate to Indian Territory west of the Mississippi River. The State of Georgia used this act as a pretext for its intrusion into the Cherokee Nation, confiscating national property, including schools, council houses, printing presses, and other community facilities and, at the same time, condoning raids into Cherokee villages and plantations by white vigilantes known as "pony clubs," a forerunner of the Ku Klux Klan later formulated in response to Reconstruction following the Civil War. No federal action was afforded the Cherokees despite treaties and Supreme Court decisions guaranteeing Indian protection under the federal role of *parens partriae*. Indeed, Georgia intensified its actions against the Cherokee Nation because they felt President Jackson condoned their efforts.[10]

Intrusions into Canada

Now a power within the Americas, the United States again had designs of controlling all of British North America. The "War Hawks," notably John C. Calhoun of South Carolina and Henry Clay of Kentucky, wanted to declare war on Great Britain under the guise of punishing them for impressing U.S. seamen but with the ultimate purpose of conquering Canada. On June 18, 1812, a divided Congress barely supported a declaration of war against Great Britain. President James Madison signed the war measure, marking the first time the United States had declared war on another nation. Any hopes of annexing Canada were quickly dashed when Canadians mustered their support for Britain and not the United States. The War of 1812 ended in a stalemate 3 years later with the Treaty of Ghent in 1815. The War of 1812 ended the use of armed conflict in order to expand northward to Canada but this issue was not settled until boundaries were finalized in the 1870s. It also provided the embarrassment of Washington, DC, being attacked, a feat not accomplished again until the September 11, 2001 terrorist attack on the Pentagon.

Essentially, the War of 1812 aided Canada in developing its own sense of self-determination given that it provided the greatest number of military forces in the conflict. The U.S. invasion of Canada also served to forge a sense of nationalism uniting an otherwise divided country. With the United States as the aggressor, both Upper Canada (English Canada) and Lower Canada (French Canada) united in repulsing U.S. forces. Indeed, many of the English Canadians fighting the United States were U.S.-born loyalists who fled during the American Revolution. The War of 1812 ended future U.S. efforts to take Canada from Great Britain, instead setting the stage for the eventual process of Canadian Confederation in 1867. G. G. Campbell notes, The War had done much to stimulate local pride and patriotism. The Bluenose had shown himself a match for his Yankee cousin when it came to seamanship—or to fighting, for that matter. Another feature of the War of 1812 was the migration of blacks fleeing the United States to Canada.

British North America was the term used for its colonies following the American Revolution. A number of significant events occurred during the period from the War of 1812 until the formation of a unified Confederation in 1867. Until this time, British North America consisted of "Lower" (Quebec) and "Upper" (Ontario) Canada and the Atlantic provinces (Nova Scotia, New Brunswick, Prince Edward Island). In 1837, a series of small-scale revolts were staged by the French Canadians in reaction to attempts toward forceful assimilation into British Canadian society. Both Quebec and Ontario had their own locally elected legislative assembly while still being ruled by crown-appointed colonial leaders, including the governor, executive council, and legislative council. At the same time, a border dispute was festering along the Maine–New Brunswick–Quebec borders. Stanley Ryerson detailed the ongoing conflict between the United States and New Brunswick in what was coined the "Aroostook War," in which the United States was attempting to annex the rich forest lands lying between New Brunswick and Quebec. The Aroostook War, also referred to as the "Pork and Beans War," was part of the mounting tensions at this time even though it was an undeclared, nonviolent border confrontation occurring at the same time as the uprising in Lower Canada. Interestingly, New Hampshire–born Daniel Webster, then U.S. Secretary of State in the Van Buren (1837–1841) administration, was a major player in negotiating the U.S. (Maine) and British North American (Quebec, New Brunswick) border, which, in the end, favored the United States (The Webster-Ashburton Treaty of 1842).[11]

The leader of the Ontario rebellion, William Lyon MacKenzie, died during the Upper Canada revolt and the attack on Toronto. The Lower Canada revolt involved French Canadians led by Louis J. Papineau and was a more substantial uprising but also was repressed, resulting in Papineau fleeing to New York State in the United States. Pierre Vallieres, leader of the *Front de liberation du Quebec* (FLQ) in the 1960s and 1970s, claimed that Papineau's real interest was to protect the interests of French elite, the patriots, at the expense of the habitants and not to usher in a popular revolution in Lower Canada. Nonetheless, French nationalism in Lower Canada (Quebec Province) led to the creation of the *Fils de la Liberte*, a group of French Catholic patriots fashioning themselves after the Sons of Liberty during the American Revolution. This movement led to the establishment of other French ethnic organizations, such as the *Institut Canadien* in 1844, Montreal's first French public library, and the newspaper *L'Avenir* in 1847. These rebellions forced the issue of the formation of a union between Upper and Lower Canada, an effort led by Britain through Lord Durham.

In 1840, the Union Bill was introduced, establishing the Province of Canada along with a cabinet-type executive accountable to the elective legislature. The Union became effective in 1848 but was still seen as an effort toward forced assimilation by the French Canadians, a fact evident in Lord Durham's report of 1839 that stated it had been a mistake to try to preserve a French Canadian nationality in the midst of Anglo–American colonies and states. The Durham report notes that in order to elevate the French Canadians from hopeless inferiority they must be given "our" English character by being engulfed in a British North American union. Hence, it would then be to their advantage to assimilate to the English-speaking majority. This Union did not address the issue of the Atlantic colonies. An alternative Union was also under consideration at this time, one with the United States, with some support from elements of both the Anglo and French Canadians, each with their own interests in mind. French Canadian radicals supported the ideological concept of ultramontanism, the idea of the supremacy of the Catholic Church over the state in Canada with submission to papal authority. In this sense, both the French and Irish Catholics agreed. But the Irish raids from the United States as well as the continued harassment of Acadian Catholics in northern New England along the international border quickly dissolved any reality of a Canadian–U.S. union.[12]

The New Frontier: Acquiring Spanish/Mexican Territory

The Adams-Onís Treaty of 1819

The role of Anglo settlers from the United States into its southern neighbor had its beginnings with the War of 1812. Although the major objective of the war was United States expansion into British Canada, Spain nervously watched as U.S. forces entered its territory in Florida and fought its last major battle in New Orleans. Stung by France's sale of its former buffer territory—the Louisiana Purchase—Spain was now compelled to populate its northeastern border as a protection from the encroaching United States. A major factor in this process was the Adams-Onís Treaty of 1819. The Treaty of Amity, Settlement, and Limits between the United States of America and His Catholic Majesty (also known as the Transcontinental Treaty of 1819, the Florida Treaty, or the Adams-Onís Treaty) ended the Seminole Wars, ceding Florida to the United States as well as establishing the Mexico–U.S. border at the Sabine River. Here, Spain paid the United States $5 million for Florida while relinquishing claims west of the Sabine River, finally ending its opposition to France's right to sell the Louisiana Territory.[13]

The treaty ended the U.S. claim that the Louisiana Purchase included Spanish-held territory up to the Rio Grande and the Rocky Mountains, including what was then Texas and New Mexico. By selling Florida and forgoing its claims to Oregon Territory in the Northwest, Spain was able to establish its claim to Texas and the New Mexico territories (including what is now Arizona, Utah, and Nevada) maintaining a buffer between the United States and its California colonies. Unfortunately, although the Adams-Onís Treaty was signed on February 22, 1819, it was not ratified until 3 years later on February 22, 1821. Mexico's independence provided the United States another opportunity to break a treaty challenging its own border agreements regarding the U.S.–Mexico border. Nonetheless, the Adams-Onís Treaty necessitated Spain's efforts to populate its territories along the

U.S. border. This endeavor opened the door to empresario contracts with U.S. expatriates.

The Empresario Land Grants

Eight months prior to independence, a number of settlers from the United States petitioned for land grants. Moses Austin was granted the first empresario permit on January 17, 1821, allowing him to settle 300 families in what is now Texas. Moses Austin left Missouri for Mexico due to the better land deals offered by Spain. In the United States, two major events precipitated the migration south to Mexico. One was the economic panic of 1819, and the other was the high cost of public land. The economic panic of 1819 resulted in the loss of numerous holdings notably in the newly opened western United States, leaving many landholders destitute and bitter. Complicating this situation was the high cost of public land. The price per acre was set by Congress at $2, payable in four installments. In 1820, the price was slashed to a dollar and a quarter per acre, but the bill had to be paid in full at the time of purchase, making these lands available only to the affluent. In Mexico, good land was available at 12.5 cents per acre with 6 years to pay. Much of this land was conveniently located in the eastern interior provinces close to the U.S. border. Texas/Coahuila was part of this territory. Mexico's independence from Spain on September 27, 1821, did not immediately alter these arrangements. But later difficulties arose due to the differences that existed between the Republic of Mexico and the United States of America. Two areas of contrast involved the issue of slavery and women's rights. Mexico outlawed slavery while continuing the Iberian legal tradition of recognizing women's property rights—events that would not occur in the United States for decades and after considerable internal conflict.

The senior Austin died during the preparations for the settlement, and his son, Stephen F. Austin, took over the responsibilities as empresario of the Austin grant. The empresario became the de facto lord or governor of his land grant, including the subcontracting families. However, neither the empresario nor the subgrantee settlers owned their land outright. Instead, empresarios were awarded a premium for each 100 families settled under their contract. Austin's premium was 23,000 acres per 100 settlers to his contracted lands. These land grants were interspersed with other elements of the Spanish frontier community, which consisted of Catholic missions, presidios (frontier garrisons), ranches, farms, and towns. The empresario grants in Texas (Coahuila and Tejas) continued following the establishment of the Republic of Mexico on September 27, 1821, with the largest owners, including Austin, Green de Witt, and Haden Edwards.

Under the Imperial Colonization Law, immigrants had to be Catholics or convert to Catholicism. Each married settler family potentially received one league (silio) of 4,428 acres of combined pastureland and farmland.

The Emerging United States and Its Expansionist Mandate

The family received one labor (177 acres) of farmland and if the new settler desired to raise cattle, then he could get 24 labors of pastureland (4,251 acres) as well. Unmarried settlers were granted one-fourth this amount. Mexico held the deed to the settler's land for 6 years. Title transfer was contingent upon all conditions being met. The Republic of Mexico continued this practice stipulated in its national decree of August 18, 1824. These conditions were then enacted by the Legislature of Coahuila and Texas on March 24, 1825. The limit of a single empresario was 800 families. The conditions of the empresarios were as follows. They were required to

- Establish boundaries of the proposed colony
- Respect the legal titles already existing in their proposed colony
- Settle the required number of families within 6 years
- Settle Catholic families of good moral character
- Prohibit criminals
- Organize and command a national militia force
- Make all official and public communications in Spanish
- After April 6, 1830, bar immigrants from adjoining countries, notably the United States of America

Although the Anglo–American immigration into Texas began with the Austin empresario during Spanish rule, the vast majority of expatriate Americans came with the Mexican Republic law of August 18, 1824, and state colonization law of March 24, 1825. A month following passage of the state colonization law in 1825, the governor of the combined State of Coahuila and Texas contracted for 2,400 American emigrant families. Two empresarios, Haden Edwards and Robert Leftwich, each contracted for the maximum 800 families. The flood of Anglo–Americans continued until 1832. Mexican empresarios joined this movement to populate Coahuila and Texas as is evident by the listing of the other land contractors of this time: de Witt, Thorn, de León, Purnell, Lovell, Milam, Wavell, Wilson, Woodbury, Vehlein, Burnet, Cameron, Exeter, Hewetson, Power, McMullen, McGloin, Vehlein, de Zavala, Dominguez, Padilla, Chambers, Filisola, Beales, and Royuela. The Beales and Royuela empresarios were the last granted under the law of March 24, 1825.

The Austin contracts were the most successful empresarios. The census of 1827 indicated the Austin colonies to be about 2,000 and 5,600 in 1831. Also successful were the empresarios of de Witt and de León. Others that had varying degrees of success were those of McMullen and McGloin, Robertson, Milan, Hewetson, Power, Zavala, Burnet, and Vehlien. And those that established no permanent settlements include Wavell, Wilson, Wilson and Exeter, Woodbury, Cameron, Dominquez, Filisola, Padilla and Chambers, Thorn, Purnell and Lovell, Bales and Royuela, Campos, Beales, and Grant.

It is estimated that the predominant Anglo–American empresarios totaled 30,000 at the time of the Texas Revolution in 1836.[14]

Mexico soon became wary of the growing Anglo–American emigrants, especially following the Fredonian Rebellion when the Edwards brothers led an uprising and declared independence in 1826. The Edwards brothers (Haden and Benjamin) were granted empresarial grants in April 1825 entitling them to settle up to 800 families in the Nacogdoches area just north of the Austin grant. Their authoritarian methods of governance alienated many of the original residents in the region, which led to a probe by the regional political leader, José Antonio Saucedo. Haden Edwards and his political machine were investigated for oppression and corruption leading to the dispatch of a Mexican military force into the region led by the military commander of Texas, Lieutenant Colonel Mateo Ahumada. The Edwards brothers mustered their own militia and declared their empresario an independent republic called Fredonia. They even appealed to the United States for assistance in their rebellion. However, their neighbors in Texas, including Anglo–Americans, Hispanics, and Native Americans, opposed the Edwards brothers' rebellion and assisted Ahumada in putting it down. The short-lived rebellion and independent Republic of Fredonia ended on January 31, 1827, when the remnants of the revolutionists fled across the Sabine River to the United States.[15]

Anglo–American emigrants benefited from the chaos during the Mexican fight for independence (1810–1821) and the aftermath of forging a viable republic. During this transitional decade, Spanish policy endured, extending the status quo for the empresarios. During the first decade of postcolonial rule, Mexico, like its neighbors to the north, encountered contravening political perspectives on how to govern the new country. The main battles were between factions supporting a monarch, a decentralized federation, or a centralized government. During the early years of independence, Mexico went from being a short-lived monarchy with Augustín de Iturbride as emperor to a republican federalist state in 1824 only to succumb to a centralized regime in 1830. With the latter came efforts to enforce the dictates of the Mexican Constitution, including in the Anglo-dominated colony of Texas. Following the Emperor's abdication and the emergence of a federal republic, Guadalupe Victoria became Mexico's first president. It was during his term that the new nation became leery of Anglo–American aggression in Texas as illustrated by the Fredonian revolt. Indeed, the impact of the Mexican Congress's curtailment of Anglo–American immigration was felt in New Mexico Territory as well. Here, the bulk of Anglo–Americans were traders without empresario status. Even then, the New Mexico delegate to the Mexican Congress, Manuel de Jesús Rada, encouraged the establishment of foreign empresarios to create factories and mines in the territory. The worsening crises in Texas obviated goodwill endeavors initiated between the United States and Mexico relevant to expanding travel and trade in New Mexico.

The Mexican Constitution and the Slavery Issue

Serving his full term, Victoria was succeeded by his secretary of war, Gómez Pedraza. Although Pedraza won the vote, he was quickly overthrown by a military coup, making Vincent Guerrero the actual ruler. Inaugurated in April 1829, Guerrero issued his decree abolishing slavery throughout the Republic of Mexico in September, sending a shock wave throughout the Anglo settlers in Texas. Texas, however, was successful in avoiding Guerrero's decree due to a clause in the colonization laws guaranteeing the settlers security of their property, including their slaves. Another military coup in January 1830 replaced Guerrero with his vice president, General Anastacio Bustamante.

President Bustamante was instrumental in getting Congress to pass a decree on April 6, 1830, that would fuel the Texas Revolution. Four of the 18 articles of the Bustamante Decree, as it came to be known, were points of contention. Article 3 proposed closer oversight of the colonies, articles 9 and 11 were designed to curb further immigration from the United States, and article 10 enforced Mexico's antislavery laws:

> Article 3. The government is authorized to name one or more commissioners who shall visit the colonies of the frontier states and contract with the legislatures of said states for the purchase, on behalf of the Federal government, of lands deemed suitable for the establishment of colonies of Mexicans and other nationalities; and the said commissioners shall make, with the existing colonies, whatever arrangements seem expedient for the security of the republic. The said commissioners shall supervise the introduction of new colonists and the fulfilling of their contract for settlement, and shall ascertain to what extent the existing contracts have been completed.

> Article 9. The introduction of foreigners across the northern frontier is prohibited under any pretext whatsoever, unless the said foreigners are provided with a passport issued by the agent of the republic at the point whence the said foreigners set out.

> Article 10. No change shall be made with respect to the slaves now in the states, but the Federal government and the government of each state shall most strictly enforce the colonization laws, and prevent the further introduction of slaves.

> Article 11. In accordance with the right reserved by the general congress in the seventh article of the law of, August 18, 1824, it is prohibited that emigrants, from nations bordering on this republic shall settle in the states or territory adjacent to their own nation. Consequently, all contracts not already completed and not in harmony with law are suspended.[16]

Ironically, in 1822, Bustamante had been a strong advocate of the Austin colony and the empresario system. Moreover, Stephen Austin continued to support Bustamante despite his 1830 decree. Bustamante's reign ended in December 1832 when Gómez Pedraza finally ascended to the presidency he had originally won in 1828. This action allowed Pedraza to serve the final 3 months of his constitutional 4-year term. More significant, however, was the ascendance of the Criollo Antonio López de Santa Anna to the presidency on April 1, 1833. He was the Mexican leader most intricately involved with Texas independence, the Mexican War, and the Gadsden Purchase. He subsequently served five terms as president within a 22-year span. Tejas Anglo–American settlers despised Santa Anna, mainly for his enforcement of Mexico's antislavery laws. Clearly, Santa Anna's efforts to consolidate his authority by changing sides once duly elected as president upset many of the Anglo–American immigrants. Santa Anna supported Pedraza's return to the presidency and used this as a vehicle for becoming the leader of the Liberal Republican Party and rising to the presidency himself. But once president, Santa Anna switched allegiances and supported the conservative Centralist Party—the party of the military and ecclesiastical aristocracy. With support of both the military and the Catholic Church, Santa Anna held considerable power. During this chaotic time, Austin was incarcerated in Mexico City and awaited trial on charges of disaffection. However, with no court willing to prosecute, Austin was released on bond on Christmas Day in 1835. He returned to Texas, and the stage was set for the Texas Revolution.

Slavery and Catholicism were the two main objections of Anglo–American immigrants in Texas, a sentiment noted by Stephen Austin in correspondence with Erasmo Sequin, a Texas representative to the federal Congress:

> There are two obstacles that retard emigration to this province and to the whole nation; one is the doubt that exists concerning the admission of slavery, and the other is religion. Many Catholics would come from Louisiana if they could bring their slaves here, but, as the greater part of their capital consists in slaves, they cannot emigrate unless they take the slaves with them.[17]

Indeed, the main reason for the separation of the Texas colony from Coahuila was the Anglo immigrants' desire to forge their own slavery laws. Austin saw the slave prerogative from an international perspective—one that favored the U.S. southern sentiments. These views were articulated in an 1835 correspondence to a friend in New Orleans:

> Texas must be a slave country. It is no longer a matter of doubt. The interest of Louisiana requires that it should be, a population of fanatical abolitionists in Texas would have a very pernicious and dangerous influence on the overgrown slave population of that state (Louisiana). Texas must, and ought to, become an outwork on the west, as Alabama and Florida are on the east, to defend the key of the western world—the mouths of the Mississippi.[18]

Seeds were sown for the Mexican War following Texas's independence. Daniel Tyler notes that events such as the Adams-Onís Treaty and the Fredonian revolt forced Mexico to place its attention on events in Texas, setting the stage for a weakened defense in its New Mexico Territory. These circumstances led to an increased illegal encroachment into this region. According to Tyler, when the Mexican Congress curtailed the activities of all immigrants from the United States with its stringent anti-immigration laws, this action ultimately contributed to the rebellion in Texas, adding to the impoverishment and isolation of New Mexico.

The Emerging Texas Republic

The Anglo–American colonists had their opportunity for rebellion when other Mexicans actively protested Santa Anna's rule throughout the country. Initially, a combination of Tejanos (Mexican Texans) and Anglo Texans participated in this protest. Leading the Tejanos faction was Austin's friend, Captain Juan N. Sequín. The majority of the Tejanos, however, remained neutral during the rebellion. Actions leading to the revolt began on December 10, 1835, when the Texans convened a General Council to select delegates to an assembly being held on March 1, 1836, at Washington-on-the-Brazos. The consultation sent Branch T. Archer, William H. Wharton, and Stephen F. Austin to the United States to solicit money, equipment, men, and support for their cause. The March convention at Washington-on-the-Brazos consisted of 41 delegates—39 Anglos and 3 native Mexicans (José Fransisco Ruiz, José Antonio Navarro, and Lorenzo de Zavala). On March 2, 1836, the convention signed their Declaration of Independence. President Santa Anna exercised his constitutional authority to put down the rebellion and subsequently took a poorly trained and armed force north to quell the rebellion in San Antonio de Béxar. The Mexican army had outmoded smoothbore muskets and a force comprised of poorly trained conscripts, political prisoners, and even Mayan Indians who were impressed into the military, few of whom understood Spanish. With this force, President General Santa Anna laid siege to the rebels' outpost in San Antonio (the Alamo) on February 23, 1836.

The Alamo was well fortified with 21 cannons, 8- to 9-foot walls, and men armed with the best firearms of the time—Kentucky long rifles. Hence, the Alamo was considered to be the best-fortified military installation between New Orleans and Monterrey, Mexico. Santa Anna's army took the Alamo but with considerable losses—estimated to be between 500 and 600 men. All 186 Alamo defenders were slain with the exception of surviving family members of Tejanos, an Anglo–American woman and her child, and one African American slave owned by defender William Barrett Travis. The Alamo fell 4 days following the Texas Declaration of Independence. The Mexican army was also quelling another revolt southeast of San Antonio at

Goliad. Some 400 Texicans (rebels) surrendered with 342 of them executed as prisoners of war.

Santa Anna left San Antonio with his weakened forces to battle the main forces of the rebel army at San Jacinto. History tells us that Santa Anna's army of 1,500 was defeated by General Sam Houston's force of 900 men, including a small Tejano force led by Juan N. Seguín. Following a short battle, Santa Anna's forces were decimated. The Anglo forces continued to hunt down and slay retreating members of the Mexican force, resulting in some 600 deaths compared to Houston's force with only eight casualties. Three weeks later, the Treaty of Velasco was negotiated with President General Santa Anna conceding Texas independence. The Mexican Congress never confirmed the treaty. Nonetheless, given that Mexico was never able to retake Texas, it enjoyed de facto status as an independent nation.[19]

Slavery and the Texas Constitution

The constitution of the Republic of Texas was based on that of the United States and certain southern states, notably Tennessee. Sam Houston, former U.S. congressman and governor of Tennessee and close friend of President Andrew Jackson, was selected as commander in chief of the revolution, and David G. Burnet became Texas's first president, leading the interim government. A Tejano, Lorenzo de Zavala, became vice president; Samuel P. Carson, secretary of state; Thomas J. Rusk, secretary of war; and David Thomas, attorney general. The constitution of the Republic of Texas had a few caveats addressing its anti-Catholic/anti-Spanish and proslavery stance.

> Article I: Section 7. The senators shall be chosen by districts, as equal in free population (free negroes and Indians excepted), as practicable; and the number of senators shall never be less than one third nor more than one half the number of representatives, and each district shall be entitled to one member and no more.
>
> Article IV: Section 13. The congress shall, as early as practicable, introduce, by statute, the common law of England, with such modifications as our circumstances, in their judgment, may require; and in all criminal cases, the common law shall be the rule of decision.
>
> Article V: Section 1. Ministers of the gospel being, by their profession, dedicated to God and the care of souls, ought not to be diverted from the great duties of their functions; therefore, no minister of the gospel, or any priest of any denomination whatever, shall be eligible to the office of the executive of the republic, nor to a seat in either branch of the congress of the same.
>
> General Provisions: Section 6. All free white persons who shall emigrate to this republic, and who shall, after a residence of six months, make oath before some

competent authority that he intends to reside permanently in the same, and shall swear to support this constitution, and that he will bear true allegiance to the republic of Texas, shall be entitled to all the privileges of citizenship.

Section 9. All persons of color who were slaves for life previous to their emigration to Texas, and who are now held in bondage, shall remain in the like state of servitude; provided, the said slave shall be the bona fide property of the person so holding said slave as aforesaid. Congress shall pass no laws to prohibit emigrants from bring their slaves into the republic with them, and holding them by the same tenure by which such slaves were held in the United States; nor shall Congress have power to emancipate slaves; nor shall any slave holder be allowed to emancipate his or her slave or slaves without the consent of Congress, unless he or she shall send his or her slave or slaves without the limits of the republic. No free person of African descent, either in whole or in part, shall be permitted to reside permanently in the republic, without the consent of Congress; and the importation or admission of Africans or Negroes into this republic, excepting from the United States of America, is forever prohibited, and declared to be piracy.

Section 10: All persons (Africans, the descendants of Africans, and Indians excepted) who were residing in Texas on the day of the Declaration of Independence, shall be considered citizens of the republic, and entitled to all the privileges of such...

Declaration of Rights: First. All men, when they form a social compact, have equal rights, and no men or set of men are entitled to exclusive public privileges or emoluments from the community.

Third. No preference shall be given by law to any religious denomination or mode of worship over another, but every person shall be permitted to worship God according to the dictates of his own conscience...

Eight: No title of nobility, hereditary privileges or honors, shall ever be granted or conferred in this republic. No person holding any office of profit or trust shall, without the consent of congress, receive from any foreign state and present, office, or emolument of any kind.[20]

The pro-United States, anti-Spanish influence is most evident in the Texas Constitution with article 4, section 13; article 5, section 1; and the first, third and eighth items of the Declaration of Rights. Anti-white sentiments, notably toward blacks and American Indians, are clearly articulated in article 1, section 7 and sections 6, 9, and 10 of the General Provisions. Although the vast majority of Tejanos absorbed into the new Texas Republic remained neutral during the conflict, they too would suffer considerable injustices at the hands of the Anglos.

Although the Alamo and the Texas revolt have been celebrated in U.S. history books, not all American leaders at the time viewed the Texas Revolution in a positive light. Former president John Quincy Adams, coauthor of the Adams-Onís Treaty of 1819, saw it as a blatant act of self-interest for slave owners and land speculators. These divided sentiments in the United States of America caused considerable unrest, which would lead eventually to the annexation of Texas, the war with Mexico, and the War between the States (Civil War). Texas's decade as an independent republic (March 2, 1836–February 18, 1846) was equally turbulent internally with sentiments oscillating between sovereignty and allegiance to the United States. This was exacerbated by the fact that from the beginning the Texas Republic had difficulty being recognized as an independent nation in its own right. Two factors played significant roles here: Mexico's congressional refusal to recognize the Treaty of Velasco and the slave issue.

Presidents Sam Houston and Mirabeau B. Lamar's contradictory political philosophies added greatly to the republic's short history. Like the United States to the north and Mexico to the south, these turbulent years were threatened by a military takeover by its own army. The human rights issue involving black slaves, Native American tribes, and the peasant Mestizos, perhaps more than anything, denied Texas the recognition it sought among the world leaders at the time. This was despite the efforts of Texas's most influential statesman during this era: Secretary of State Stephen F. Austin. The internal conflict even resulted in the republic's first chief justice, James Collinsworth, committing suicide. In addition to the controversy around slavery, the Texas Republic continued to claim territory well beyond that agreed upon by the Treaty of Velasco.

The U.S. intervention was considerable during this time, and the eventual annexation of Texas is widely attributed to the influence of Sam Houston, former governor of Tennessee, U.S. Congressman, and friend and ally of Andrew Jackson. Indeed, the United States stood ready to protect the Texas Republic in the event of an invasion by Mexico. Even then, the Texas problem played itself out in the United States, contributing to two wars—the war with Mexico and the War between the States, the latter being the bloodiest conflict in the 19th century.[21]

Prelude to the U.S. Civil War: Annexation of Texas

The annexation of Texas began with Sam Houston's second term as president of the republic in 1841. Even his archrival, former president Mirabeau B. Lamar, eventually came to support annexation to the United States mainly for the purpose of protecting the institution of slavery and to keep Texas from becoming a British protectorate. Annexation was initially rejected by the U.S. Senate in June 1844 but became a major issue in that year's presidential elections. James K. Polk won election by supporting the annexation issue, and Congress followed suit by passing the annexation resolution on February 28, 1845. Texas, under President Anson Jones, accepted annexation in October 1845, and Texas formally became part of the United States on February 19, 1846.

Annexation sowed the seeds of war with Mexico. Following years of diplomacy, Great Britain convinced Mexico to acknowledge the independence of Texas under the proviso that it not annex itself to any country—notably the United States. The manifested cause of the Mexican–American War was the border dispute between Texas and Mexico with Mexico claiming the Nueces River, as stipulated by the Treaty of Velasco, and the United States the Rio Grande. In January 1846, President Polk sent General Zachary Taylor across the Nueces River for the purpose of establishing military posts along the Rio Grande. In April of that year, Mexican troops crossed the Rio Grande, clashing with U.S. troops. President Polk reacted quickly, requesting Congress declare war with Mexico. Congress concurred and war was officially declared May 13, 1846. Mexico reciprocated 10 days later, initiating the 2-year conflict known as the Mexican War in the United States and as the War of Northern Aggression or the United States War against Mexico in Mexico.

Polk's War and a Divided Nation

Clearly, the United States was divided over this blatant act of American imperialism under the guise of Manifest Destiny. It became clear that the United States was willing to forcefully take what it could not obtain through negotiations—a process already in place with the forceful removal of Indian tribes in the southeastern states. Mexico rejected offers to buy the adjacent northern Mexican territories of New Mexico and California. This followed the failure by the United States to expand its northern perimeter to the 49th parallel of the Alaskan border under the Buchanan-Pakenham Treaty of 1846 that awarded Great Britain all of Vancouver and the United States the Puget Sound—concessions that avoided yet another war with Great Britain. Polk's administration figured it was easier to fight a struggling third-world country like Mexico instead of one of the colonial superpowers of the time. Connor and Faulk attribute the Mexican–American War to blatant imperialism:

> The origins of the war between the United States and Mexico, 1846–48, remain controversial even today (1971). To most Mexicans the issue is simple—the United States fought Mexico in order to acquire the territory now called the American Southwest, including both Texas and California. Simple imperialism. To many Americans it is the same—the late Robert Kennedy once referred to the war as one of the most disgraceful episode in the American past.[22]

What the acquisition of this new territory did do was ignite the slave debate in the United States and pave the way for the more devastating conflict—the Civil War. Slavery and expansionism were the predominant issues that split U.S. support for the war with Mexico. Slavery exploded in Texas following statehood, increasing from 30,000 in 1845 to 182,566 in 1860. At the time Texas succeeded from the Union, black slaves made up more than 30% of the state's population. Indeed, the slave issue reflected the deep divisions in the United States at the time of Polk's presidency. Of the two major parties, the Democrats were proponents of Manifest Destiny, providing strong support for the annexation of both Texas and the Oregon Territory. The Whigs, on the other hand, held a more conservative and cautious view on expansionism, supporting the status quo of strong federalism and local autonomy. These differences were played out in the election of 1844. Henry Clay, the Whig candidate, lost to James Knox Polk, the dark horse Democratic candidate, who ran on a platform of territorial expansionism under the guise of Manifest Destiny. Imbedded in this dilemma was the slave controversy. Hence, the Democrats came to be seen as being proslavery and pro-expansionist, and the Whigs were viewed as being leery of rapid expansion, fearing that it would ultimately lead to a stronger centralized form of government and expand slavery into the newly acquired territories. Yet, Polk's expansionist interpretation of Manifest Destiny found support in both his cabinet and the Congress with the Democrats holding a 144 to 77 majority in the House and a 30 to 24 lead in the Senate. With this mandate, the war with Mexico soon followed as did a major reconfiguration of U.S. political parties.

Even with congressional support for territorial expansionism, slavery, and the war with Mexico, the Democrats themselves were divided as was the country. Serious factions emerged between the North and South. The Wilmot Proviso attempted to bridge these differences. Initiated by northern Congressmen and presented by David Wilmot, a freshman Democratic congressman from Pennsylvania, the amendment was attached to a war appropriation bill. It was designed to make Texas the last slave state:

> Provided, territory from that, as an express and fundamental condition to the acquisition of any the Republic of Mexico by the United States, by virtue of any treaty which may be negotiated between them, and to the use by the Executive of the moneys herein appropriated, neither slavery nor involuntary servitude shall ever exist in any part of said territory, except for crime, whereof the party shall first be duly convicted.[23]

The Wilmot Proviso subsequently passed the House of Representatives in both 1846 and 1847 but never was approved by the Senate. The provision was negated by the Compromise of 1850 and was ultimately struck down by the U.S. Supreme Court in the 1857 Dred Scott case.

The war with Mexico spelled the demise of the Whig Party and the emergence of the Republican Party. The Whigs were heavily represented in the Northeast with Boston the center for its Conscience Whigs, who viewed war, slavery, and the southern political structure as obstacles to both democracy and Christianity. Schroeder notes that these reformers "interpreted the Mexican War in moral terms as an aggressive, unjust, and unholy war to extend the heinous institution of slavery."[23] Nonetheless, the Whigs nominated Zachary Taylor, a southern slaveholder, as their candidate for the 1848 presidential contest. Although Taylor won the election, it further alienated the northern Conscience Whigs and some northern Democrats, leading to the proliferation of break-off political parties ultimately welded into the Free Soil Party. The Free Soil Party was initiated by the Wilmot Proviso and drew its membership from abolitionists from both the Whig and Democratic parties. The party believed in slave-free territory, free labor, free speech, and freedmen. They held their first party convention in 1848 with their leaders, Salmon P. Chase and John P. Hale. Hale's former friend and colleague, Franklin Pierce, on the other hand, adamantly supported Southern sentiments, including slavery.

The split between Pierce and Hale came about with the 1844 election of James Polk as U.S. president. Although the New Hampshire Democratic Party supported Texas annexation, Hale went against the state Democratic platform by proposing a resolution in the U.S. House of Representatives urging the creation of two states out of the former Texas Republic: one slave and one free. The resolution was soundly defeated and upset the state's Democratic Party chairman, Franklin Pierce, who set the stage for Hale's expulsion from the Democratic Party. This action effectively ended the close personal and political relationship between Pierce and Hale. Thus, the annexation of Texas raised the issue of slavery to a prominent level in U.S. politics with Franklin Pierce siding with the South and John P. Hale becoming the first U.S. Senator to speak against slavery.

Franklin Pierce and John P. Hale also differed on the war with Mexico. Although Pierce initially turned down a military cabinet position offered by President Polk, he enlisted in the militia as a private knowing that he would rapidly advance in rank due to his political stature and his father's previous military status. He quickly advanced to the rank of colonel and made brigadier general within a year's time. General Pierce served with General Winfield Scott and was wounded at the Battle of Churubusco, hence earning the needed national recognition for his eventual nomination as the Democratic presidential candidate in the election of 1852. Pierce was nominated on the 49th ballot running against both his former commanding general, Winfield Scott, and his Bowdoin classmate, John P. Hale, as well as Sam Houston, twice elected president of the Republic of Texas. Pierce won by supporting the Compromise of 1850. He was seen as a northern candidate with southern sympathies.

John Parker Hale, on the other hand, not only opposed the annexation of Texas, he opposed the war with Mexico. He was adamantly opposed to

Polk's war, making his sentiments known in a January 6, 1848, speech to the U.S. Senate:

> [W]hen we speak of the causes of this war, I must avow my conviction, beyond a cavil of doubt, to be, that it lies in the avowed policy of the American Government—a policy which was avowed four years ago—to make the extension of human slavery one of its primary motives of action. And when I say this, let me not be misunderstood. I refer to the principle avowed in the diplomatic correspondence which preceded the annexation of Texas to the United States... Was not annexation itself an act of War? War was existing between Mexico and Texas at the time. By the very fact of annexing to ourselves one of the belligerent nations we incurred the responsibility of fighting her battles; although, even after that, subsequent history has demonstrated that, owing to the feeble and distracted state of Mexico, the most ordinary prudence on the part of the Executive might and probably would have avoided flagrant war... The taking possession of Texas was of itself an act of War.[24]

The war with Mexico (Mexican–American War) of 1846–1848 led to the signing of the Guadalupe Hidalgo Treaty on February 2, 1848, which was proclaimed July 4, 1848. Santa Anna, in his fourth term as president of Mexico, was another casualty of the war, fleeing the country once again. The terms of the treaty formally ended Mexico's claim to Texas while expanding U.S. Territory to the Pacific Ocean with the acquisition of New Mexico and the upper California territories. In all, Mexico was forced to cede 55% of its territory—now the states of Arizona, California, and New Mexico and parts of Colorado, Nevada, and Utah. The United States, in turn, paid Mexico $15 million in compensation for damages incurred during the war. The Treaty of 1848 also established the Rio Grande as the official southern border for the State of Texas.[25]

The war with Mexico also provided the Mormons legitimacy for their future colonies in Utah, Arizona, and Nevada. They had provided a battalion early in the war (the First Iowa Volunteers) and patrolled the western Mexican territories. Apparently, the United States welcomed any assistance in its westward expansion, and the Mormons provided a willing group to explore this region. Although never engaging in any battles, they gained acclaim for their grueling 2,000-mile patrol from Council Bluffs, Iowa, to the coastal cities of San Diego and Los Angeles in California. Ostensibly, the Mormons used this trek as a reconnaissance for their future homeland, quickly laying claim to Utah and considerable portions of Arizona, Nevada, and even New Mexico; and providing for a political, religious, and economic monopoly that exists to the present. However, their attempt to create a separate autonomous state out of this territory, Deseret (Mormonese for honeybee), was unsuccessful. This territory was to include all the lands surrendered by Mexico in 1848 between the California Territory and New Mexico Territory (the current states of Arizona and New Mexico).[26]

The war with Mexico also provided the United States with a fresh crop of military leaders, many of whom went on to fight in the Civil War: Ulysses S. Grant, Ambrose Burnside, Stonewall Jackson, George Meade, and Robert E. Lee. It also established a generation of U.S. presidents and presidential candidates, including Zachary Taylor, Franklin Pierce, Winfield Scott, Ulysses S. Grant, and Jefferson Davis. Andrew Jackson could be added to this list given his intrusions into Spanish Florida during the War of 1812. Indeed, the U.S. political leadership for much of the 19th century had a strong military component, a factor in its aggressive expansionism and interventionism under the guise of Manifest Destiny. Mexico had little choice but to militarize its own political leadership as a defense against the United States. Indeed, the U.S. Civil War threatened the stability of all of North America at that time. The constant threat of U.S. intervention made the situation in Mexico so grave that its long-serving president during this time, Porfirio Díaz (1877–1911), expressed this dilemma as such: "*Probre México! Tan lejos de Dios, y tan cerca de los Estados Unidos* [Poor Mexico! So far from God, and so close to the United States]."

The Unresolved Slavery Issue

The Treaty of Guadalupe Hidalgo did not resolve all outstanding issues existing between the United States and Mexico. If anything, it exacerbated the unresolved slavery issue in the United States, ultimately leading to the U.S. Civil War (War between the States). Certainly the treaty did not provide adequate protection to either Mexican residents or Native Americans who traditionally inhabited the former Mexican Territory ceded in 1848. Mexican Americans were regulated to second-class status much like blacks, and some of the most intense Indian Wars and ethnic cleansing occurred in the former Mexican Territory under U.S. possession. New Mexico Territory was especially problematic to the U.S. expansionists in that it was the exception to the overall plan of getting the most land from Mexico with the fewest number of Mexican inhabitants. Texas and California fit this format with Anglo-Americans readily outnumbering their Mexican counterparts, thereby making the white supremacy component of Manifest Destiny an easy doctrine to impose and enforce.

To many expansionists, New Mexico Territory (Arizona and New Mexico north of the Gila River) was merely an obstacle to reaching the riches of California. Texas had already attempted to include the eastern portion of the state in its territory. New Mexico Territory was problematic in that it had a substantial number of Mexican colonists along with an established Spanish Catholic form of governance. The territory had some 60,000 Indian-Spanish Mestizo settlers along with 15,000 Pueblo Indians—long recognized as first Spanish and later Mexican citizens. It is estimated that there were fewer than 1,000 Euro–Americans in the territory in 1848. This meant that the United States was responsible for nearly 100,000 colonial subjects in this territory alone. Not counted in this mix were the numerous unrecognized Native American groups, collectively labeled as "savages" (Apache, Navajo, Ute, Comanche, Cheyenne, Cayuga, and Arapaho).

Under the Treaty of Guadalupe Hidalgo, those colonial residents recognized by Mexico at the time as citizens had to be protected and provided for. Reluctant to transfer U.S. citizenship to those holding Mexican citizenship at the time of the treaty signing, three options were offered the captured residents of New Mexico Territory. One, the Mestizo population could elect to relocate to Mexico south of the newly established border. Only about 4,000 chose to do so, and even then, they may have again been in a difficult position with the 1854 Gadsden Purchase. A second choice was that of de facto dual citizenship by formally retaining their Mexican citizenship by proclaiming such before a local judge (these were Mestizo judges). Finally, all others would be presumed U.S. citizens. The fact that so many colonized Mestizos chose the option of retaining their Mexican citizenship provided the small Anglo–American faction with greater power proportionately to their numbers. And federally recognized U.S. citizenship is a far weaker legal status than state citizenship.

Laura E. Gómez provides an interesting thesis on how the United States avoided protracted guerrilla war in New Mexico Territory by allowing the existing ruling Spanish–Indian Mestizo leaders to claim off-white status, equating them politically but not socially or morally with the white supremacy dictum of Manifest Destiny. In doing so, the United States was able to break the coalition of Mestizo Pueblo Indian resisters to U.S. occupation. According to Gómez's research, the Mexican empresario land grants in New Mexico Territory went to light-colored (off-white) people. The workforce also consisted of Mestizos. The upper-class Mestizo also had a tradition of keeping captured Native American women and children, mostly Navajo, as domestic servants, doing so in spite of the 1821 Plan de Iguala declaring all inhabitants of the new Mexican Republic as "equal citizens" and the specific tenets of 1829 abolishing black slavery in Mexico. There were fewer than two dozen blacks in the entire territory at the time of federal territorial recognition in 1850. At any rate, a well-established form of civil and religious order was operating in New Mexico Territory at the time it was declared a U.S. federal territory in 1850.[27]

Given the cost of the Mexican War itself, the U.S. Government was not financially fit to attempt a costly regime change in the New Mexico Territory. Instead, it used its successful Indian policy of divide and conquer, devising its plan of providing the ruling Mestizos political parity with U.S. Congressional oversight. This quid pro quo arrangement for "near white" status was contingent upon the disenfranchisement of the Pueblo Indians, thus dividing the Pueblo–Mestizo resistance. Gómez makes it clear that the "off-white" status afforded the existing ruling Mestizos in the New Mexico Territory was not to be confused with social recognition as whites or even as being on par with the status of other white citizens of the United States. The Mestizos's main purpose was to maintain calm among the existing Mexican populace. And for the remainder of the 19th century, the Mestizo elite represented the majority of all legislative and elective positions, especially in what is now the State of New Mexico. By providing order among the significant Mestizo population, the U.S. Government could more effectively wage its wars on the non-Pueblo tribes, quelling the Navajo in 1863 and the Apache in 1886. Anglo–American oversight kept the Mestizo elite under tight control, limiting their power and authority in order to maintain peace and harmony among the Hispanic population while suppressing the Pueblo tribes. Indeed, the most powerful territorial positions were presidential appointments, which included the territorial governor, territorial secretary, and the three justices of the territorial supreme court. For the most part, these positions were filled by outside Anglos. Although Anglos eventually came to comprise the majority of the populace in New Mexico, the state still has the highest proportion of Hispanics (of Mexican descent) in the United States (estimated to be between 40% and 45%).

The Road to Political Disorganization Following the Mexican War: Whigs Exit, Republicans Emerge

In the United States, a divided nation weakened the traditional Democratic Party and wiped out the Whigs while, at the same time, creating a new political party: the Republicans. The antiwar Whigs had their last candidate elected president in the elections of 1848. Antislavery Conscience Whigs bolted from their party along with disenchanted northern Democrats, forming a new, third party: the Free Soil Party. The Free Soil Party chose the former Democratic candidate, Martin Van Buren, as their candidate. Their platform was based on an opposition to the expansion of slavery to the newly acquired western territories. Southern Whig, slaveholder, and Mexican War hero Zachary Taylor won the 1848 election. However, Taylor soon lost much of his southern support when he allowed New Mexico and California to draw up their own constitutions, and both territories chose to prohibit slavery.

Dissatisfaction over the prohibition of slavery in New Mexico and California strained the delicate balance established by the 1820 Missouri Compromise with Southerners clamoring for secession. Added to the turmoil was Texas's claim to all lands extending to Santa Fe. In an attempt to salvage the Union, a number of influential congressional leaders, notably Henry Clay, Daniel Webster, John C. Calhoun, and Stephen Douglas, forged a compromise that got Texas to fall back into its original boundaries while the territories of New Mexico, Arizona, and Utah agreed to suspend the slave issue until statehood. California, on the other hand, would preserve its slave-free status, and the slave trade would be abolished in the District of Columbia while preserving its slaveholding status.

The most controversial element of the Compromise of 1850 was the Fugitive Slave Act. This act attempted to curtail the Underground Railroad for slaves attempting to escape north. Under the law, all U.S. citizens were required to assist in the recovery of fugitive slaves. Without proper judicial oversight, even free blacks were captured and sent south to be enslaved. The compromise was only a temporary solution—one that actually served to widen the gap between slaveholders and abolitionists.[31] The slave issue, exacerbated by the annexation of Texas and the subsequent War with Mexico, also accentuated festering religious biases stemming from newly arrived immigrants, leading to the emergence of the American Party. A number of nativist (Protestant) political parties emerged during the early years of the U.S. republic that were openly anti-immigrant, especially against Roman Catholics. One, the Order of the Star Spangled Banner, took on the moniker "the Know Nothing Party" due to its pat response when inquiries were made concerning its political platform and mandate. The Know Nothing Party initially targeted Irish Catholics following their mass migration to the United States after the potato famine in Ireland. Clearly, this situation merely exacerbated the anti-Catholic sentiments long held in the northeastern United States toward the French in general and French Canadians in particular.

The Know Nothing Party adapted as its influence spread to the newly acquired western territories following the Treaty of Guadalupe Hildago. Fueling the anti-Catholic, anti-Irish sentiments of the Know Nothing Party was the role of the Irish conscript who joined the Mexican forces during the war with Mexico. Most notable was the Saint Patrick Battalion, comprised of mainly Irish immigrants who deserted from the U.S. Army to fight on the Mexican side. Most were killed at the Battle of Churubusco with rumors of surviving POWs being tortured and executed by U.S. forces.[28]

During the Pierce presidency, United States expansionism continued with the purchase of more Mexican Territory and tacit support for armed intervention in Latin America. The gunboat diplomacy initiated by Pierce's predecessor, President Millard Fillmore, came to fruition with the signing of the U.S.–Japan Treaty of Kanagawa on March 31, 1854, forcing Japan to open its ports to American and European trade. This action inadvertently introduced yet another player into the fierce colonial wars that continued to rage during the 19th and 20th centuries, culminating in World War II.

Pierce's presidency witnessed continued raw expansionism under the guise of Manifest Destiny with armed interventions into Mexico and Latin America by American filibusters. Most notable was William Walker, a medical doctor and lawyer from Nashville, Tennessee, whose forces first raided

Baja, California, and Sonora state in an attempt to carve another independent republic out of Mexico with Walker anointed president of the Republic of Sonora. Mexican resistance forced Walker's regime to retreat, resulting in a brief trial for Walker followed by an acquittal. Walker's next adventure was to lead an American force of mercenaries in Nicaragua where he successfully defeated the Nicaraguan National Army and captured the capital of Granada in 1855. With support from American business leaders who wanted to construct a rail link in Nicaragua connecting the Atlantic and Pacific oceans and proslave groups in the United States, Walker represented a group that wanted to expand slavery in Latin America by overthrowing the governments of Costa Rica, El Salvador, Guatemala, and Honduras and establishing white Anglo-Saxon Protestant (WASP) administrations. One of Walker's first acts as president of Nicaragua was to rescind the county's 1824 emancipation edict, making slavery legal. Franklin Pierce readily recognized Walker's regime in Nicaragua, lending tacit support to this plan. Walker later crossed Cornelius Vanderbilt, curtailing his efforts to build the east–west rail link and leading to Walker's exit from Nicaragua. Walker was later captured by the British Navy entering Honduras (Belize) and instead of returning him to the United States, where he was seen as a southern hero, they turned him over to local authorities, who executed him on September 12, 1860.[29]

The Ostend Manifesto and Gadsden Purchase

The Ostend Manifesto was yet another example of attempts at raw expansionism during the Pierce administration. The Ostend Manifesto represented a clandestine plot hatched by proslavery leaders in the Pierce administration, initiated by his secretary of state, William L. Marcy. Here, the U.S. diplomats to Britain (James Buchanan), France (John Y. Mason), and Spain (Pierre Soulé) met with Spanish officials in Ostend, Belgium, in an attempt to force Spain to sell Cuba to the United States for a sum of $120 million. Once acquired, it would then be added to the Union as a slave state. The U.S. delegation made it clear that Cuba would be taken by force if they did not agree to this plan. The document, along with its intention of Cuba becoming a U.S. slave state, was leaked and met with fierce opposition from the Free Soilers, who termed the clandestine plot the Manifesto of Brigands. President Pierce and Secretary of State Marcy quickly backtracked, and the manifesto offer was withdrawn.[30]

Pierce was successful, however, in purchasing additional lands south of the U.S.–Mexico western border articulated in the 1848 Treaty of Guadalupe Hidalgo. This became known as the Gadsden Purchase. Named after Pierce's U.S. minister (ambassador) to Mexico, James Gadsden, the purchase's official name is the Treaty of La Mesilla of December 30, 1853. Ostensibly, the purchase of more than 45,000 square miles at a cost of $15 million was to settle the suspended Bartlett-García Conde Compromise designed to resolve errors in the original map. The major boundary error following the Treaty of Guadalupe Hidalgo was the inclusion of the city of El Paso within the territory acquired by the United States. The purchase actually represented a continuation of the efforts to expand the slaveholding territory associated with the South. It was, in effect, a diluted model of the ill-fated Ostend Manifesto.

James Gadsden was an unabashed capitalist whose major interest was completing a southern east–west rail route. Born in South Carolina, Gadsden's previous roles included being President Monroe's agent in charge of removing Florida's Seminole Indians onto reservations. His blatant conflict of interest in the Gadsden Purchase was his role as president of the consolidated South Carolina, Louisville, Charleston, and Cincinnati railroads, which wanted to construct a rail line to the Pacific Ocean in an attempt to beat northern rail efforts to connect the east with California. The purchase became necessary for Gadsden's plan when engineering studies indicated that the most efficient route was one south of the Gila River delineating the southern U.S.–Mexico border emerging from the 1848 Treaty of Guadalupe Hidalgo. An additional gain was the rich Santa Rita copper mines that were originally mined by Native Americans before the advent of Europeans and continue to be mined today by Phelps Dodge Company.[31]

The Gadsden Purchase also provided the United States an opportunity to renege on one of the critical agreements in the 1848 settlement—that of providing Mexican residents protection from attacks from Indian tribes residing in the newly acquired U.S. Territory. It also imposed upon Mexico provisions for a railroad across the Isthmus of Tehuantepec for mainly U.S. purposes. Here, article 2 of the Treaty of La Mesilla voided article 11 of the Treaty of Guadalupe Hidalgo, and article 8 gave the United States further rights of intrusion into Mexico for American self-interest.

> Article II (Gadsden Purchase). The government of Mexico hereby releases the United States from all liability on account of the obligations contained in the eleventh article of the treaty of Guadalupe-Hidalgo; and the said article and the thirty-third article of the treaty of amity, commerce, and navigation between the United States of America and the United Mexican States concluded at Mexico, on the fifth day of April, 1831, are hereby abrogated.

> Article XI (Treaty of Guadalupe-Hidalgo). Considering that a great part of the territories, which, by the present treaty, are to be comprehended for the future within the limits of the United States, is now occupied by savage tribes, who will hereafter be under the exclusive control of the Government of the United States, and whose incursions within the territory of Mexico would be prejudicial in the extreme, it is solemnly agreed that all such incursions shall be forcibly restrained by the Government of the United States whensoever this

may be necessary; and that when they cannot be prevented, they shall be punished by the said Government, and satisfaction for same shall be extracted in the same way, and with equal diligence and energy, as if the same incursions were mediated or committed within its own territory, against its own citizens.

It shall not be lawful, under any pretext whatever, for any inhabitant of the United States to purchase or acquire any Mexican, or any foreigner residing in Mexico, who may have been captured by Indians inhabiting the territory or either of the two republics; nor to purchase or acquire horses, mules, cattle, or property of any kind, stolen within Mexican territory by such Indians.

And in the event of any person or persons, captured within Mexican territory by Indians, being carried into the territory of the United States, the Government of the latter engages and binds itself, in the most solemn manner, so soon as it shall know of such captives being within its territory, and shall be able so to do, through the faithful exercise of its influence and power, to rescue them and return them to their country, or deliver them to the agent or representative of the Mexican Government. The Mexican authorities will, as far as practicable, give to the Government of the United States notice of such captures; and its agent shall pay the expenses incurred in the maintenance and transmission of the rescued captives; who, in the mean time, shall be treated with the utmost hospitality by the American authorities at the place where they may be. But if the Government of the United States, before receiving such notice from Mexico, should obtain intelligence, through any other channel, of the existence of Mexican captives within its territory, it will proceed forthwith to effect their release and delivery to the Mexican agent, as above stipulated.

For the purpose of giving to these stipulations the fullest possible efficacy, thereby affording the security and redress demanded by their true spirit and intent, the Government of the United States will now and hereafter pass, without unnecessary delay, and always vigilantly enforce, such laws as the nature of the subject may require. And, finally, the sacredness of this obligation shall never be lost sight of by the said Government, when providing for the removal of Indians from any portion of the said territories, or for its being settled by citizens of the United States; but on the contrary, special care shall then be taken not to place its Indian occupants under the necessity of seeking new homes, by committing those invasions which the United States have solemnly obliged themselves to restrain.

Article VIII (Gadsden Purchase). The Mexican Government having on the 5th of February, 1853, authorized the construction of a plank and railroad across the Isthmus of Tehuantepec, and to secure the stable benefits of said transit way to the persons and merchandise of the citizens of Mexico and the United States, it is stipulated that neither Government will interpose any obstacle to the transit of persons and merchandise of both nations; and at no time shall higher charges be made on the transit of persons and property of citizens of the United States than may be made on the persons and property of other foreign nations, nor shall any interest in said transit way nor in the proceeds thereof, be transferred to any foreign government.

The United States, by its agents, shall have the right to transport across the isthmus, in closed bags, the mails of the United States not intended for distribution along the line of communication; also the effect of the United States Government and its citizens, which may be intended for transit, and not for distribution on the isthmus, free of customhouse or other charges by the Mexican Government. Neither passport nor letters of security will be required of persons crossing the isthmus and not remaining in the country.

When the construction of the railroad shall be completed, the Mexican Government agrees to open a port of entry in addition to the port of Vera Cruz, at or near the terminus of said road on the Gulf of Mexico.

The two Governments will enter into arrangements for the prompt transit of troops and munitions of the United States which that Government may have occasion to send from one part of its territory to another, lying on opposite sides of the continent.

The Mexican Government having agreed to protect with its whole power the prosecution, preservation and security of the work, the United States may extend its protection as it shall judge wise to it when it may feel sanctioned and warranted by the public or international law.[32]

This land grab added Yuma, California; Tucson, Nogales, Wilcox, and Douglas in Arizona; and Lordsburg, Deming, Columbus, Mesilla, and Santa Rita in New Mexico; as well as numerous other villages and tribal homelands to the United States. The United States also added insult to injury with article 8, for not only did the United States wage war on Mexico to steal more than half of its territory, it now had the audacity to demand free passage across the isthmus so that the eastern part of the country could trade and communicate with the newly acquired western territories. The eventual digging of the Panama Canal made this item moot in the long run. It did, however, establish a precedent regarding free travel across the international border for Americans and later, in 1929, made it illegal for Mexicans to traverse the border to enter the United States without its permission.

Regarding local tribes, some of the fiercest Indian warfare occurred in this newly acquired territory in violation of the 1848 treaty relevant to Mexico's confirmation of citizenship to Native Americans with its 1821 constitution. Instead, the United States waged a war of genocide on Indians in the southwestern United States, treating them as less-than-human pests that needed to be removed. These tribal wars raged on both sides of the border and were not resolved until the surrender of Geronimo in 1886 and the forced removal and imprisonment of the entire Apache band to a prison in Florida. However, all three major players in this deal were eventually discredited. James Gadsden was recalled as Minister to Mexico for his conflict of interest in the purchase. He died in 1858 never realizing his dream of a southern transcontinental rail route. Indeed, the Civil War ended the efforts for a southern route to be the first transcontinental route. Congress authorized funding in 1862 for a northern route going from Omaha, Nebraska, in the East to Sacramento, California, in the West. The Union Pacific and Central Pacific railroads met at Promontory Point, Utah, on May 10, 1869, and the Southern Pacific line from New Orleans to California was not completed until 1883. Antonio López de Santa Anna again disgraced his country, this time during his fifth, and last, term as president. He was again exiled first to Colombia and, later, the Virgin Islands. He returned to Mexico in 1874 impoverished and died in 1876. Franklin Pierce served a single term as U.S. president and became the only sitting president to seek and not receive his party's nomination for a second term. Pierce died an alcoholic in 1869 at age 64.[33]

Pierce was replaced with a true southern sympathizer, his minister (ambassador) to England, James Buchanan. Social conditions in the United States continued to deteriorate with the 1857 Dred Scott decision, John Brown's attack on Harper's Ferry in 1859, and South Carolina's ordinance of secession from the Union. During this time, the new Republican Party emerged, drawing from the many splinter groups for membership, most notably the American Party. The ensuing War between the States (U.S. Civil War) became the deadliest conflict of the 19th century, splitting the nation for more than a century until the civil rights movement and resulting laws enacted in the mid-1960s. But the United States was not alone; conflict was contagious throughout North America. Conflict in Canada resulting from the 1849 Union Bill led to the establishment of its current form of government with the British North American Act creating the Dominion of Canada in 1867. This act attempted to resolve the wide cultural, social, and religious differences between Anglo Canadians and French Canadians.

In Mexico, with Santa Anna's despotic rule finally ended, Mexico turned to a full-blooded Native American as its leader. Benito Pablo Juárez assumed the presidency on January 19, 1858, following his release from prison, and in his capacity as chief justice. Juárez's government was recognized by the United States in April 1859. He was elected as president of Mexico in the elections of 1861 and served until 1863. One of his major accomplishments in office was to challenge the role of the Catholic Church. This action plus his suspension of payments on the nation's national debt led to France declaring war against Juárez on April 16, 1862. Napoleon III's forces captured Puebla in May of that year, and Napoleon proclaimed his relative Maximilian von Hapsburg emperor of Mexico. This Catholic colonial force ruled from 1864 until 1867, leading to Mexico's own civil war known as the War of Reform with its most famous battle being the Cinco de Mayo battle against Maximilian's forces. Juárez's forces finally won, putting Maximilian and his principal followers before firing squads. Juárez was again elected president of Mexico in 1867, serving until his death in 1872. Juárez continues to be revered by Mexico's indigenous peoples and its substantial Mestizo population. Nonetheless, the emerging conflicts in both the United States and Mexico and between these two neighboring countries intensified along their borders until the Second World War.[34]

The Monroe Doctrine and Imperial Designs: 1865–1917

In 1823, the United States proclaimed that it was the premier colonial authority in the Americas, and European powers henceforth would not be permitted to intervene in the affairs of the western hemisphere countries. This unilateral declaration became known as the Monroe Doctrine, and it carried with it serious implications for Latin America later in the 19th century and thereafter. Mexico was the first country to feel the full impact of Manifest Destiny and the intrusions of the Monroe Doctrine. This process began with the United States recognizing the Republic of Texas after the Anglo–American settlers broke away from Mexico over the slave issue in 1836. When Mexico became independent from Spain in 1821, it outlawed slavery to the dismay of the American empresarios. Nine years later, in 1845, the United States admitted Texas as a slave state, setting the stage for initiating a war with Mexico the following year. The United States felt that this was sufficient provocation for Mexico to declare war, but they did not take the bait. It was the United States that declared war over a seemingly minuscule incident involving the death of a few American soldiers in a disputed piece of land claimed by both Mexico and Texas. The war with Mexico (1846–1848) took half of Mexico and expanded the United States from the Atlantic Ocean to the Pacific Ocean, again doubling its size with the acquisition of what are now the states of New Mexico, Arizona, Colorado, Nevada, California, and parts of Utah and Wyoming. Reparations to Mexico for this territory were established at $15 million of which only $3 million was actually paid; the rest was paid to Americans who were allowed to file damage claims against Mexico resulting from the war America started. And Mexicans who stayed in the newly acquired U.S. Territory became secondary citizens, especially those of mixed Spanish and Indian blood, the Mestizos.

Obviously, the Monroe Doctrine did not deter European interference in the region, especially Mexico, when in 1861 the Tripartite Convention of London authorized the armed intervention in Mexico with forces from Britain, France, and Spain using this mandate to recover an 82-million-peso debt. The United States could do little about this given that it was preoccupied with its own Civil War at this time. Even then, Britain and Spain pulled out of Mexico in 1862 leaving only French forces there. Under these circumstances, the Archduke Maximilian was made the European dictator of Mexico in 1864. But Napoleon III could not afford to continue supporting Maximilian; therefore, in 1866, he withdrew French troops from Mexico,

The Emerging United States and Its Expansionist Mandate

resulting in Maximilian's defeat and execution in 1867, again freeing Mexico for U.S. exploitation.

This was also the time of the U.S. Civil War of 1861–1865, which no longer was just a battle over slavery, but also a conflict regarding the transformation of America from a rural to an industrialized society. The conflict not only pitted the landed gentry of the southern plantation society against the industrialization occurring in the north, but how these competing social models would impact the newly acquired western lands. In this sense, the Emancipation Proclamation can be seen as a side issue. When President Lincoln issued the Emancipation Proclamation freeing slaves throughout the United States on January 1, 1863, there were nearly four million black slaves in the United States residing in 15 of the 34 states. However, limited resources were allocated following the end of the war to resocialize or integrate the emancipated freedmen and their families into the larger dominant society. But with the need to continue the Indian Wars to rid the west and southwest of its indigenous Indian tribes, coupled with a marked reduction in military force following the Civil War, reconstruction was short lived in the South, effectively ending by the mid-1870s. President Lincoln also took advantage of the South's declaration of independence to enforce the Homestead Act in May 1862. It favored giving land to Union veterans flooding Indian Territory in the West with an armed and trained force to combat the Indians that also claimed this land. More than 285 million acres of contested land, 10% of the entire United States, was settled under the Homestead Act.[35]

The withdrawal of U.S. occupation forces from the vanquished South, along with the failure of the Freedmen's Bureau to incorporate lasting changes within the South, set the stage for extralegal actions by southern whites directed against the newly freed blacks, resulting in a United States version of apartheid. The resulting enforced caste system created in the post–Civil War South led to a new type of race discrimination with the emergence of Jim Crow laws, which separated white and black facilities, including schools. It also allowed for a vigilante-type of racist justice known as lynching administered by the ruling whites and their de facto police: the Ku Klux Klan (KKK). Blacks were publically mutilated and hanged by white mobs without the protection of the police or the courts. This process went on for 100 years until the U.S. Civil Rights laws of the mid-1960s.[36]

Canadian Challenges during the Monroe Doctrine Era

British North America was the term used for its colonies following the American Revolution. A number of significant events occurred during the period from the War of 1812 through the formation of a unified Confederation in 1867. Until this time, British North America consisted of "lower" (Quebec) and "upper" (Ontario) Canada and the Atlantic provinces (Nova Scotia, New Brunswick, Prince Edward Island). In 1837, a series of small-scale revolts were staged by the French Canadians in reaction to attempts toward forceful assimilation into British Canadian society. Both Quebec and Ontario had their own locally elected legislative assembly while still being ruled by crown-appointed colonial leaders, including the governor, executive council, and legislative council. At the same time, a border dispute was festering along the Maine–New Brunswick–Quebec borders. Stanley Ryerson detailed the ongoing conflict between the United States and New Brunswick in what was coined "the Aroostook War," where the United States was attempting to annex the rich forest lands lying between New Brunswick and Quebec. The Aroostook War, also referred to as the "Pork and Beans War," was part of the mounting tensions at this time even though it was an undeclared, nonviolent border confrontation occurring at the same time as the uprising in Lower Canada. Interestingly, New Hampshire-born Daniel Webster, then U.S. Secretary of State in the Van Buren (1837–1841) administration, was a major player in negotiating the U.S. (Maine) and British North American (Quebec. New Brunswick) border, which, in the end, favored the United States (the Webster-Ashburton Treaty of 1842).[37]

The leader of the Ontario rebellion, William Lyon MacKenzie, died during the Upper Canada revolt and the attack on Toronto. The Lower Canada revolt involved French Canadians led by Louis J. Papineau, and was a more substantial uprising but also was repressed, resulting in Papineau fleeing to New York State in the United States. Pierre Vallieres, leader of the *Front de liberation du Quebec* (FLQ) in the 1960s and 1970s, claimed that Papineau's real interest was to protect the interests of the French elite, the patriots, at the expense of the habitants, and not to usher in a popular revolution in Lower Canada. Nonetheless, French nationalism in Lower Canada (Quebec Province) led to the creation of the *Fils de la Liberte*, a group of French Catholic patriots fashioning themselves after the Sons of Liberty during the American Revolution. This movement led to the establishment of other French ethnic organizations, such as the *Institut Canadien* in 1844, Montreal's first French public library, and the newspaper *L'Avenir* in 1847. These rebellions forced the issue of the formation of a union between Upper and Lower Canada, an effort led by Britain through Lord Durham.

In 1840, the Union Bill was introduced, establishing the Province of Canada along with a cabinet-type executive accountable to the elective legislature. The Union became effective in 1848 but was still seen as an effort toward forced assimilation by the French Canadians, a fact evident in Lord Durham's report of 1839 that stated it had been a mistake to try to preserve a French Canadian nationality in the midst of Anglo–American colonies and states. The Durham report notes that in order to elevate the French Canadians from hopeless inferiority they must be given "our" English character by being engulfed in a British North American union. Hence, it would then be to their advantage to assimilate to the English-speaking majority. This Union did not address the issue of the Atlantic colonies. An alternative Union was also under consideration at this time, one with the United States, with some support from elements of both the Anglo and French Canadians, each with their own interests in mind. French Canadian radicals supported the ideological concept of ultramontanism, the idea of the supremacy of the Catholic Church over the state in Canada with submission to papal authority. In this sense, both the French and Irish Catholics agreed. But the Irish raids from the United States as well as the continued harassment of Acadian Catholics in northern New England along the international border quickly dissolved any reality of a Canadian–U.S. union.[38]

The Fenian Challenge

Indeed, the Irish rebels, known as "Fenians," inadvertently played an important role in helping forge a confederation unifying all of Canada. The Fenians did this with their ill-fated raids on British North America following the U.S. Civil War. The Fenian Brotherhood was one of many revolutionary groups following the Potato Famine that supported an independent Irish Republic. It was the outgrowth of the 1848 insurrection by a group calling itself Young Ireland, which was quickly put down by the British. One of its members, James Stephen, fled to Paris and a decade later returned to Dublin where he began to organize the secret revolutionary society known as the Irish Republican Brotherhood. The Irish Republican Brotherhood drew considerable support in Ireland during the depression of 1860.

A colleague of Stevens's from the Young Ireland movement, John O'Mahony, fled to the United States about the same time Stevens fled to France. He then began to organize the substantial Irish ethnics in the United States in support of Steven's group, calling the U.S. branch the Fenian, after the legendary Irish warriors called Fianna. Drawing on the large Irish population in the United States, the Fenian Brotherhood grew rapidly in America, especially from the discharged and mostly unemployed soldiers following the conclusion of the U.S. Civil War. Now the plan was to attack and capture the British North American colonies and trade them back to England in exchange for an independent Irish Republic. These plans became more of a reality once Stephen escaped capture in Ireland and fled to the United States to join O'Mahony's faction. A split soon occurred between Stephen and O'Mahony as to where the attacks would occur.

O'Mahony was replaced by the more aggressive William Randall Roberts, who planned to attack New Brunswick along the U.S. Maine border versus Stephen's plan to attack Ontario. The Roberts group included U.S. Civil War Brigadier General "Fighting Tom" Sweeny and began with raids into New Brunswick. This was a wake-up call for New Brunswick, especially for Lieutenant Governor Arthur Hamilton Gordon, whose duties also placed him in charge of the militia. Gordon renovated the hapless militia into a three-tier formation, including the "home guards" who were well-trained, regular militia serving in a voluntary capacity. They augmented the British Forces under the command of Major General Charles Hastings Doyle in fighting the Fenian invasion. Once it became clear that the large Irish population of New Brunswick was not going to join the invading American Fenians, the Stephens faction, under General Samuel Spear, attacked Ontario from New York State with the main battles at Ridgeway and Fort Erie in 1866. The Fenian raids only ended when the United States finally enforced the laws of neutrality ending the cross-border raids under the direction of President Andrew Johnson and the command of Major General George Meade.

The initial tacit approval of the Fenian raids by the United States reflected a de facto policy of Manifest Destiny that was endorsed in the 1850s during the presidency of Franklin Pierce through the administration's encouragement of American Filibusters, armed private armies, to instigate insurrections in Mexico and Central America. These tensions were part of a greater U.S. plan to also annex southwestern Ontario as well as parts of western British North America. With the independent Irish Republic movement, these filibusters now attacked across the northern U.S. border, again with well-armed American mercenaries, including high-ranking Civil War officers. General Sweeny, the Fenian Secretary of War, was able to continue his career in the U.S. Army until his retirement in 1870. The people of British North America reacted to the Fenian threat by coming together as a cohesive unit overcoming the previous divisions that were obstacles to Confederation. This was a prime example of Simmel's theorem: "out-group hostility increased in-group cohesion."

Robert Dallison, in his 2006 book *Turning Back the Fenians: New Brunswick's Last Colonial Campaign*, summarizes the role of these invasions on Canadian unity. Essentially the Fenian crisis gave the people of British North America a common and shared military experience along with a distrust of the United States, enhancing their sense of community and loyalty and removing the major obstacles, at least temporarily, that existed between the various ethnic and sectarian groups. Moreover, Lieutenant Governor Gordon's reorganization of the militia into small but active volunteer forces provided the model for Canadian defense that has carried on to the present. This coming together of the various factions in New Brunswick led both Queen Victoria and Lieutenant Governor Gordon to now support confederation and a union of the Atlantic Provinces. Dallison notes, "Without New Brunswick, there would have been no Confederation, and without Confederation there would be no modern Canada. Canada is the real legacy of the Fenian crisis of 1866. Even then, Prince Edward Island and

Newfoundland chose to remain British colonies keeping alive the plan for some in the United States for their annexation."[39]

Dominion of Canada

In 1867, the British North American Act (Constitution Act), expanded the Canadian Union of 1840, creating the Dominion of Canada, consisting of the provinces of Quebec, Ontario, Nova Scotia, and New Brunswick. French Canadians made up 80% of Canada at this time. The British North American Act reduced some of the harshness of the Ex-Quebec Act by recognizing the French language and allowing each province certain powers, such as control over education. This led to Canada's contrasting educational system with each province dictating the direction of its schools, notably if they were to be French Catholic or English Protestant. The British North American Act also divided powers between the federal and provincial governments. Quebec Province retained its French administrative and Napoleonic civil traditions including socioeconomic and cultural affairs. The parliamentary system also provided universal suffrage for all male citizens 18 or older. The crown-recommended, federally appointed Governor General for Canada and the Provincial Lieutenant Governor posts were mainly ceremonial with the real political authority vested in the respective prime ministers.

The act also established the Court of Appeals, the highest provincial judicial authority. This system provided the legal mechanism used by French Canadians in their numerous efforts at secession from Canada in the 20th century. Hence, the British North American Act did not reduce the intensity of conflict that existed between the dominant British Canadian administration and the French and Indians. The Dominion of Canada only included the eastern provinces with the exception of Newfoundland and Prince Edward Island. The western territories were still considered British colonies, but Canada was worried about U.S. intentions of annexing these territories following the establishment of territorial governments in Dakota, Montana, and Idaho as well as the purchase of Alaska in March 1867. These fears led to pressures toward incorporating portions of Canada West into the Confederacy, notably British Columbia and Manitoba, those territories being eyed by the United States for annexation.[40]

The geopolitical mix at this time was the continuing battle between Canada's French Catholics and its British Protestants as well as constant threats from the United States to annex western Canada and/or Prince Edward Island and Newfoundland in the east. The Liberal-Conservative Coalition, put together in 1854 by British leader John A. Macdonald and French leader Georges Cartier, which ultimately forged the Dominion Act, was being threatened by the conflict in Canada West. Ironically, Macdonald apparently was proslave and a Confederate sympathizer who, as attorney general of Canada

West during the U.S. Civil War, refused to prosecute Confederate operatives (Copperheads) who used Canada as a base for raids in Vermont and New York as well as for planning the assassination of President Lincoln. His racism aside, Macdonald became the first Canadian Prime Minister (1867–1873) and provided strong support for the Confederation and the Canadian Union.

On the other hand, W. L. Mackenzie, mayor of Toronto, infuriated U.S. slaveholders when he publically condemned slavery in the United States, a sentiment that encouraged the use of Canada as the last station on the Underground Railroad, which brought some 30,000 black slaves to freedom. The United States still harbored hard feelings toward Britain for supporting the Confederacy during the 1861–1865 war. The tacit support by the postwar administrations of both Andrew Johnson and U. S. Grant of Fenian and other filibusters caused trouble along the Canadian border, hastening the need for Canada to bring its western territories into the Confederation and to consolidate its reign from the Atlantic to the Pacific. If the South was able to secede from the U.S. Union, the U.S. Secretary of State publically advocated the annexation of all of Canada as compensation for losses to the Confederacy. The main vehicle for the consolidation of the west with the rest of Canada was the completion of the transnational Canadian Pacific Railroad. The last spike was driven on November 7, 1885. The United States had completed its transcontinental railroad more than 16 years earlier, on May 10, 1869, opening up the west south of the Canadian border.

Louis Riel and the Indian/Métis Rebellions

The Red River, only 70 miles from Minnesota in the United States, became the focus of cross-border tension, resulting in an armed uprising by the *Métis*, those Canadians of mixed European (mostly French) and Aboriginal descent. They were descendants of men who came to the area to work for the Hudson Bay Company (HBC), married Indian women, and lived among the indigenous tribes of the area for generations. These Métis settlements wanted to maintain their frontier lifestyle once these lands were brought into the Confederation. Initially, most of the Red River's population wanted to be a crown colony rather than part of Canada, but under the leadership of Louis Riel, the Métis established a de facto provisional government, challenging the envisioned onslaught of Anglophone Protestant settlers from Ontario who would take their land.

The Métis National Committee stopped a survey party from partitioning the former HBC lands into English-style square-shaped lot allotments, insisting instead that the new province use the Quebec-like seigniorial system because most of the long-term residents of the area were of French Canadian descent. Moreover, they did not hold title to the HBC land on which they traditionally resided and would have had to compete with Anglos from Ontario

The Emerging United States and Its Expansionist Mandate

for allotments. Another problem was that provisions in the HBC buyout were made for tribal lands, but no such arrangements were made for the Métis, who were considered nonstatus as well as any of their full-blooded wives.

Consequently, the Métis blocked the nonbilingual Lieutenant Governor designate, William McDougall, from entering the territory from the United States on November 2, 1869. The Métis also seized Fort Garry on the same day, resulting in the Red River Rebellion. The Red River Rebellion illustrated the ethnic and sectarian divide that was challenging the new Canadian Confederacy and the delicate balance forged by Prime Minister John A. Macdonald with the French Canadian leader, Georges Cartier, in his Liberal-Conservative Coalition. The main protagonists were the French Catholic Canadians and the Calvinist Scotch–Irish settlers. Louis Riel came to represent the French Canadians, and Thomas Scott became the poster child for the anti-Catholic Calvinists. The *Dictionary of Canadian Biography* describes Thomas Scott as a Presbyterian and zealous Orangeman and a member of the 49th Hastings Battalion of Rifles at Stirling. Scott was captured by the Métis forces, escaped, and later attempted to storm Fort Garry under the leadership of Major Charles Arkoll Boulton.

Although all other captives were eventually released and/or pardoned by the Métis, Scott remained a belligerent prisoner and was executed by firing squad on March 4, 1870, making him a cause célèbre for the Orangemen of English Canada. Scott's execution was a miscalculation by the Métis, delaying the eventual entry of Manitoba into the Confederation but without the bicultural and bilingual provisions sought by the Métis National Committee and ending any hopes for a Quebec West province. The execution of Thomas Scott also forced Louis Riel into exile across the border in the United States. Nonetheless, the Manitoba Act of May 12, 1870, formally admitted Manitoba into the Canadian Confederation with Louis Riel now viewed as "The Father of Manitoba." The new Lieutenant Governor, Adams George Archibald, brought along elements of the Canadian militia to quell any further outbursts from within Canada West as well as to keep the Fenians and filibusters from coming across the U.S. border and causing trouble. British Columbia followed suit a year later.[41]

The transcontinental railroad exacerbated the conflict in Canada West, especially between the new, mainly English-speaking settlers and the French Canadians, who hoped to create another French Catholic province in the west. Included in this mix were the Cree and Blackfoot First Nations Indian tribes. Anglo settlers soon flooded the region, displacing both the Métis and indigenous tribes, killing off the buffalo, stealing tribal lands, and forcing them into Saskatchewan Territory. The situation worsened when the federal government reneged on its treaty obligations, causing dire conditions among the First Nation people as well as the Métis and leading to the Northwest

Rebellion of 1885. Riel was asked to return from the United States to lead his people in this second rebellion. Again, the Métis and their First Nation confederates formed a provisional government, now in Saskatchewan, and fought a number of small skirmishes, including the Battle of Duck Lake, the Battle of Fish Creek, and the Battle of Batoche. The armed Métis rebellion was short lived due to the rapid deployment of the militia under Major General Frederick Dobson Middleton, which arrived in less than 2 weeks via the nearly completed trans-Canada railroad. On May 15, 1885, Riel surrendered, but his First Nation allies held out until June 3 at the Battle of Loon Lake. The Canadian Indians, like their kin in the western United States, were waging a losing battle against the onslaught of white settlers determined to occupy their land and destroy their lifestyle.

Louis Riel, although a dual U.S.–Canadian citizen, was charged with treason. The trial went forward despite cries for amnesty or at least a change of venue for this trial. But due to pressure from the Anglo-Canadians, especially from Calvinist Ulstermen, Prime Minister Macdonald ordered the trial to be held in Regina where Riel was tried before a jury of six English and Scottish Protestants from the area. The trial started on July 28, 1885, and lasted 5 days. The jury found Riel guilty of treason but recommended mercy. Nonetheless, the judge, Hugh Richardson, sentenced him to death. Circumstances surrounding Louis Riel's mental state during the conflict were offered as reasons for appeal before both the Court of Queen's Bench of Manitoba and the Judicial Committee of the Privy Council. All appeals were denied. Macdonald upheld the execution order, and Riel was hanged for treason on November 16, 1885.

Many felt that he was actually executed in retaliation for Thomas Scott's execution in 1870. Riel's execution had significant repercussions for Macdonald and the Conservative Party as well as for Canadian nationalism, setting the stage for the French–Anglo sectarian divisions that were to follow. Quebec province no longer was a passive partner of the Conservative majority, resulting in the creation of a new French Nationalist Liberal government led by Honore Mercier. Although John A. Macdonald held on to power into his 70s and died in office in 1891, the stage was set for a divided Canada along sectarian lines. In 1890, Riel's province, Manitoba, with its now English Protestant majority, established a single, state-supported school system abolishing Catholic separate schools, violating the intent of the 1870 settlement. Mercier's pro-Catholic Quebec was met with the rise of the ultra-Protestant movement in Ontario. But the pendulum swung from the extremes back to the middle by 1896 with both Anglo Conservatives and French Liberals seeking middle ground in order to preserve Macdonald's nationalistic efforts. With the 1896 Remedial Bill, education became a right of the province and not the federal government. In 1896, Wilfred Laurier became the first French Canadian Prime Minister with his Liberal party leading Canada until Britain's entry into the World War I. He died in 1919.[42]

Turbulence in Mexico: The Road to Revolution

Following the Gadsden Purchase, Mexican liberals finally gained the upper hand. In 1855, they staged yet another revolt known as the Ayutla Revolution, which was successful in ridding Mexico of President Antonio López de Santa Anna for good. Now the liberals, led by Benito Juárez, the only full-blood Indian to govern Mexico, assembled to construct the 1857 Constitution, which called for a democratic republican form of government, one that supported protection from the dismantling of communal lands. However, the conservative elite hit back before these elements of the Constitution could be put into effect, inviting Maximilian of Hapsburg to intervene into Mexican politics and assuring him the role of Emperor. What ensued was known as the War of Reform, which included General Porfirio Díaz's defeat of Napoleon III's forces at Puebla on May 5, 1862—an event celebrated to the present as the Cinco de Mayo day of celebration. Eventually, the liberals won over the conservatives, resulting in Maximilian's death at the hands of General Díaz in 1867.

The Reign of Porfirio Díaz: America's Favorite Despot

The Porfiriato Setting the Stage for the Mexican Revolution

The long reign of Porfirio Díaz, known as the Porfiriato, lasted from 1872 until he was exiled to Paris on May 25, 1911, in the midst of the Mexican Revolution that began in 1910. Díaz, a general under President Juárez during the rebellion against Archduke Maximilian, first made a name for himself as part of the May 5, 1862, defeat of Napoleon III's troops at Puebla—a major event in Mexican history celebrated to this day as *Cinco de Mayo*. Díaz was also involved in the final defeat and execution of Maximilian in 1867. Díaz and Juárez later had a falling out over the 1871 presidential elections won by Juárez, which paved the way for his administration following the death of Díaz on July 9, 1872. Confirmed as president in 1877, Díaz began his long tenure as de facto head of Mexico.

Díaz had support from the United States because of the lessening of border tensions and the opening up of Mexican resources and markets for U.S. capitalist endeavors. During the Porfiriato era, Mexico had a semblance of political stability and economic growth. The national debt was paid, and the national treasury had some $70 million worth of cash reserves at the end of Díaz's tenure in 1911. This prosperity for big business and the upper classes came at a price, one that eventually led to the revolution of 1910. The indigenous Indians and poor lower-class Mestizos suffered under the classist and racist policies of the Porfiriato era. These practices, however, further endeared Díaz to U.S. political and business interests.

Essentially, Díaz was an ideal partner for both U.S. and European capitalists opening up Mexico's resources for their exploitation and profit. This economic environment included cheap labor, significant tax breaks, and favorable judicial responses that favored foreign interests as well as those of the elite *cientificos*. Consequently, notable capitalists, such as William Randolph Hearst, invested heavily in mines (gold, silver, zinc, lead, and copper), petroleum, and textiles while amassing large land holdings along with the elite Mexican *cientificos*. The Díaz administration facilitated these foreign endeavors by constructing a rail system from southern Mexico to the United States, providing a means of transporting minerals and products out of Mexico. The rail system also provided greater access to low-cost Mexican laborers by allowing for the better distribution of this available labor resource. Toward this end of appeasing foreign interests, peasant lands and Indian collectivities were taken for these enterprises or in order to create massive haciendas. Taking a chapter from U.S. Indian policy, Díaz abrogated Spanish laws protecting Indian lands and peasant collective farms. This process forced Indians and peons to continue to live on their former land and compelled them to work for the new landowners. This bondage of the impoverished peasants was further welded by forcing the peons to purchase all essentials from the hacienda store, thereby forcing them into debt—a debt passed on from generation to generation and among hacienda owners, making these workers virtual slaves. Another facet of *cientifico* control was maintained by keeping the peons ignorant by denying them any education—a model borrowed from the American slave plantations. At the time of the revolution in 1910, 3% of the population owned 95% of functional land in Mexico.

An outgrowth of the Díaz administration was the emergence of a middle class comprised of clerks, teachers, small businessmen, and legal and clinical practitioners. Creating a wedge between the elite *cientificos* and the large peon/peasant class, this group by virtue of its limited influence also felt alienated by the government. During the Díaz administration, there was in effect a caste-like system in which the upper echelons of loyal *cientificos* continued to hold all important and profitable positions in Mexican society. Clearly, the prosperity of the Díaz era did little to increase the quality of life for the rank-and-file Mexican worker and his or her family. Even in foreign-based enterprises, Mexican workers earned less than workers from the United States employed at the same facility. Concern over the double-wage system led to strikes in mines and to the bloody suppression of the Mexican workers. Borrowing techniques from the Texas Rangers, these strikers were brutally suppressed by government goon squads called *rurales*. Garner, in his book on Porfirio Díaz, notes that in the Cananea mining strike of 1906 the Mexican government allowed the mine's U.S. owners to bring in U.S. police and vigilantes to quell the strike and attack Mexican workers, doing so under the pretense of protecting U.S. lives and property. This became a common Manifest Destiny theme that later played out numerous times in U.S. interventions in Central America and continues to the present. The harsh responses to labor strife were precursors to the Mexican Revolution:

> The first flashpoint was the mining town of Cananea in Sonora, which was, in effect, a U.S. company town belonging to the Cananea Consolidated Copper Company. A protest over wage differentials between the 6,000 Mexican employees and their 600 U.S. counterparts led to a riot in which company guards fired on the workforce. The excessive use of force was compounded by the permission granted to the company by the governor of Sonora, Rafael Izábal, to allow 260 Arizona rangers to cross the border to restore order in what was widely criticized at the time as an open violation of Mexican sovereignty. A year later, strikes at Mexico's textile mills were also brutally suppressed by troops and *rurales*, resulting in striking workers killed and five union leaders executed. These actions merely solidified the solidarity of the workers and their membership in the Great Circle of Free Workers, which comprised mainly female workers—a force to be reckoned with in the festering revolution. These were workers in the textile mills of Puebla, Tlaxcala, and Veracruz who called for a number of strikes over pay and working conditions. Their actions were met with lockouts and firings. Harsh treatment by the government extended beyond striking workers. Manzanarez notes that law and order under the Díaz administration came at a high price. Civil liberties and rights were suppressed for the majority of Mexicans, especially for those of Indian descent. This double standard of justice was based upon the *cientificos*' belief that the indigenous and the poor lower-class Mestizos were morally inferior. From this, Manzanarez concludes, "The Porfirian society was not only classist, but racist too."[43]

Ironically, Harris notes that Díaz's effectiveness in controlling crime along the border led to the disbanding of the Texas Rangers's notorious Frontier Battalion and to the relegation of the Rangers to a state police force providing assistance to local law enforcement agencies. The Mexican Revolution changed the status quo when the war threatened the borderland area. By 1901, the Texas Rangers had become the personal police force for the reigning governor, serving to protect the large landowners and the railroad tycoons. In this sense, they served a similar function as their counterparts in New Mexico and Arizona, intervening in labor disputes and quelling strikes. Díaz's administration inadvertently helped set the stage for further U.S. expansionism—an extension of Pierce's interpretation of Manifest Destiny and the Monroe Doctrine. Following Maximilian's defeat, Díaz postponed Mexico's revolution by toning down the anti-Catholicism fervor initiated by Benito Juárez, thus giving the impression of appeasing the Indian and Mestizo who held their lands in communal holdings. Nonetheless, Díaz shared the U.S.' view of American Indians—that they were racially inferior and a significant burden to modernization and progress. Díaz's policies of the 1880s and 1890s included harsh penalties against protests as well as the revision of colonization laws allowing the Mexican elite and white foreigners, notably Protestants, to obtain large tracts of land that formerly were held by the Catholic Church and peasant communities. Hence, some two million acres of communal Indian lands went to large landholding corporations.[44]

With a peaceful northern border, one heavily policed by friendly Díaz forces, the United States was again free to strike against Spanish holdings in the Americas and beyond. The pretense for the Spanish-American War was the mysterious sinking of the gunboat USS *Maine* in Havana harbor on February 15, 1898. It set the stage for U.S. military intervention against the remaining Spanish holdings in the Americas and beyond. This intervention included Cuba and Puerto Rico as well as Spanish holdings in the Pacific—the Philippines, Carolina, and the Marshall and Mariana Islands, which included Guam. President McKinley's war concluded with a treaty with Spain, signed in Paris on December 10, 1898. The Spanish-American War made McKinley a national hero along with his Assistant Secretary of the Navy Theodore Roosevelt, who both agitated for this conflict. When war appeared inevitable, Theodore Roosevelt resigned his administrative position for the brevet military rank of lieutenant colonel and command of a volunteer regiment of cowboys, the Texas Rangers, and Ivy League friends. His unit was coined the First United States Voluntary Cavalry, also known as the Rough Riders.

Nonetheless, the Teller Amendment to the congressional approval for the war in April 1898, precluded the United States or any other foreign country from colonizing Cuba. The exception was that section captured in the first military action in Cuba by the U.S. Marines: Guantanamo Bay. The United States has held a perpetual, irrevocable lease on this portion of Cuba since 1903. The Paris treaty expanded U.S. holdings to include Puerto Rico, Guam, and the rest of the Mariana, Carolina, and Marshall Islands. And the United States forced Spain to relinquish the Philippine Islands for $20 million, much like it did in the Gadsden Purchase nearly a half-century earlier. The purchase of the Philippine Islands, however, was contested by its indigenous peoples, leading to the Philippine-American War of 1899–1900. The new acquisitions in the Pacific, including the annexation of Hawaii in 1898, led to considerable resentment among the Japanese, who felt that Asia was its own to colonize, as well as the eventual U.S. involvement in the Second World War. Moreover, as with the war with Mexico, this latest episode of U.S. imperialism provided the proving ground for a number of military and political leaders during the 20th century, notably, Theodore Roosevelt, who used his Rough Rider fame to become governor of New York, vice president, and president; brevet Major John Pershing, who rose to the highest U.S. military rank of general of the armies after a career that included leading a regiment of black "Buffalo Soldiers" (hence his nickname: "Black Jack") and heading the Punitive Expedition into Mexico in 1916–1917 and the American Expeditionary Force in the First World War; and Douglas MacArthur, who served as second lieutenant under his father, Major General Arthur MacArthur, in the Philippine-American War, and who became a highly decorated general in the First World War and a five-star general during the Second World War.[45]

Seeds of Mexican Discontent

Although most Mexicans were probably not much interested in the geopolitics of the time, U.S. imperialism in Spanish-held territories had to worry some of the elite within Mexico. Ai Camp, in his book *Politics in Mexico*, offers more compelling grassroots reasons for the anti-Díaz revolution. Although Díaz did much to improve the overall Mexican economy, the wealthy elite, both at home and abroad, were the main benefactors. Conspicuously absent from these capitalistic gains were the laboring Mestizos and the native Indians. These were the same groups that strongly supported Díaz when he succeeded the popular indigenous President Juárez. His political machine included executive control of the national police and the army, a brute force governing mechanism that was an integral part of Mexican politics until the 1940s. The political manipulation of national elections existed until the 21st century. By placing increasingly more power in the hands of the elite, Díaz managed to reverse the decentralization trend begun by President Juárez. Indeed, over its 30 years of influence, the Porfiriato reverted back to the old Spanish authoritarian and paternalistic model that excluded the masses from meaningful enfranchisement.

After three decades of abuse, Mexicans revolted over the exploitations of Mestizo and Indian peasants as well as the restrictions placed upon the new, emerging middle class. The Maderista Revolt against the Díaz regime was launched on November 10, 1910, by Francisco Madero, a Mexican of high status and wealth. Francisco Madero ran against Díaz in the 1910 elections and was subsequently arrested, escaped from jail, and fled to the United States. On November 10, 1910, Madero and his forces crossed into Mexico from the United States at Piedras Negras in the State of Coahuila. Two popular revolutionary leaders emerged during the early years of the revolution: Emiliano Zapata, a Mexican Indian, and Francisco Pancho Villa, a Mestizo. In May 1911, Madero's forces took Ciudad Juárez, the critical border town linking El Paso, Texas, with Mexico. This event led to the Treaty of Juárez in which Díaz agreed to resign and leave the country. On May 25, 1911, General Victoriano Huerta escorted Díaz to a German ship for exile to France, leaving his vice president, Francisco Leon de la Barra, to take over as interim president and setting the stage for Madero's election as Mexico's president in November 1911. Madero's reign was short lived. He and his vice president, Pino Suarez, were assassinated in a coup d'etat led by General Victoriano Huerta in 1913. In July 1914, Huerta was forced into exile, and the revolution took on new dimensions with the forces of Generals Carranza and Obregón (Constitutionalists) now fighting the popular forces of Emiliano (Emilio) Zapata and Francisco (Pancho) Villa (Conventionists). The Constitutionalists represented a strong Mexican federal government free of U.S. controls but one that maintained the status quo of a highly stratified social structure, and the Conventionists wanted an autonomous country but with a redistribution of the land and a return to the communal village system. Zapata was assassinated under orders of General Pablo Gonzalez, and Pancho Villa's forces raised havoc in northern Mexico, finally lending his support to President-Elect Adolfo de la Huerta in 1920.[46]

The Texas Rangers's Reign of Terror: Prelude to Pancho Villa's U.S. Raid

Benjamin Heber Johnson, in his 2003 book *Revolution in Texas*, documented the Texas Rangers's active involvement in vigilantism directed against Tejanos:

> Tejanos paid a high price for the newfound unity of Anglo south Texans... Those suspected of joining or supporting the raiders constituted the most obvious of targets, as they had from the uprising's beginning. Ethnic Mexican suspects were lynched after nearly every major raid in 1915. Shortly after the attack on the Norias ranch house, for example, unknown assailants killed three Tejanos... presumably for suspicion of aiding or participating in the attack. The Texas Rangers who had arrived after the fight might have been responsible. In any event, the Rangers's actions encouraged such measures: the next morning, they posed with their lassos around the three corpses, and the picture soon circulated as a postcard.[47]

U.S. soldiers, who were not permitted by military law to execute their prisoners, often turned Mexican or Tejano suspects over to local sheriffs or the Texas Rangers, knowing that they would execute them without a trial. In a battle on September 28, 1915, the Texas Rangers and raiders fought near Ebenoza, in Hidalgo County. Following the clash, the Texas Rangers took and hanged over a dozen prisoners, leaving the bodies to rot with empty beer bottles stuck in their mouths. Relatives did not dare to bury their dead because of the fear of being targeted for death themselves by the local sheriff or Texas Rangers. Many felt that the official death count of 300 was low. A local paper, the *Regeneración*, put the count closer to 1,500. U.S. Army scout Virgil Lott notes, "How many lives were lost can not be estimated fairly for hundreds of Mexicans were killed who had no part in the uprising, their bodies concealed in the thick underbrush and no report ever made by the perpetrators of these crimes."[48]

The Texas Rangers's reign of terror in south Texas had its effect on the Tejanos with many fleeing across the border never to return. This was what the large Anglo landowners wanted. Indeed, Robert Kleberg, manager of the King Ranch, wanted martial law enforced in south Texas with Mexicans and Tejanos placed in concentration camps. He further suggested, "When a certain man [who] is discovered to have taken part in a bandits' raid is captured or killed in such a raid, his brothers, half-brothers, and brothers-in-law are assumed to be guilty and are immediately arrested or killed." It should be noted that the King Ranch increased its holdings under Kleberg from 500,000 acres in 1885 at the time of the death of founder Richard King to nearly 1.25 million acres. Much of this land was stolen from Mexican and Tejano owners at the time of the 1848 Treaty of Guadalupe Hidalgo and given to Anglos such as King by white-run courts. The King Ranch was run with sharecropper labor, and its owner had a keen interest in keeping the former Hispanic owners as subservient laborers indebted to the company store. Toward this end, the Texas Rangers acted as the King Ranch's private police force, harshly punishing any uppity Mexican. Interestingly, this program of ethnic cleansing and the forced displacement and elimination of Mexicans and Tejanos in south Texas has only recently been widely discussed despite an investigation by the Texas House in 1919 looking into the deaths of some 5,000 people of Mexican descent by the Texas Rangers and local law enforcement officers doing the dirty work of Anglo landowners. A positive outcome was that this extreme action of targeting Hispanics resulted in an effort to organize Mexican Americans into a viable political entity, leading to the creation of the League of United Latin American Citizens (LULAC). The racist behavior of the Texas Rangers, coupled with U.S. interference in the Mexican Revolution, were major factors in General Villa's raid on the Army base in Columbus, New Mexico.

Pancho Villa's Raid on the United States

The massacre of Mexicans and Mexican Americans (Tejanos) by the Texas Rangers in south Texas and across the border had a negative impact in Mexico itself with U.S. residents targeted by Mexican forces. These actions were often sanctioned by General Pancho Villa, who dominated the revolutionary forces in northern Mexico. Ironically, General Villa was the only revolutionary leader not to openly condemn President Wilson's action of sending U.S. troops into Mexico and seizing Veracruz in 1914. Nonetheless, the harsh treatment of Hispanics following the ill-fated *Plan de San Diego* soured Villa. As a result, he engaged in cross-border raids—the most notable being the 1916 raid on the U.S. Army base at Columbus, New Mexico. Villa, long alienated from the Carranza administration, was also upset that President Wilson now formally recognized Carranza as the legitimate leader of Mexico. General Villa believed that Wilson had made an agreement with Carranza allowing Mexico to become a de facto U.S. protectorate, thus allowing for a return to the Díaz status quo. Two months earlier, on January 11, 1916, Villa's troops stopped a train at Santa Ysabel, Chihuahua, Mexico, and executed 17 Texas mining engineers who were invited by President Carranza to reopen the Cusihuiriachi mines in Mexico. In reaction to this act, U.S. vigilantes killed another 100 or so Mexican Americans.

On March 9, 1916, Villa and 485 troops made an early morning raid on the 13th U.S. Cavalry at Camp Furlong near Columbus, New Mexico, former Mexican Territory until the Gadsden Purchase. The raid had a dramatic effect on U.S.–Mexican relations because of its audacity and not due to U.S. casualties with only 10 enlisted men and eight civilians killed. The aftermath of the raid had far more devastating consequences for Mexicans and Mexican Americans. James Hurst, in his work on the Villista prisoners, indicates that some scholars contend that abuses occurred immediately following the raid with U.S. soldiers indiscriminately killing anyone who looked Mexican during the so-called hot pursuit led by Major Frank Tompkins's forces. Tompkins justified the "hot pursuit" into Mexico and the slaughter of up to 100 Mexicans by claiming that these casualties were part of the raiding party. President Wilson's reaction was one of intervention into Mexico under U.S. unilateral authority inherent in the Monroe Doctrine.

President Wilson sent up to 12,000 army troops under Brigadier General John J. "Black Jack" Pershing in an 11-month punitive expedition. In listing all U.S. forces involved in the punitive expedition, two National Guard units, the First New Mexico Infantry National Guard and the Second Massachusetts Infantry National Guard, were among the forces mustered for this action. Although the Posse Comitatus Act restricted the National

Guard for use only by the authority of the governor of a state unless authorized by the president pursuant to the Insurrection Act, this represented a new era in U.S. national defense. These two National Guard units remained on the U.S. side of the border during the punitive expedition, providing a supportive function. The concept of a federally mobilized National Guard greatly aided in the expansion of the U.S. Army for the First World War via the Defense Act of 1916. This also put an end to volunteer regiments, such as the Rough Riders, which were often poorly trained with allegiance only to their politically appointed leaders.

The expedition brought considerable hardships to Mexicans in the area but never completed its original mission of capturing General Villa. The punitive expedition not only raised havoc among the rural, poor Mexicans in northern Mexico, it clashed with Carranza's government force on June 20, 1916, in the town of Carrizal where dozens were killed. Anticipating a full-fledged war with Mexico, Congress passed the National Defense Act in June 1916 authorizing doubling the size of the U.S. Army and authorizing the president to federalize the National Guard. Following its passage, President Wilson activated some 75,000 National Guardsmen into federal service to serve along the U.S.–Mexico border.[49]

Harsh Treatment of the Villista Prisoners

Although Mexico showed compassion for U.S. prisoners of war (POWs), the United States did not reciprocate in kind. In the Columbus, New Mexico, raid seven Mexican soldiers were captured, tried in civilian courts, and sentenced to death by hanging. Racial sentiments played a major role here as they did in south Texas. With anti-Mexican sentiment running high among Anglo-Americans in New Mexico, especially in the southern part bordering Mexico, the Deming, New Mexico, courts labeled the captured prisoners bandits. Another 19 soldiers were captured by Pershing's troops in Mexico, and they also were charged with murder and tried in civilian courts. Six Mexican soldiers were executed (hanged) in June 1916, and six of the seven captured in the Columbus raid eventually received full, complete, and unconditional pardons from New Mexico Governor Lorrazolo in November 1920. His decision was influenced by the 1907 Hague Convention concerning the laws and customs of war on land. These rules were adopted in response to the brutal treatment of the Boer (Dutch) by the British in South Africa during the Boer War and the atrocities attributed to U.S. troops in the Philippines in the aftermath of the Spanish-American War. But once freed by the governor, they were rearrested by the Luna County sheriff and again charged with murder. They were sentenced to prison terms in a violation of the U.S. Constitutional guarantee against double jeopardy.[50] The Texas Rangers, other state militias, and the National Guard were established mainly to rid the country of its nonwhite peoples, a trend that continued in the segregated south until Congress passed the U.S. Civil Rights laws in the mid-1960s. Even then, de facto racism within U.S. law enforcement continues to the present. A look at the use of police and the military to control American Indians illustrated this unique American phenomenon.

Policing American Indians: Boundary Maintenance through Laws and Force

Introduction

Following the U.S. Civil War, Congress ended treaty-making through the Indian Appropriations Act of 1871, setting the stage for the post–Civil War militaristic tendency toward Indian policies. A year later, President Ulysses S. Grant proposed his *peace policy* whereby he established the concept of forced accommodation of American Indians via missionary groups being entrenched in Indian Country, notably within the emerging militarized concentration camps set up to better control the Indians as well as to provide more of their treaty and traditional lands for white settlement. On March 3, 1871, the U.S. House of Representatives expanded its role over Indian Country matters by eliminating the U.S. Senate from its traditional role as the sole authority over ratifying Indian treaties. Now, any "agreements" with tribes required ratification by both houses of Congress. Executive orders and Congressionally determined federal statutes now became the new norm for dealing with American Indians, effectively eliminating tribes from having a voice in U.S. Indian affairs. These new political avenues did much to obviate existing treaties. By reversing the long-held colonial tenet of the *aboriginal right of occupancy*, the United States could now unilaterally classify uncooperative tribes as well as individual Indians as outlaws, renegades, and/or savages (enemy combatants, to use contemporary terminology), allowing them to be hunted down and destroyed like dangerous criminals by the military, militias, and vigilantes. The idea of full assimilation for American Indians was never part of the peace policy or any U.S. Indian policy. Even the concept of *accommodation* with a shared but separate social structure was never intended as a viable plan. Indian Wars continued despite the new peace policy, especially with the Apache of the Southwest and the Plains Indian tribes. These policies did much to increase the level of conflict, making a mockery of President Grant's so-called *peace policy*. The dual policy of demonizing American Indians who wanted to maintain their traditional ways and customs along with the invasion of religious groups mandated to educate, domesticate, and otherwise "civilize" the tribes, set forth the era of competing physical genocide by the U.S. military and the onslaught of cultural genocide and Christian ethnocentrism by church groups. Hence the Indian Wars lasted from the 1860s until the Wounded Knee massacre of December 29, 1890.

The ever-changing landscape of Indian Country in the United States, involving treaties, removal, allotment, Termination and Relocation, and eventually a degree of self-determination extends from the colonial era to the mid-1970s. During this time, an internal battle raged between military and civilian authorities over who would manage Indian Country. Racist leaders prevailed in both camps with generals such as Sheridan, Sherman, Crook, and (brevet) Custer eager to hunt down Indians deemed "renegades." They competed with often-corrupt politically appointed Indian Agents and/or condescending religious zealots for control over the spoils that could be gained from federal contracts awarded for the care of Indian tribes forced (incarcerated) onto reservations that were virtually concentration or internment camps. Included in this mix were *agent provocateurs* eager to ignite hostilities between Indians and whites, including those intruding into the so-called protected tribal domains in Indian Country. Neither the U.S. Army nor the Indian Agents were interested in preserving the traditional cultures of the tribes they oversaw. Indeed, the U.S. Army was bent on physical genocide, and their civilian counterparts were engaged in cultural genocide. The idea of accepting American Indian culture and traditions as equal to those of the dominant white society was destroyed with removal of the Five Civilized Tribes in the 1830s, a process that continued until the 20th century and with new ramifications in the 1950s under Termination and Relocation. The use of Indian scouts by the U.S. Army and Indian police by civilian agents emerged during the second half of the 19th century during the second phase of the U.S. Indian Wars (1865–1890).

U.S. Army and the Indian Wars of 1865–1891

The Indian Wars began during the colonial era and continued off and on up to the U.S. Civil War. Nonetheless, the longest U.S. official war was the Indian Wars that began during the Civil War and lasted until the 1890s. During this time, the U.S. Army's official Indian Campaign Medal was awarded for service in enumerated campaigns or against hostile Indians or in any other action in which the United States troops were killed or wounded between 1865 and 1891. The eligible campaigns during the Indian Wars include the following:

- Southern Oregon, Idaho, northern California, and Nevada between 1865 and 1868

- Against the Comanche and confederate tribes in Kansas, Colorado, Texas, New Mexico, and Indian Territory between 1867 and 1875
- Modoc War between 1872 and 1873
- Against the Apaches in Arizona in 1873
- Against the Northern Cheyenne and Sioux between 1876 and 1877
- Nez Perce War in 1877
- Bannock War in 1878
- Against the Northern Cheyenne between 1878 and 1879
- Against the Sheep-Eaters, Piute, and Bannocks between June and October 1897
- Against the Ute in Colorado and Utah between September 1879 and November 1880
- Against the Apaches in Arizona and New Mexico between 1885 and 1886
- Against the Sioux in South Dakota between November 1890 and January 1891
- Against hostile Indians in any other action in which U.S. troops were killed or wounded between 1865 and 1891

The Indian Campaign Medal was issued only once regardless of how many battles or campaigns a soldier was involved in. However, a silver citation star was attached to the medal for meritorious or heroic conduct. This was the predecessor to the Silver Star, currently the third highest military award for heroism. Eleven troopers were awarded the silver citation between 1865 and 1891. The highest U.S. military award, the Congressional Medal of Honor, however was also awarded during the Indian campaigns. Like many other military awards, the Indian Wars Medal was not authorized until 1907, the same time that the War Department created the Civil War Campaign Medal. These medals were awarded retroactively.

The post–Civil War and Indian Wars era provided the United States with its first permanent four-star general, U.S. Grant, in 1866. The Confederate Army, however, created the four-star general for Robert E. Lee, but this was considered a brevet rank like many of the generals of the Union, including George Armstrong Custer. When U.S. Grant became president of the United States, the sole four-star general rank was passed on to William T. Sherman and then to Philip H. Sheridan, who were leaders during the Indian Wars in the West. Ironically, William *Tecumseh* Sherman was named after the great Indian warrior. Although the Indian Campaign Medal only covers battles and encounters between 1865 and 1891, the U.S. Army documents numerous battles between the Mexican War of 1846–1848 and the U.S. Civil War (1861–1865), including fights in the 1850s with the Apaches and Utes in New Mexico Territory; the Yakima, Walla Walla, and Cayuse in the northwest;

Sioux in Nebraska; Cheyenne in Kansas; and Comanche in Oklahoma and Kansas. During the Civil War, the U.S. Army pursued the Sioux in Minnesota in 1862 during the Great Sioux Uprising and in campaigns in the Upper Missouri River region in 1863–1864. The difference following the Civil War was the division of the western United States into combat regions like the U.S. military did a century later during the Vietnam War. The major structure for frontier defenses was the division of the western areas into the Department of Dakota, Department of the Platte, Department of the Missouri, Department of Texas, Department of Arizona, Department of California, and the Department of the Columbian. During the Indian Wars, the generals of the Army were Major General Winfield Scott (Indian Removal; Mexican War), Major General George B. McClellan, Major General H. W. Halleck, General Ulysses S. Grant, General William T. Sherman, General Philip H. Sheridan, and Lieutenant General John McAllister Schofield in addition to five subordinate major generals and 16 brigadier generals and numerous colonels and lieutenant colonels. The U.S. Adjutant General was the administrative officer of the army.[51]

During the U.S. Civil War, Confederate prisoners of war (POWs) were recruited to fight Indians in the west for the Union forces. Here, southern POWs were offered the opportunity to join the Union to fight in the western Indian Wars with the promise that they would not be fighting fellow confederates. These "galvanized Yankees" had to swear allegiance to the Union and would receive a full pardon in exchange for their successful service with the U.S. Army. Freedmen, liberated former black slaves, were also recruited by the U.S. Army to fight in the Indian Wars. They became known as "Buffalo Soldiers," a name given them by the Indians because of their bravery and similarity between the hair and color of black soldiers. The Buffalo Soldiers, like the Galvanized Yankees, were enlisted men led by white Northern officers. The Buffalo Soldiers fought in the Indian Wars and the Spanish-American War, producing 23 Medal of Honor recipients for their valor.[52]

General John "Black Jack" Pershing, leader of U.S. forces during World War I and later named General of the U.S. Armies—the highest military rank in the United States (a status shared only with George Washington). This rank warrants four gold stars, outranking the silver five stars created during World War II and ended with the death of Omar Bradley in 1981. Pershing was one of the officers in charge of Buffalo Soldier units during both the Indian Wars and in the Spanish-American War, hence his nickname, Black Jack. Interestingly, George Armstrong Custer, former brevet major general during the Civil War, was offered the higher rank of full colonel if he led a Buffalo Soldier unit. He declined; hence his lower rank of lieutenant colonel. Pershing led the 1916 U.S. punitive expedition into Mexico following

General Villa's attack on a U.S. Army base in Columbus, New Mexico, transforming the U.S. Army into a mechanized force.[53]

Indian Police and Policing Indian Country: Military versus Civilian Jurisdictions

The practice of using Indian scouts usually involved employing traditional enemies, such as Custer's use of Crow scouts in his battles with the Sioux and Cheyenne or the use of same tribe Indians who were lured into service because they were "progressives" who wanted to be on the winning side as illustrated by General Crook's Apache scouts. In some instances, Indian scouts also served as Indian police. At any rate, the Indian scout held more status and was better paid than his Indian police counterpart. Indian law enforcement, regardless if it was imposed by the Army or civilians, relied on the unique judicial and administrative rules that governed Indian Country, a process that evolved rapidly from the earlier Trade and Intercourse Acts. In the early years, the War Department provided the enforcement arm in Indian Country, and the Indian Agent, later upgraded to the title of Commissioner of Indian Affairs in 1832, determined which issues required adjudication. The regulation of non-Indians within federally protected Indian Country was first established by Congress in 1817 with the Federal Enclaves Act, also known as the General Crimes Act. The purpose of this act was to extend federal law into Indian Country given that the federal government held exclusive jurisdiction in Indian Country.[54]

At the same time, Indian tribes were struggling for legal parity during this era of diminished tribal authority and increased control and regulations placed upon them, a process that was clearly one-sided with whites having a substantial legal advantage over Indian clients. A landmark case reflecting this dilemma was that of Standing Bear who filed a writ of habeas corpus before the federal courts questioning his forced incarceration in Indian Territory (Oklahoma). His tribe, the Ponca, was removed from its traditional home in eastern Nebraska so as to make room for the forceful removal of the Santee (Dakota) Sioux following the uprising in Minnesota in the early 1860s, which led to the largest federally sanctioned execution in the United States with 38 Sioux warriors hanged together on December 26, 1862.[55]

Standing Bear and his followers left the horrid conditions of their new reservation in Oklahoma and headed home to Nebraska, now the home of the interned or removed Santee Sioux. The group was subsequently arrested by General Crook's forces, and it was at this time that Standing Bear presented his habeas corpus writ to the U.S. Circuit Court, District of Nebraska. In a landmark decision, Judge Elmer S. Dundy, on May 12, 1879, ruled in Standing Bear's favor, essentially granting American Indians the official status of *human beings (persons)* albeit not U.S. citizens. American Indians no longer had to be referred to as bucks, does, and fawns in official military reports, but rather as men, women, and children.[56]

The Federal Enclaves Act was subsequently replaced with the Assimilative Crimes Act of 1825, the Major Crimes Act of 1885, and Public Law 280 in 1953. The Assimilative Crimes Act stipulated that offenses in Indian Country, although still under federal jurisdiction, would now use state or territorial statutes and sentences as a guide for federal jurisdiction, mainly for offenses committed in Indian Country by non-Indians. Tribal customs and traditions remained the mainstay for intratribal matters. Thus, the local, state, or territorial laws where the reservation was located would be used by the federal government for those crimes not specified by federal code. Although the intent was for tribal justice to operate within Indian Country for crimes by Indians against Indians, the white Indian Superintendent held virtual absolute authority in dealing with all issues within his authority. Most significantly, he had the resources of the U.S. Army at his disposal as an enforcement agent. In the constant friction between the U.S. Army and the Department of the Interior, Indian Agents began creating their own reservation police forces. Thomas Lightfoot, the Indian Agent for the Iowa, Sac, and Fox tribes in southeastern Nebraska, is credited with the movement to recruit Indians as police in Indian Country outside the Five Civilized Tribes who continued to use their police and court systems once removed to Indian Territory, doing so in 1869. Three years later, in 1872, the military special Indian Commissioner for the Navajos organized a horse cavalry of 130 Navajos to guard the newly drawn up reservation following the Navajo's return from incarceration at Fort Sumner (the *Long Walk*, 1863–1868). Meanwhile, the Cherokee Nation created the position of High Sheriff in 1875.[57]

At about the same time, Indian Agent John Clum was experimenting with his own Indian police force on the San Carlos (Arizona) Reservation. Clum did this mainly as an attempt to wrest civilian control from the military in Indian Country given that he subscribed to the cultural genocide policy spelled out in Grant's Quaker or Peace Policy in which church groups were incorporated to teach the heathen Indians the superiority of Christianity. Although not entirely successful, agents Clum and Lightfoot were successful in establishing a parallel Indian police, albeit poorly paid and trained, in Indian Country. The Apache police, as did many of their colleagues in other tribes, also served as scouts when operating with the U.S. Army.[58]

Two years following the Cherokee initiative and those of Indian Agents Clum and Lightfoot, U.S. Indian Commissioner Ezra A. Hayt officially petitioned the U.S. Congress for authorization for more Indian police on reservations. Based on Commissioner Hayt's recommendations, the U.S. Congress, in 1879, authorized pay for 430 Indian privates supervised by 50 white officers. Forty-three men served on the Indian police in Indian Territory (Oklahoma), a vast territory providing each police officer a 712-square-mile jurisdiction.

Moreover, the Indian police had to work with the U.S. Marshals and other police in bringing law to this vast haven for outlaws. Indian police were greatly restricted by the U.S. Congress. Indian police actually acted under the direction of the white Indian Agent administering his form of marshal law as against enforcing written federal, state, or territorial laws. Congress deliberately set the pay for Indian police way below that of others working for the government in Indian Country. They were paid $5 per month and had to provide their own horses, guns, and other equipment needed for the job. Indian teamsters and Indian scouts were earning three times that amount and with better benefits. As late as 1906, Indian police earned only $20 per month. A further stigma was that Congress would only authorize the use of poorly maintained, used pistols fearing that if they had rifles they could use these in a rebellion.[59]

Congress also forced them to wear gray uniforms like those of the defeated Confederate soldiers instead of the Union blue worn by soldiers and even Indian scouts. Hagan notes that pistols that wouldn't fire, starvation wages, and shoddy uniforms plagued Indian police while, at the same time, forcing them to be janitors and handymen to the Indian Agent. Clearly, the Indian police were used to enforce and protect the administration of the white Indian Agent in charge of the reservation. Agent John Clum's success was that he was able to consolidate the five Apache agencies in Arizona Territory into one large concentration at San Carlos, appeasing both the federal government, making it easier to hunt down "hostile" Apache, and the local white settlers, notably the "Tucson Ring," which benefitted from having the Apache being restricted to one area. Altruism or compassion for Apache culture never entered into the equation. Indeed, it was clear that the appointment of Indian police and Indian judges by Indian Agents was a clear attempt to abrogate traditional tribal authority and traditions and to replace these with Euro–American ways.[60]

As could be expected, some of the Indian police were also outlaws or accused of crimes, as was Sixkiller. Bob Dalton, of the infamous Dalton gang, served as a U.S. Deputy Marshal and as chief of the Osage police. He was forced out of these positions when he and his family were exposed as bootleggers. He then used his talents in robbing banks and trains. On the other hand, police heroism was exemplified in Sam Sixkiller, son of Redbird Sixkiller, former High Sheriff of the Cherokee Nation and later a captain in the Union Agency Indian police, and U.S. Deputy Marshall, who was killed in the line of duty in the streets of Muskogee in 1886. Both Dalton and Sixkiller illustrate the turbulent situation in Indian Country where lawlessness prevailed and agent provocateurs agitated Indian unrest, setting the stage for another unique chapter in American jurisprudence, that of the *court of no appeal.*[61]

Indian Territory became a haven for outlaws following the U.S. Civil War gaining the titles "robbers roost" and "the land of the six-shooter." In

The Emerging United States and Its Expansionist Mandate

an attempt to bring some justice to the territory, a unique form of justice prevailed, one in which the U.S. District Judge performed both the petit court and appellate court functions, hence federal courts of no appeal. Judge Isaac Parker, the "hanging judge," best illustrates this phenomenon. He was appointed to the U.S. Court for the Western District of Arkansas at Fort Smith with jurisdiction over all of Indian Territory (Oklahoma). Judge Parker became known as the hanging judge, and this image eventually led to changes. In 1883, the U.S. Congress split up his district, assigning the western half of Indian Territory to the U.S. Judicial District of Kansas and the southern region to the Northern District of Texas. In 1889, Congress acted to abolish the circuit court powers of the district courts with all capital cases tried before a U.S. court requiring review of an appellate court before judgment could be exercised. State law replaced territorial jurisprudence when Indian Territory became the State of Oklahoma in 1907. This still gave Judge Parker authority over the Five Civilized Tribes. He was appointed at age 35 and served in this capacity for 21 years (1875–1896) adjudicating 13,490 cases with 344 capital offenses of which 160 were sentenced to death. Shirley describes Parker's judicial reign as follows:

> The death penalty was prescribed more often and for more flagrant violations of law than anywhere on the American continent. That Judge Parker's administration was stern to the extreme is attested by the fact that he sentenced 160 men to die and hanged 79 of them. His court was the most remarkable tribunal in the annals of jurisprudence, the greatest distinctive criminal court in the world; none ever existed with jurisdiction over so great an area, and it was the only trial court in history from the decisions of which there was, for more than fourteen years, no right of appeal. ...In cases of homicide, his tribunal functioned as a circuit court, and federal statutes made no provision for having his findings reviewed by the Supreme Court of the United States. To that extent his court was greater than the Supreme Court, for it possessed both original and final jurisdiction. His decisions were absolute and irrevocable.[62]

The U.S. Marshal represented the federal law enforcement presence in Indian Country because the 1804 Congress designated the southern Mississippi Valley the Territory of Orleans and provided it with a U.S. district court along with a U.S. Marshal's office. President Thomas Jefferson appointed Francis J. L. D'Orgenay, a Creole, as marshal of the territory, making him the first "western" marshal. Among the duties of the western marshals was policing the vast territory obtained under the Louisiana Purchase, including all the Indian tribes located in this newly acquired Indian Country. Although tribes addressed their own internal disputes, the 1834 Indian Intercourse Act extended the general laws of the United States into Indian Country where Indian/white cases were now brought before the U.S. courts of Missouri and the Territory of Arkansas. Here, the U.S. Marshal and his deputies, supported by the U.S. Army, had the primary duty of enforcing federal laws as well as acting as officers of the federal court. Judge Parker relied on the U.S. Marshal and his deputies to police his vast jurisdiction as did other federal judges in Indian Country. Sixty-five deputy U.S. Marshals died during the 20-year tenure of Judge Parker carrying out his law in Indian Territory. Of these noted lawmen was Marshal Crawley P. Dake's deputy, Virgil Earp in Tombstone, who also presided over the Lincoln County War and the pursuit of Billy the Kid, and Marshal Zan L. Tidball, Marshal of Arizona Territory during the Geronimo and San Carolos episodes.[63]

In 1883, the Courts of Indian Offenses were established under the influence of President Chester A. Arthur's Secretary of the Interior, Henry M. Teller. Teller approved a *Code of Indian Offenses* designed to prohibit American Indian traditional ceremonial activities throughout Indian Country, notably traditional customs, dances, and plural marriages, which then could be prosecuted by the Courts of Indian Offenses. These courts also adjudicated minor offenses in Indian Country already defined by the Federal Enclaves and Assimilative Crimes Acts. The idea behind the Courts of Indian Offenses was to appoint "progressive" Indian judges, those dedicated to the promotion of Euro-American customs as against traditional "heathenish" practices. One of the most notable and colorful Indian judges was Quanah Parker who was appointed in 1886 to the First Court of Indian Offenses for the Kiowa and Comanche. He was later dismissed for continuing to practice certain traditional practices.[64]

During this time, the Crow Dog incident was progressing through the U.S. courts. Preliminary to this case was the strong anti-Indian sentiment in the United States fueled by Custer's Last Stand at Little Big Horn in 1776. The Crow Dog case was equally sensational in that it involved the killing of federally sponsored Sioux leader Spotted Tail by a former Indian police chief, Crow Dog. Both were Brule Sioux from the Rosebud Reservation in South Dakota just north of the Nebraska border. Given that the newly established Courts of Indian Offenses only dealt with minor cultural infractions and were not in effect at the time of the incident, the murder of Spotted Tail was left to be handled by tribal custom and protocol. Spotted Tail was the head chief of the Brule at the time of the treaties of the 1860s that established the Great Sioux Reservation and was favored by the U.S. Government because he kept the Brule Sioux out of the 1876 uprising that led to Custer's defeat. Crow Dog was a traditional Sioux and respected warrior and leader of the Big Raven Band. He was a close associate of Crazy Horse and accompanied him when he surrendered in 1877. He was also a close associate of Sitting Bull.

Both Spotted Tail and Crow Dog were vying for leadership positions in the new Rosebud agency carved out of the once-promised Great Sioux Reservation. The federal government favored Spotted Tail who they saw as a "progressive" Indian to Crow Dog who remained a "traditionalist." These ideological differences aside, the actual altercation leading to Spotted Tail's demise was most likely over a woman, Light-in-the-Lodge. Accordingly, Spotted Tail was seen as attempting to entice Light-in-the-Lodge away from her disabled elderly husband, and Crow Dog took it upon himself to right this wrong. On August 5, 1881, the 47-year-old Crow Dog shot 58-year-old Spotted Tail as they approached each other on a road near the agency. Because this was seen as an intratribal matter, it was presumed to be exempt from federal or territorial jurisdiction under the existing Federal Enclaves/General Crimes Act regulating Indian Country. The matter was subsequently resolved in a traditional fashion between the respective clans representing both Spotted Tail and Crow Dog with the Crow Dog clan compensating Spotted Tail's clan with a restitution of $600, eight horses, and a blanket.

Although this restored balance to the Brule Sioux, it did not resonate well with the federal Indian Agents and the U.S. Army. Crow Dog was then arrested under the orders of Indian Agent John Cook. Crow Dog was brought to Fort Niobrara in Nebraska for trial with the blessings of the U.S. Attorney General. At the federal trial, Crow Dog was portrayed as a bad Indian like his colleagues Crazy Horse and Sitting Bull, deserving to be executed for his crime. Given these sentiments from the prosecution, there was little doubt that the all-white male jury would find Crow Dog guilty of capital murder and sentenced by Judge G. C. Moody to be executed by hanging. In his appeal (remember, Indians are now "persons"), the First Judicial District Court of Dakotas upheld his sentence with G. C. Moody again presiding. The case then went to the U.S. Supreme Court (something that would not have happened in Judge Parker's jurisdiction). Its December 17, 1883, decision, *Ex parte Crow Dog*, upheld Crow Dog's petition and had him released from incarceration. Essentially the U.S. Supreme Court agreed with Crow Dog's contention that there were no federal laws relevant to his case and that the District Court did not have jurisdiction in an internal tribal case.[65]

The U.S. Congress responded to the Crow Dog decision by passing the Major Crimes Act in 1885. This represented a significant encroachment on tribal authority, providing overlapping jurisdiction with the Federal Enclaves Act by applying federal jurisdiction to any offender in Indian Country. U.S. Marshals could now arrest Indians and non-Indians alike for major offenses in Indian Country, subsequently bringing them before a federal court for adjudication. The original seven major crimes outlined in this law were murder, manslaughter, rape, assault with intent to kill, arson, burglary, and larceny. These soon became known as the seven index crimes. The Major Crimes Act was challenged in 1886 in *United States v. Kagama* but upheld by the U.S. Supreme Court. In March 1893, U.S. attorneys were provided original jurisdiction in representing all federal Indian wards of the United States.[66]

This policy clearly established the superior weight of the U.S. and white interest in Indian Country. An obvious problem with the law was that

American Indians did not have equal weight before the courts, especially when cases were being adjudicated before a white judge and jury. Keep in mind that it would be another 39 years before American Indians were granted federal citizenship. Even then, this did not guarantee equal legal status in local jurisdictions, notably those in which American Indians did not enjoy state citizenship. This practice continued until the Eisenhower administration and the imposition of Public Law 280 unilaterally (without tribal consent or input) allocating certain states primary legal authority in Indian Country existing within their boundaries. Clearly, the imposition of white-dominated law enforcement in Indian Country set the stage for *allotment* and the end of Indian Territory and other land areas set aside specifically for American Indians through treaties.[67]

J. Edgar Hoover, the former head of the Federal Bureau of Investigation (FBI) used the Major Crimes Act to expand the authority of the FBI throughout the United States. The index crimes provided the basis for federal data collection presented in the Department of Justice's annual *Uniform Crime Report: Crimes in the United States* with the FBI director (Hoover) taking credit as the author. Eventually, the seven major crimes were expanded to 13 offenses, including carnal knowledge of any female not his wife, not yet age 16 (statutory rape); assault with the intent to commit rape; incest; assault with a dangerous weapon; assault resulting in serious bodily injury; and robbery—many of these mere refinements of the original seven index crimes. The Major Crimes Act allowed for the FBI to have jurisdiction in Indian Country beginning with it origin in 1908. However, J. Edgar Hoover did little to publicize the presence of the FBI in Indian Country until it took on the American Indian Movement (AIM) in 1973 on the Pine Ridge Reservation in what became known as "Wounded Knee II."[68]

Allotment involved dividing up tribal lands into individual and family allotments of homestead acres (40 to 160 acres) with the excess or *surplus* lands opened up to white settlers to homestead. Moreover, Indian lands not actively being tilled were to be managed by the U.S. Department of the Interior with monies made from leases (made to white ranchers and mining, petroleum or uranium, or timber corporations) to be held in a government fund known as the Individual Indian Money (IIM) trust. The General Allotment Act (Dawes Act) was passed on February 8, 1887, over the objections of Henry M. Teller, the 15th U.S. Secretary of the Interior (1882–1885) and former U.S. Senator from Colorado and who was otherwise a strong proponent of "civilizing the savages." He feared that allotment was designed to end the communal ownership of Indian lands and treaty obligations with the manifest purpose of opening Indian Country to white settlers and homesteaders. His prophecy was correct. Indian-owned land under allotment decreased from 138 million acres in 1887 to 48 million acres in 1934. The Dawes Act was followed by a number of similar acts leading to the State of Oklahoma and dissolving of Indian Territory—the promised refuge for removed tribes. In order to better police the evicted Indians, the U.S. Congress, in July 1892, authorized the president to appoint U.S. Army personnel as Indian Agents. The 1898 Curtis Act effectively destroyed tribal governments while opening tribal lands to outside mineral and timber exploitation. In May 1906, the Burke Act reduced the length of federal protection for Indian allottees, making their holdings ripe for white exploitation as Henry Teller feared. In March 1907, the Lacey Act authorized the Individual Indian Money (IIM) trust, giving the Department of the Interior the Indians right to unilaterally to Indian allotments. Less than a year later, Oklahoma became the 46th U.S. state. Following the First World War, in which American Indians served honorably, the U.S. Congress finally conferred federal citizenship to all American Indians in 1924. Dramatic changes were imposed on the indigenous peoples at the hands of the United States from the period of the U.S. Civil War up to the First World War. Rounded up, hunted down, and forced onto reservations so that whites could have their lands and resources was the norm during this era.[69]

North America and the Neocolonial Conflicts of the 20th Century

4

Introduction

The early 20th century saw a significant influx of non-British immigrants from Europe needed to fuel its rapid industrialization, much of it related to the transformation of the U.S. military from the horse era to the new mechanized services. Moreover, the mobilization of white males into the Army provided an impetus for freedmen and their families to trade their sharecropper existence for jobs in the industrial centers of the northern states. Both the newly arrived immigrant and the black migrants found this transition to be troublesome once the white soldiers returned home following the conclusion of the First World War. At the same time, anti-Indian sentiments were also expressed, resulting in further land grabs, treaty violations, and ill treatment at the hands of the U.S. Government. Efforts to restore Indian rights and protection occurred during the Great Depression and World War II but faced a reversal during the post–WWII "communist fear" era of conservative Republicans.

Canada, during this same era, had its own problems, especially with French Canadians and its WWI draft as well as the massive migration from Quebec to New England. Regarding its indigenous populations, the dominant English Canadian government often parroted the United States, including forcing American Indian children into boarding schools. The post–WWII era saw serious threats of Quebec succession, including terrorist acts. Mexico's post-revolution era saw the entrenchment of the Institutionalized Revolutionary Party (PRI) whose actions were also often guided by the U.S. Government.

The United States and Its "Indian Problem": Changing Boundaries and Identities

Allotment: Dismantling Indian Country

Once the U.S. Congress passed the Major Crimes Act of 1885, the wheels of Indian cultural genocide went into effect. "Allotment" was a policy designed to take away the promised massive Indian Territory created with the Louisiana

Purchase in 1803. The main purpose was to dissolve the aboriginal communal ways of shared property, thereby forcing Indians to comply with the Euro-American concept of individually owned property. The caveat here was that American Indians could then be easily exploited by corrupt whites, including government agents given that American Indians had little standing before the white courts. Through the division of communal tribal lands into individual Allotments, supposedly protected by federal trust agreements, tribal authority would be greatly diminished. Moreover, "excess" or "surplus" lands could be given to white settlers:

> Whenever any Indian, being a member of any band or tribe with whom the Government has or shall have entered into treaty stipulations, being desirous to adopt the habits of civilized life, has had a portion of the lands belonging to his tribe allotted to him in severalty, in pursuance of such treaty stipulations, the [white] agent and superintendent of such tribe shall take such measures, not inconsistent with law, as may be necessary to protect such Indian in the quiet enjoyment of the lands so allotted to him.[1]

The protective trust aspect of Allotment failed, and many allotted plots were taken over by unscrupulous whites in collusion with the white-run courts, resulting in a substantial number of non-Indians living within the tribal boundaries yet not subject to tribal authority. In the end, more than 60% of Indian Country (federally protected reservations), some 86 million acres, was lost during the Allotment era, 1886–1934.

Wilcomb E. Washburn of the Smithsonian Institution, in his work *The Assault on Indian Tribalism*, contends that Allotment reflected the growing frustration by the United States over the Indian problem. In an effort to find a solution that would placate whites, a number of options were floated for serious consideration: (1) renege on existing treaty obligations and pursue an intense program of physical genocide; (2) preserve the status quo and all treaty obligations to protect Indian Country from unwanted white encroachment; (3) entice tribes to agree voluntarily to individual Allotments of land and the adoption of "civilized" ways, for example, to become farmers; (4) destroy tribal authority and force Allotment upon Indians as well as to subject them to the larger dominant society's laws; or (5) take whatever actions were deemed necessary to appease the demands of white settlers, farmers, ranchers, miners, and railroad companies for coveted tribal resources. The last option was what eventually emerged regardless of how it was presented to the tribes, the nation, or the world.[2]

Interestingly, the General Allotment Act initially exempted the Five Civilized Tribes (Cherokee, Creek, Choctaw, Chickasaw, and Seminole) as well as the Osage, Miami, Peoria, Sac, and Fox in Indian Territory as well as the Seneca Nation of New York Indians and the Sioux Nation in Nebraska. But it soon became apparent that this ruse was yet another deception in establishing a federal policy intended to eventually eliminate the Five Civilized Tribes and the others initially exempt from this policy. Indeed, in 1891, the Dawes Act was amended to allow leasing of Indian Allotments under government supervision, a process that was taken unilaterally without the consent of the Indian owners. Moreover, Indians were legally prohibited from entering their leased lands by the whites who contracted with the government for these rights.

In 1893, a new effort was made to eliminate the Five Civilized Tribes with the authorization of the Commission to the Five Civilized Tribes (Dawes Commission). The 1894 Dawes Commission report, chaired by Henry L. Dawes, called for the destruction of the Five Civilized Tribes, claiming that they were not worthy of self-government and, at the same time, praising the Protestant religious groups who attempted to "civilize" the Cherokee, Choctaw, Chickasaw, Creek, and Seminole. The final step in dismantling the governments of the Five Civilized Tribes came with the Curtis Act of June 28, 1898, that, in effect, prohibited aggrandizement of lands and abolished tribal courts and institutions, forcing Allotment throughout Indian Territory.[3]

The U.S. Supreme Court upheld the Curtis Act in 1899 in *Stephen v. Cherokee Nation*. And in 1901, the U.S. Congress granted citizenship to all Indians in Indian Territory by amending the Dawes Act. This did not provide Indian landowners equal status before the U.S. Courts. This placed Indian defendants and plaintiffs at a considerable disadvantage given that they no longer had recourse with the now-dissolved tribal courts. In 1898, U.S. federal courts held exclusive jurisdiction over all civil and criminal cases in Indian Territory. Between the enactment of the Curtis Act in 1898 and Oklahoma (formerly Indian Territory) statehood in 1907, many Indian Allotments were stolen from the indigenous allotters through a widespread conspiracy of unsavory "boomers" (white settlers) and discriminatory courts.

In 1919, all Indian veterans of World War I could apply for U.S. citizenship, providing that they initiated this action. On June 2, 1924, nearly 60 years after blacks (freedmen) were granted citizenship, all Indians born within the United States were granted *citizenship*:

> That all non-citizen Indian born within the territorial limits of the United States be and they are hereby declared to be citizens of the United States: Provided, That the granting of such citizenship shall not in any manner impair or otherwise affect the right of any Indian to tribal or other property.[4]

Reorganization

The exploitation of American Indians occurred on a grand scale, placing them in greater economic peril during the Great Depression. Attempts were made during Franklin D. Roosevelt's administration with enactment of "Reorganization"—the Wheeler-Howard Act of 1934, also known as the Indian Reorganization Act (IRA). Reorganization represented a 180 degree turnabout to the devastation created by Allotment. The impetus for change stemmed from a report conducted by the Brookings Institution titled *The Problem of Indian Administration*, authored by Lewis Meriam, hence, *The Meriam Report*. The 2-year Brookings Institution study resulted in a dismal portrayal of the shocking social and economic conditions among American Indians living under federal protection. The Meriam Report recommended individualized support for American Indians through education and job training without the religious conversion component of past reservation so-called "educational programs."[5]

The Meriam Report set the stage for the appointment of the first seemingly progressive Indian Commissioner, John Collier. Appointed by President Roosevelt in 1933, Commissioner Collier wasted no time in initiating New Deal relief programs among American Indians. Another outgrowth of the Meriam Report was the Johnson-O'Malley Act, which was passed 2 months prior to the Reorganization Act (IRA). This act allowed for federal monies being allocated to states and territories for the provision of educational, medical, and social welfare services to Indians living off of protected Indian lands.[6] Although the IRA provided for annual funding for special Indian education, its most significance element was the prohibition of Allotment. The IRA also provided funds and governmental assistance for the purpose of expanding Indian trust lands as well as provisions relevant to tribal organization and incorporation. In 1936, the IRA provisions were extended to those Indians who suffered most from Allotment: the Indian residents of Oklahoma. The downside of Indian Reorganization was that tribes had to adopt an American-style constitution. Sections 16–18 provided the framework for tribal government, a process modeled on the U.S. legislative format. Although limited in its jurisdictional scope, tribal government became the norm, if only because it was compulsory for continued federal support. The standard tribal or band constitution spelled out the governmental structure and its respective authority as well as allowances for developing tribal-specific amendments. The constitution also specified eligibility standards (blood degree) for tribal membership. Under this system, tribal leaders (Chiefs, Vice Chiefs, Presidents, Governors) and tribal council members needed to be elected by popular vote for a specific term. This system continues to the present.[7]

Termination/Relocation

Following the Second World War, Republicans again gained control of the Presidency and U.S. Congress allowing, once again, for a conservative

North America and the Neocolonial Conflicts of the 20th Century 105

anti-Indian backlash. These harsh policies were part of the Cold War anti-communism environment that prevailed in the United States during the nuclear bomb era. These fears surfaced within Indian Country with President Eisenhower's appointment of Dillon Myer, the former head of the Japanese-American Relocation Camps during the Second World War. *Termination* started with House Concurrent Resolution 108, passed on August 1, 1953. With it, the U.S. Congress attempted to terminate federal supervision over American Indians, ending treaty provisions, hence subjecting them to the same laws as non-Indians:

> Whereas it is the policy of Congress, as rapidly as possible, to make the Indians within the territorial limits of the United States subject to the same laws and entitled to the same privileges and responsibilities as are applicable to other citizens of the United States, and to grant them all of the rights and prerogatives pertaining to American citizenship; and Whereas the Indians within the territorial limits of the United States should assume their full responsibilities as American citizens.[8]

This sudden, unilateral change in U.S. Indian policy was strongly opposed by the vast majority of American Indians. Nonetheless, all Indian tribes in California, Florida, New York, and Texas, along with the Flathead Tribe of Montana, the Lkamath Tribe of Oregon, the Pottawatomie Tribe of Kansas and Nebraska, the Chippewa Tribe of Turtle Mountain Reservation in North Dakota, and the Menominee Tribe of Wisconsin, were slated to be the first groups subjected to Termination.

Ironically, certain elements of the IRA set the stage for the devastating methods employed during the Eisenhower era to again dissolve Indian Country and impose the capitalist economic model on this historically harmonious, cooperative tribal system. The vehicle here was the option provided to tribes to incorporate. Those selecting this option had their tribal status transformed into that of a business corporation in which enrolled members constituted shareholders. A clause in the tribal corporation choice was for the tribe to terminate federal supervision and protection. Clearly, few tribal groups were adequately schooled in the economic and legal intricacies associated with corporate America, and conflicts soon emerged as to what authority the tribal corporation had relevant to bringing suit or being sued in civil litigations in a system dominated by whites.

These and other legal issues in Indian Country led to the establishment of the Indian Claims Commission, a process that actually began under the Truman administration. Truman's Hoover Task Force Commission recommended cuts in the Bureau of Indian Affairs (BIA) as a means of curtailing domestic spending in order to fund postwar rehabilitation programs for the defeated Axis nations, notably Germany and Japan. Ironically, these savings were to be at the expense of American Indians and their tribal holdings and traditional ways. This process began with the Zimmerman Plan of 1947 in which William Zimmerman, Assistant Commissioner of Indian Affairs, had tribes ranked according to what his office considered to be their readiness to survive the removal of federal trust and be subject to state tax codes.

Donald Fixico, in his book *Termination and Relocation: Federal Indian Policy, 1945–1960*, notes that the Zimmerman Plan clearly provided the blueprint for the federal government to abrogate its trust responsibilities in Indian Country. Hence, the Indian Claims Commission was created by Congress in order to begin the process of buying off tribes. This act served to spur American Indians to organize to better represent their interests, which, up to this point, were determined solely by white administrators and politicians. Indian veterans of the Second World War established the National Congress of American Indians (NCAI) in a reaction to the trend toward dissolving federal protection of lands and minerals being sought by western state conservatives, notably the Mormons. Unforeseen by politicians was the fact that the American Indian population had grown since the massive deaths during the Indian Wars. Indeed, population growth along with advances in mass communication and inadvertent intertribal interaction due to the Great Depression programs, Civilian Conservation Corps and Works Projects Administration, and service during World War II and the Korean conflict contributed to a new phenomenon—that of *Pan-Indianism*.[9]

Attempts at reversing the IRA began in 1945 with John Collier's resignation as Indian Commissioner and gave conservative Republicans further incentives when Felix Cohen left the Interior Department in 1948. The recommendations of the 1949 Hoover Commission provided the final justification to dissolve Indian Country. President Truman also contributed to this dismal process by appointing Dillon S. Myer, in 1950, as Commissioner of the Bureau of Indian Affairs (BIA). As mentioned earlier, Myers was the notorious director of the War Relocation Program during the Second World War. President Eisenhower's replacement for Myers, Glenn L. Emmons, was a white New Mexico rancher and businessman who shared Myer's plan of eliminating federal responsibility for Indian Country and opening up these lands to white exploitation. Public Law 280 was a tool designed to further place Indian Country under the control of states.

Public Law 280, also passed in 1953, augmented Termination by extending state jurisdiction over offenses committed by Indians in Indian Country (federal Indian reservations). Again, a number of states were targeted for the initial stage of this experiment: California, Minnesota, Nebraska, Oregon, and Wisconsin. Like Termination, Public Law 280 was yet another unilateral Congressional action enacted without the consent of the tribes.[10]

Clearly, Public Law 280 was a prelude to Relocation, the compliment to Termination, in the continued efforts of those bent on Indian cultural genocide—notably Western politicians, ranchers, miners, oil and coal, forest interests, and the Mormons. This plan was to entice young adult Indians off the reservation into magnet urban areas. The intent of Relocation was to separate subsequent generations from their traditional language, culture, and customs. Essentially the hopes of the anti-Indian whites was that by relocating these young adults to urban Indian ghettos, they would lose their "Indianism"—hence, a final solution to the U.S. Indian problem, which had plagued it from the country's inception in 1776.

Initiated in 1954, thousands of Indians were directly assisted to relocate, a process described by the American Indian Historical Society:

> Religious groups and white controlled humanitarian organizations generally embodied the worst of the growing paternalism towards the Natives. Finally, the federal government, jockeying precariously between policies of assimilation and the growing recognition that the tribes simply would not disappear together with their unique cultures, originated what has become known as the "Relocation Program." Indians were induced to go to the cities for training in the arts of the technological world. There they were dumped into housing that in most cases was ghetto-based, into jobs that were dead-end, and training that failed to lead to professions and occupations. The litany of that period provided the crassest example of government ignorance of the Indian situation. The "Indian problem" did not go away. It worsened. The policies of the Eisenhower administration, which espoused the termination of federal-Indian relationships, was shown to be a failure, a gross injustice added to a history of injustice.[11]

Relocation survived, creating large urban populations of marginal Indians—individuals who are Indian in appearance but not in culture. They hold membership in neither the larger dominant society nor in their particular traditional culture. Termination, however, began and ended with the failed Minominee experiment. This economic model sent the tribe deeper into poverty when the state and unsavory outsiders exploited the tribe in the name of capitalism. Altogether, some 190 tribes were affected, including 1,362,155 acres in Indian Country and 11,466 tribal members, resulting in the shrinkage of federal Indian trust lands by 3.2%. Common to these Termination acts was the transformation of land ownership patterns from one of communally held tribal lands to a corporate or capitalist design. Tribal lands were appraised and sold by the U.S. Government to a non-Indian bidder, often involving collusion, and the proceeds were then assigned to the tribe minus the processing fees determined by the Secretary of the Interior, thus ending the trust responsibility. To fill the gap created by federal withdrawal of services and protection, state jurisdiction was imposed on the tribes with state legislatures and county boards given the authority to impose their influence in the areas of law, education, land use, religion, and social and economic issues. This authority was granted via Public Law 280. Moreover, all exemptions from state taxing authority ended with Termination, and at the same time, all special federal programs to tribes were discontinued, placing the tribal members at the mercy of the white-dominated political and law enforcement apparatus. The plan of Termination was the end of any degree of tribal sovereignty. A dire failure, Termination ended with the Menominee Restoration Act of 1973. Yet, the provisions put in place by Public Law 280 continue unabated.[12]

The backlash to Termination and Relocation led to increased tribal activism. Many urban Indians felt that the federal government deliberately caused chaos in Indian Country by playing tribes against one another, causing dissent within the ranks of the National Congress of American Indians (NCAI). This dissatisfaction led to the creation of the National Indian Youth Council (NIYC) in Gallup, New Mexico, in 1961. The NIYC's membership was more radical than the more traditional leaders of NCAI. Indeed, the NIYC birthed the more radical American Indian Movement (AIM). The NIYC represented the new pan-Indianism that now included those American Indians born off the reservation in urban Indian ghettos created by Relocation. The NIYC's offspring, AIM, gained more notoriety than any Indian movement since the Ghost Dance movement of the late 19th century, which resulted in the Wounded Knee massacre in 1890.

AIM was the Indian counterpart to ethnic countercultural movements of the 1960s and 1970s, such as the Black Panthers and La Raza. AIM was born in the urban Indian ghetto of Minneapolis in 1968 as a result of the failed Relocation program. AIM is perhaps best known for its involvement in the Pine Ridge Reservation occupation of Wounded Knee, the area where Big Foot's party was massacred on December 29, 1890. Here, AIM assisted Lakota tribe members who were attempting to remove Dick Wilson, the BIA-backed tribal leader who had his own private police force known as the Guardians of the Oglala Nation (GOON) squad. AIM leader Russell Means and a contingent of Sioux and other AIM followers seized the area around the Wounded Knee massacre site for 71 days. During this time, the U.S. military, FBI, and local and tribal police fired more than 500,000 rounds of ammo into the AIM fortification resulting in the death of two occupying Indians and an FBI agent. More than 1,000 protesting Indians were arrested for this action, and many others hid on other reservations throughout Indian Country.

As a reminder that U.S. Indian policies had not changed much since the end of the Indian Wars, the next 3 years witnessed FBI and local police harassment of young Indians throughout Indian Country and in the Indian urban ghettos. American Indians refer to this era as the "FBI's Reign of Terror." The FBI's actions emboldened Wilson's GOON squads, resulting in 61 unresolved homicides among AIM supporters. It was these circumstances that resulted in the murder of two FBI agents, Jack R. Coler and Ronald A. Williams, on June 16, 1975, when they encountered a large contingent of AIM supporters at the Jumping Bull Ranch on Pine Ridge. Three Indian suspects, Robideau, Butler, and Peltier, were charged with the FBI agents' deaths. Robideau and Butler stood trial and were acquitted, but Peltier, a top AIM official, fearing summary execution by government agents, fled to Canada.

After an intense international manhunt, Leonard Peltier was captured in Canada, extradited, and convicted of the FBI agents' death by an all-white jury. Despite serious questions about his involvement in the murders and judicial improprieties in his trial, he is serving two life sentences at the federal military prison at Leavenworth, Kansas. The irony is that the Wounded Knee II battle occurred in the same region as the Crow Dog situation in the 1880s and under similar circumstances. Both situations pitted traditional Indians against a U.S.-backed puppet government (Spotted Tail, Dick Wilson) and then used the resulting unrest as a pretext for more intense police actions in Indian Country. These situations during the 1960s and 1970s fostered Congressional action in the form of the American Indian Policy Review Commission, leading to a greater degree of Indian self-determination.[13]

Indian Self-Determination and the New Federalism for Indian Country

The American Indian Police Review Commission set the stage for the contemporary scene in Indian Country. The crises involving Indian Country and Indian activism led certain members of Congress to question the status of Indian affairs in the early 1970s. A leading proponent of the Review Commission was James Abourezk, the U.S. Senator from South Dakota. This comprehensive review addressed the following areas of Indian affairs: (1) trust responsibility and the federal–Indian relationship, including treaty review; (2) tribal government; (3) federal administration and structure of Indian affairs; (4) federal, state, and tribal jurisdiction; (5) Indian education; (6) Indian health; (7) reservation development; (8) urban, rural nonreservation, terminated, and non-federally recognized Indians; and (9) Indian law revision, consolidation, and codification. The commission's mandate and general recommendations were presented in the final report:

> This final report of the American Indian Policy Review Commission represents 2 years of intensive investigative work encompassing the entire field of Federal-Indian relations. The last such investigation occurred almost 50 years ago. The conclusions of that investigation and its condemnation of the policies which had governed Federal administration over the preceding 50 years

brought an abrupt shift in the statutory policies governing the Federal-Indian relations, a complete repudiation of the policies which had controlled from the late 1800's to the mid-1930's. And yet the American Indian today finds himself in a position little better than that which he enjoyed in 1928 when the Meriam Report was issued. …The relationship of the American Indian tribes to the United States is founded on principles of international law. It is a political relation: a relation of a weak people to a strong people; a relationship founded on treaties in which the Indian tribes placed themselves under the protection of the United States and the United States assumed the obligation of supplying such protection. It is a relationship recognized in the law of this Nation as that of a domestic, dependent sovereign. …The fundamental concepts which must guide future police determinations are:

1. That Indian tribes are sovereign political bodies, having the power to determine their own membership and power to enact laws and enforce them within the boundaries of their reservations, and
2. That the relationship which exists between tribes and the United States is premised on a special trust that must govern the conduct of the stronger toward the weaker….

Certain broad concepts have been agreed upon which we believe should guide future policy in relationship to the trust doctrine:

1. The trust responsibility to American Indians extends from the protection and enhancement of Indian trust resources and tribal self-government to the provision of economic and social programs necessary to raise the standard of living and social well being of the Indian people to a level comparable to the non-Indian society.
2. The trust responsibility extends through the tribe to the Indian members, whether on or off the reservation.
3. The trust responsibility applies to all United States agencies and instrumentalities, not just those charged specifically with the administration of Indian affairs…

Finally, Indian project initiatives must be encouraged through a program, planning, and budget process which is guided by Indian priorities rather than to satisfy the needs of a self-perpetuation bureaucracy.

It is the conclusion of this Commission that:

1. The executive branch should propose a plan for a consolidated Indian Department or independent agency. Indian programs should be transferred to this new consolidated agency where appropriate.
2. Bureaucratic processes must be revised to develop an Indian budget system operating, from a "zero" base, consistent with long-range Indian priorities and needs. Those budget requests by tribes should be submitted without interference to Congress.

3. Federal laws providing for delivery of domestic assistance to State and local governments must be revised to include Indian tribes as eligible recipients.
4. To the maximum extent possible, appropriations should be delivered directly to Indian tribes and organizations through grants and contracts, the first obligation being to trust requirements.[14]

An important outcome of the Review Commission was the establishment of the post of Assistant Secretary for Indian Affairs under the Secretary of the Interior. This idea was first put forth by President Richard Nixon, but it took the impact of the American Indian Policy Review Commission's Final Report recommendations for this action to take place during President Jimmy Carter's administration. This action essentially established what is now commonly known as the "Indian Desk" in the Department of the Interior. The assistant secretary is traditionally an enrolled American Indian, and his or her main responsibility is to run and oversee the Bureau of Indian Affairs (BIA).[15]

Two days following the authorization of the comprehensive American Indian Policy Review Commission, the U.S. Congress passed the Indian Self-Determination and Education Assistance Act, laying the foundation for the new era of Indian self-determination. A major element of this act was its provision for tribes to contract to run their own education and health programs and to have greater control over curriculum matters.

> An Act to provide maximum Indian participation in the Government and education of Indian people; to provide for the full participation of Indian tribes in programs and services conducted by the Federal Government for Indians and to encourage the development of human resources of the Indian people; to establish a program of assistance to upgrade Indian education; to support the right of Indian citizens to control their own educational activities and for other purposes.[16]

Not everyone was pleased with the movement toward Indian self-determination. Those states and industries that benefited most from Termination and exploitation of resources in Indian Country were the most displeased. Indeed, most Western states were in favor of full state rights over Indian Country regardless of whether they were included in the Public Law 280 Termination scheme. Representing themselves as the Council of State Governments, they presented their objections to the findings of the American Indian Policy Review Commission in September 1977, known as the Meeds minority report. Those opposed to the Review Commission in Congress proposed legislation that would further open up Indian Country for continued exploitation by non-Indian interests. Charles Wilkinson, in his 2005 book *Blood Struggle*, describes the conservative anti-Indian movement within the U.S. Supreme Court. Here, tribal sovereignty was assailed with respect to tribal self-determination and tribal authority to tax oil and gas companies that had lucrative deals with the U.S. Department of the Interior to exploit natural resources in Indian Country with impunity from prosecution by tribal governments.

Wilkinson cites the *Merrion v. Jicarilla Apache* case, which went to the U.S. Supreme Court in 1982. This case favored the tribes in their efforts to earn revenues in order to provide governmental services to their people. The Supreme Court decided that tribes must have similar flexibility to other sovereign governmental entities in order to generate monies for municipal services. Justice Thurgood Marshall, the first black to serve on the U.S. Supreme Court, wrote the decision, noting the dire needs within Indian Country are great in comparison to the big corporations exploiting resources in Indian Country; therefore, they should be subject to tribal fees. Wilkinson noted that these favorable sentiments within the U.S. Supreme Court changed drastically once William Rehnquist arrived on the bench in 1972. The U.S. Supreme Court then began its conservative, anti-Indian and prostate rights, a sentiment echoed by both Antonin Scalia upon his appointment in 1986 and Clarence Thomas in 1991.[17]

Indian self-determination was also countered with increased federal criminal jurisdiction, especially following the Wounded Knee II incident. In the Indian Crimes Act of 1976, the Major Crimes Act of 1885 was expanded beyond the original seven index crimes to include exclusive federal jurisdiction over the following offenses committed within Indian Country: murder; manslaughter; kidnapping; rape; carnal knowledge by a man of any woman, not his wife, who had not attained the age of 16 (statutory rape); assault with intent to commit rape; incest; assault with intent to commit murder; assault with a dangerous weapon (aggravated assault); assault resulting in serious bodily injury (aggravated assault and battery); arson; burglary; robbery; and larceny. These offenses now fall under the jurisdiction of the Federal Bureau of Investigation (FBI) where they are adjudicated within the federal court system (Federal District Courts). Moreover, in 1978, in *United States v. Wheeler*, the U.S. Supreme Court upheld the right of the FBI and federal courts to charge Indian defendants with a major crime (felony) even when tribal courts had already ruled on the same incident as a lesser offense (misdemeanor) within their jurisdiction subjecting Indians within Indian Country to double jeopardy, a blatant violation of the United States Bill of Rights. Also in 1978, in *Olipnant v. Suquamish Indian Tribe*, the U.S. Supreme Court ruled that tribal jurisdiction did not extend to non-Indians in Indian Country opening tribal lands to non-Indian offenders much like what existed in Indian Territory during the 19th century. These restrictions on tribal courts and law enforcement continued until 1991 when the U.S. Congress finally curtailed the U.S. Supreme Court interventions by strengthening tribal criminal jurisdiction with passage of Public Law 102-137, Criminal Jurisdiction over Indians. And in 1993, Congress passed the Indian Tribal Act of 1993, which attempted to bring tribal codes up to those of the Anglo-based U.S. system in general. With this 1993 act came a new support system known as the Office of Tribal Justice Support. Taken together, these efforts have resulted in an increase in the number of tribal courts within Indian Country.[18]

Indian Religious Freedom

Traditional spiritualism is the foundation of Indian culture as it is for most societies. It has been assaulted since the colonial days with these attacks forming the basis of cultural genocide. Rooted in the cooperative aboriginal harmony ethos, traditional spiritualism was seen as the antithesis of the Euro–American Protestant ethic and as the force that kept the American Indian cultural ways alive. Attempts to extinguish native languages, rites, and customs were harsh with the dominant white cultural ways deemed superior. Clearly, white supremacy is the main tenet of Manifest Destiny and the ethnocentric policies that have surfaced in order to justify the harsh treatment of the indigenous population of the Americas. Although the military, militias, and police were responsible for carrying out physical genocide against American Indians, Christian churches (Catholic, Protestant, Mormon) were the soldiers of cultural genocide surrounding the ever-diminishing Indian Country in the United States and Canada.

Although the military long ago withdrew from reservations (to be replaced by the FBI), the churches remain as the cultural police with the mandate of curtailing any aboriginal regression in Indian Country. Indeed, the first thing one is likely to see upon entering an Indian reservation are the numerous churches surrounding all the entries, like the walls of a fort. Even then, aboriginal ways have survived to the present. As physical genocide and ethnic cleansing were not able to wipe out the American Indians, neither were attacks on their spirituality able to totally destroy their culture. French, in a study of the Appalachian Cherokees (Eastern Band) in the 1970s, when the reservation population was about 8,000 enrolled members, found that there were 27 churches on or close to the main portion of the reservation (Qualla Boundary): 21 Baptist, one Methodist (with three satellites), one Pentecostal Holiness, one Church of God, one Episcopal, one Latter Day Saints (Mormon), and one Roman Catholic.[19]

In 1978, the U.S. Congress passed the American Indian Religious Freedom Act (AIRFA), thus formally putting an end to the days of incarcerating Indian children in religious-run boarding schools. A companion to the Indian Religious Freedom Act, passed a year later in 1979, was the Archaeological Resources Protection Act. This act finally recognized Indian burial sites as sacred places, just as burial sites are for non-Indians. For centuries, the looting of Indian sites, including burial sites, has been a lucrative cottage industry with the U.S. Government and major colleges, universities, and museums being the main culprits in this market. Displaying Indian artifacts, including skeletal remains, did not rise to the same level of repulsion and illegality as grave robbing non-Indians. This act recognized that "existing Federal laws do not provide adequate protection to prevent the loss and destruction of these archaeological resources and sites resulting from uncontrolled excavations and pillage."[20] Even then, non-Indians could still apply to the Federal land manager for a permit to excavate or remove any archaeological resource located on public land or in Indian Country. Since passage of this law, tribes have fought to have artifacts, including body parts, returned to the custody of the tribe. Religious artifacts are returned for spiritual rituals, and body parts are finally given a traditional burial. Nonetheless, Indian sites continue to be exploited to fuel the lucrative market in such items. Valuable artifacts being excavated today for profit include the burial bowls of the Mimbres and Anasazi tribes located in sites in Arizona and New Mexico.[21]

A strong proponent of Indian religious freedom was Rueben Snake, Jr., who fought for federal recognition of the Native American Church (NAC) and its ritual use of peyote. Toward this end, he established the Native American Religious Freedom project with the Native American Rights Fund (NARF). These efforts, with the assistance of both Peterson Zah, then president of the Navajo Nation, and U.S. Senator Daniel K. Inouye, chairman of the Senate Committee on Indian Affairs, resulted in 12 Congressional hearings recommending the acceptance of the use of peyote by the NAC. These recommendations were initially blocked by President George H. W. Bush but were later made into law by President William J. Clinton. With President Clinton's signature, House Resolution 4230 became Public Law 103-344, amending the 1978 Religious Freedom Act to legally protect the use, possession, or transportation of peyote in all 50 states and Washington, DC. President Clinton also signed a directive in 1994 providing for the distribution of eagle feathers for American Indian religious purposes. It authorized the Department of the Interior to maintain an adequate refrigerated repository of eagle feathers available to qualified Indian spiritual leaders.[22]

New Federalism and Indian Child Welfare

Another well-meaning initiative during the early self-determination years was passage of the Indian Child Welfare Act of 1978. The basic thrust of this act was in reaction to programs that sanctioned white adoptions of Indian children, including the Mormon school-year resocialization scheme. This act addressed increasing concerns within Indian Country over the BIA and state authority allowing these adoptions and placements to occur without tribal authority. Now, tribes would have a say in getting Indian children placed with Indian families or with tribal-run foster care facilities. The Department of the Interior was also authorized to provide grants to Indian tribes for the establishment and operation of Indian child and family service programs on or near the reservation.[23]

Absent from the 1978 Indian Child Welfare Act were federal protections against Indian child abuse, including compulsory reporting laws that were imposed on all state jurisdictions at this time. These changes would come only following the Special Committee on Investigations of the 101st Congress in a 1989 report, *A New Federalism for American Indians*. The committee's executive summary spells out the nature and extent of these abuses of Indian children:

> The Committee found that the BIA also permitted a pattern of child abuse by its teachers to fester throughout BIA schools nationwide. For almost 15 years, while child abuse reporting standards were being adopted by all 50 states, the Bureau failed to issue any reporting guidelines for its own teachers. Incredibly, the BIA did not even require a minimum background check into potential school employees. As a result, the BIA employed teachers who actually admitted past child molestation, including at least one Arizona teacher who explicitly listed a prior criminal offense for child abuse on his employment form.

> At a Cherokee Reservation elementary school in North Carolina, the BIA employed Paul Price, another confessed child molester—even after his previous principal, who had fired him for molesting seventh grade boys, warned BIA officials that Price was an admitted pedophile. Shocked to learn several years later from teachers at the Cherokee school that Price continued to teach despite the warning, Price's former principal told several Cherokee teachers of Prince's pedophilia and notified the highest BIA official at Cherokee. Instead of dismissing Price or conducting an inquiry, BIA administrators lectured an assembly of Cherokee teachers on the unforeseen consequences of slander.

> The Committee found that during the 14 years at Cherokee, Price molested at least 25 students while the BIA continued to ignore repeated allegations—including an eyewitness account by a teacher's aide. Even after Price was finally caught and the negligence of BIA supervisors came to light, not a single official was ever disciplined for tolerating the abuse of countless students for 14 years. Indeed, the negligent Cherokee principal who received the eyewitness report was actually promoted to the BIA Central Office in Washington—the same office which, despite the Price case, failed for years to institute background checks for potential teachers or reporting requirements for instances of suspected abuse. Another BIA Cherokee school official was promoted to the Hopi Reservation in Arizona without any inquiry into his handling of the Price fiasco.

Meanwhile at Hopi, a distraught mother reported to the local BIA principal a possible instance of child sexual abuse by the remedial reading teacher, John Boone. Even though five years earlier the principal had received police records of alleged child sexual abuse by Boone, the principal failed to investigate the mother's report or contact law enforcement authorities. He simply notified his superior, who also took no action. A year later, the same mother eventually reported the teacher to the FBI, which found that he had abused 142 Hopi children, most during the years of BIA's neglect. Again, no discipline or censure of school officials followed: the BIA simply provided the abused children with one counselor who compounded their distress by intimately interviewing them for a book he wished to write on the case.

Sadly, these wrongs were not isolated incidents. While in the past year the Bureau has finally promulgated some internal child abuse reporting guidelines, it has taken the Special Committee's public hearing for the BIA to fully acknowledge its failures.[24]

Both Prince and Boone were white teachers and both were eventually convicted and sentenced to prison in North Carolina. In reaction to the select committee's findings, Congress passed the Indian Child Abuse Prevention and Treatment Act of 1990. This bill established mandatory reporting procedures for certain professionals working in Indian Country by amending Title 18 of the U.S. Code (USC), providing criminal penalties for failure to report cases of child abuse or neglect—holding Indian Country to the same rules regulating child protection as had long been held in all state jurisdictions. Child abuse reporting was the major element of the Indian Child Protection and Family Violence Prevention Act. The law

1. Requires that reports of abused Indian children are made to the appropriate authorities in an effort to prevent further abuse
2. Authorizes such actions as are necessary to ensure effective child protection in Indian Country
3. Establishes the Indian Child Abuse Prevention and Treatment Grant Program to provide funds for the establishment on Indian reservations of treatment programs for victims of child sexual abuse
4. Provides for the treatment and prevention of incidents of family violence
5. Authorizes other actions necessary to ensure effective child protection on Indian reservations[25]

The next critical epoch for American Indians in the United States as well as their counterparts in Canada and Mexico was passage of the North American Free Trade Agreement (NAFTA) in 1994 and the changes this brought to the traditional culture of Mexican Indians and mixed-blood peasants (Mestizos) as well as cross-border visits among the tribe with transborder reservations. Further challenges to border security followed with the terrorist attacks on the United States on September 11, 2001. Again, the border and Indian groups came under increased scrutiny. The balance between border security, homeland security, and free cross-border trade poses challenges that continue to the present. These issues are discussed in the following chapter.

Extending the Monroe Doctrine in the 20th Century: Hemispheric Exploitation and Cold War Fears

The United States engaged in conflicts outside its borders during the years between the two World Wars and the Cold War era of the second half of the 20th century. The era between the World Wars is characterized by the use of the Monroe Doctrine and the U.S. military, notably the U.S. Marines, in providing protection for U.S. businesses located in Mexico and South and Central American nations. Here, the U.S. military often served as the private police force for big U.S. corporations. Indeed, the U.S. Marine Corps was widely used between the Spanish-American War and World War II as the U.S. international police force.

During the Haitian campaign, Marine noncommissioned officers (NCOs) were also awarded commission ranks in the Haitian national police (*Gendarmerie d' Haiti*), commanding local police in enforcing the laws of the country. While a major (0–4) in the U.S. Marine Corps, Smedley Butler was in charge of the *Gendarmerie d' Haiti* with the brevet rank of major general. At the same time, the mix of military and local law enforcement agencies in domestic affairs was extended beyond Indian Country during the Prohibition era. Again, Smedley Butler played a military police role when he was loaned to Philadelphia from the U.S. Marine Corps to serve as the Director of Public Safety from 1924 to 1925 to enforce federal prohibition laws. The use of the military in domestic law enforcement outside Indian Country did not occur again until President Eisenhower deployed the Army Airborne to protect black children from the forces of segregation in Arkansas (local, county, and state police and the National Guard) in 1958. Eisenhower was also instrumental in federalizing the National Guard in order to countermand Southern governors using it as their segregation police force. Later, when he was one of the highest ranked generals in the Marine Corps (major general), Smedley Butler commented on the use or misuse of the U.S. military in foreign affairs at a speech he made to the American Legion in 1931, just prior to his retirement:

War is a racket. Our stake in that racket has never been greater in all our peace-time history. It may seem odd for me a military man, to adopt such a comparison. Truthfulness compels me to. I spent 33 years and 4 months in active service as a member of our country's most agile military force—the Marine Corps. I served in all commissioned ranks from a Second Lieutenant to Major General. And during that period I spent most of my time being a high-class muscle man for big business, for Wall Street and for the bankers. In short, I was a racketeer for capitalism... Thus I helped make Mexico and especially Tampico, safe for American oil interests in 1914. I helped make Haiti and Cuba a decent place for the National City Bank boys to collect revenues in. I helped in the raping of a half a dozen Central Republics for the benefit of Wall Street. The record of racketeering is long. I helped purify Nicaragua for the international banking house of Brown Brothers in 1901–1912. I brought light to the Dominican Republic for American sugar interests in 1916. I helped make Honduras "right" for American fruit companies in 1903. In China in 1927 I helped see to it that Standard Oil went its way unmolested. During those years, I had, as the boys in the back room would say, a swell racket. I was awarded with honors, medals, promotions. Looking back on it I might have given Al Capone a few hints. The best he could do was to operate his rackets in three city districts. We Marines operated on three continents. ... We don't want any more wars, but a man is a damn fool to think there won't be any more of them. I am a peace-loving Quaker, but when war breaks out every damn man in my family goes. ...No pacifists or Communists are going to govern this country. If they try it, there will be seven million men like you to rise up and strangle them. Pacifist? Hell, I'm a pacifist, but I always have a club behind my back.[26]

Concerns over international worker protests, anarchism, communism, and the nationalization of Mexico's petroleum industries during the Great Depression, coupled with the apparent success of fascism in Italy, Germany, and Spain, led to a movement by big business in the United States to introduce its own form of fascism. The fear of communism led to a right-wing swing by the captains of U.S. capitalism leading to the creation of the American Liberty League to challenge Franklin D. Roosevelt's New Deal initiatives. Anti-Semitism, isolationism, and profascist sentiments in the United States during the early stages of President Roosevelt's presidency were obstacles to the President's later efforts to help the Allies before the United States entered the war. During this time, there were serious efforts to remove him from office and replace America's democracy with a fascist government. The plot to overthrow President Roosevelt was initiated during his first 100 days of the New Deal in 1933 by an affiliate of the Ku Klux Klan, the American Liberty League. This movement was financed and organized by some of the richest and most powerful people in the country: Irene DuPont (founder of the America Liberty League); Grayson Murphy (Director of Goodyear, Bethlehem Steel, and associated with J. P. Morgan banks); William Doyle (American League official); John Davis (former Democratic presidential candidate); Al Smith (co-director of the American Liberty League); John J. Raskob (DuPont official and former chairman of the Democratic Party); Robert Clark (leading Wall Street banker and stockbroker); and Gerald MacGuire (affiliate of Clark and official of the American Legion). Other business leaders behind this scheme were Henry Ford, John D. Rockefeller, and John and Allen Dulles.

The plan for this quiet revolution was to get U.S. Marine Corps General Smedley Butler, son of a U.S. Congressman and one of the most respected military figures of the time, to muster support not only from the standing military, but from the two Congressionally recognized veteran's organizations: the Veterans of Foreign Wars (VFW) and the American Legion. Butler was chosen because the successes abroad were due to the abilities of Benito Mussolini, Adolph Hitler, and Francisco Franco to play to the sentiments and support of their World War I veterans. The first action of the new fascist U.S. regime was to restore the gold standard. But not only did General Butler refuse to participate; he reported this plot to both President Roosevelt and the U.S. Congress.

A special Congressional committee was formed to investigate Nazi propaganda activities, and it looked at Butler's accusations in 1934 and provided a sanitized report that left out the names of prominent business and political leaders with no action taken against the plotters. The main reason for little action was that these individuals were the President's social peers and he did not want to publically embarrass them. This same oversight committee changed its name to the House Un-American Activities Committee (Dies Committee), which changed course dramatically from looking at fascism to policing communist activities (red-baiting). The link between organized labor and anti-Communism sentiments was furthered with passage of the Taft-Hartley Act in 1947. With this act, the U.S. Congress restricted union activities by allowing states to pass "right-to-work" laws. The Taft-Hartley Act provided the textile industry of New England an opportunity to break the yoke of unionism, a strong incentive to move to "right-to-work" states in the South, such as the Carolinas, with a cheaper labor force.[27]

Under the guise of fighting Communism, the United States extended its clandestine operations in the Americas, again using the Monroe Doctrine as the legitimizing mandate for these incursions. U.S. corporate interests in South and Central America led to numerous human rights violations during the 1970s and 1980s, including the infamous overthrow and assignation of Chile's freely elected president, Salvador Allende Gossens in 1973. This action resulted in the U.S. support of the fascist military dictator General Augusto Pinochet, whose administration is linked to the disappearance (execution) of thousands of Chileans during his rule from 1973 until 1990. Pinochet's brutality gained international attention when Spain attempted to extradite him for human rights violations. One of the concerns of the families of the detained and disappeared was the illegal adoption of the children of those slain by Pinochet's protégés.

Although U.S. interventions occurred numerous times during the 19th and early 20th centuries, a permanent military presence began in 1903 under President Theodore Roosevelt for the protection of American interests in the development of the Panama Canal. A geographic command of the U.S. Army was created in July 1917 known as the Panama Canal Department. Forty years later, after the Second World War, President Truman authorized the Unified Combatant Command for policing the Americas south of the U.S. border. On June 6, 1963, the notorious United States Southern Command (USSOUTHCOM) emerged with the mandate to enforce the Monroe Doctrine in 32 nations (19 in Central and South America and 13 in the Caribbean), as well as 14 American and European territories. The training arm of the USSOUTHCOM is the U.S. Army School of the Americas (SOA). The SOA existed under this name from its inception in 1946, until it was repackaged in 2001, as the Western Hemisphere Institute for Security Cooperation. Located at Fort Benning in Columbus, Georgia, it is, along with the Inter-American Air Forces Academy, the primary training facility for Latin American military students for the preservation of the dictates of the Monroe Doctrine. Graduates of the SOA are responsible for some of the worst human rights abuses in the Americas. The rationale for this level of brutality was kept secret until the SOA's curricula was disclosed when their training manual surfaced and was publicized. The SOA clearly promoted techniques that violated human rights and democratic standards. These disclosures were a major source of embarrassment to the United States resulting in the pretense of closing the SOA in 2001, only to have it surface again as the Western Hemisphere Institute for Security Cooperation.

One of the most notorious anti-Communist plans supported by the USSOUTHCOM was Plan Condor, a program of political repression and state terror and assassinations under the mandate of eliminating Marxist subversion, for example, democracy. These programs operated in Argentina, Chile, Uruguay, Paraguay, Bolivia, Brazil, Ecuador, and Peru with assistance from the U.S. Central Intelligence Agency (CIA). Torture and assassination techniques were taught these various military personnel at the U.S. Army School of the Americas. Pinochet's coup in Chile represented only one of these CIA-supported programs. Argentina's Dirty War, in which the "enemies of the state" (leftist dissidents; union members; peasants, metizos, and Indians; priests and nuns; students and teachers; intellectuals; and suspected guerillas) were bound and thrown out of helicopters into the ocean. Brazil's Black Hand, among other infamous programs attacking citizens of their own country, abounded during the years of U.S. support from the Eisenhower administration through 1978 and again under Ronald Reagan's administration from 1981 until 1989. Henry Kissinger, advisor to both the Nixon and

Ford administrations, was a strong proponent of CIA and USSOUTHCOM activities.[28]

The era of secret U.S. involvement in Latin America began with the Truman administration but was accelerated during the Eisenhower administration with the support of the Dulles brothers, the same ones who were complicit in the attempt to overthrowing Franklin D. Roosevelt. John Foster Dulles was Eisenhower's Secretary of State, and Allen Dulles headed the CIA. Under the Eisenhower and Reagan administrations (1952–1990s) were the CIA-supported death squads; resulting in hundreds of thousands of deaths contributing to the current economic and political unrest in many of these countries today. The countries most affected today include Honduras, Guatemala, and El Salvador. During this time, the U.S. military also invaded Grenada and Panama in the name of protecting U.S. citizens and preserving capitalism in the region. Indeed, President Ronald Reagan intervened in South and Central America on behalf of corporate America more than any post–World War II leader. Reagan's enforcement of the Monroe Doctrine included Jacksonian-like extralegal methods, including lying to Congress and the public regarding these activities, including the Iran-Contra Affair. Here, the Reagan administration illegally sold U.S. weapons to America's sworn enemy, Iran, for monies to illegally fund the Nicaraguan contras, the rebel force attempting to overthrow the elected socialist government.[29]

Justice Issues: The Role of De Facto Discrimination

Having covered the trials and tribulations concerning American Indian justice, we have to go back to the U.S. War between the States (Civil War) of the mid-19th century to better understand the complexities of current race and ethnic discords, notably those affecting blacks. Attempts at maintaining the privileges of whites continued following the U.S. Civil War with political actions challenging the advances put forth by the Thirteenth, Fourteenth, and Fifteenth Amendments. These efforts to undermine federal authority and responsibility under Reconstruction began immediately with President Lincoln's vice president and successor, Andrew Johnson (1865–1869). Johnson was impeached by the U.S. Senate but not removed from office for violating the U.S. Constitution by removing Secretary of War Edwin M. Stanton from office, thereby obstructing the implementation of the Reconstruction Act. A southern Democrat born in North Carolina and representing Tennessee as both the governor and later a senator, his prejudices against blacks were well known. He served out the remainder of Lincoln's second term following the President's assassination and later returned to the U.S. Senate (U.S. Senators were appointed by their state delegations until passage of the Seventeenth Amendment in 1913 which called for direct election by the voters). Even then, de facto support for Jim Crow was actually an agreement between

Republicans who wanted to stay in office following U.S. Grant's administration and southern Democrats. Murphy, Fleming, and Barber note that Jim Crow discrimination emerged during the disputed Hayes-Tilden presidential compromise of 1877, that allowed the Republicans to retain the White House in exchange for ending Reconstruction in the South. This was done by transferring federal civil protection for the newly freed blacks to state authority, which would be run by whites.

Thus, although efforts to undermine the rights of blacks were often associated with the dismal presidency of Andrew Johnson, the deal for Jim Crow discrimination was actually secured during the administration of President Rutherford B. Hayes (1877–1881), leading to confirmation in the 1896 U.S. Supreme Court in *Plessy v. Ferguson* (163 U.S. 537, 1896). Here, the separate-but-equal Jim Crow laws in the South were upheld by the U.S. Supreme Court when it stated that racial segregation did *not* violate the Fourteenth Amendment's equal protection clause. The Jim Crow debacle was later reversed through the school integration rulings in *Brown v. Board of Education* (347 U.S. 483, 1954) and later with passage of the U.S. Civil Rights Acts of 1964.

The problems associated with Jim Crow laws that led to the landmark civil rights decisions of the 1950s and 1960s were clearly instituted under President Woodrow Wilson whose presidency legitimized segregation, including banning blacks from attending Princeton when he was the school's president. Wilson viewed blacks in condescending and paternalistic terms. His view of African Americans did not vary considerably from that of his opponents in the presidential election of 1912: Theodore Roosevelt (1904–1908) and William Howard Taft (1908–1912). The main difference is that Wilson formally instituted segregation at the federal level, transcending the mostly parochial practices of the Southern states. Once elected, Wilson appointed five conservative southerners to crucial cabinet posts: treasury, agriculture, attorney general, secretary of the navy, and postmaster general. Clearly, these appointees were willing agents of white supremacists, notably the National Democratic Fair Play Association. Collectively, their actions resulted in the segregation of federal workers along with the removal of any blacks in supervisory positions over whites. Wilson's racist sentiments were expressed on February 18, 1915, when he held a private viewing for his cabinet members and their families of the inflammatory film *The Birth of a Nation*, an anti-black film produced by two of his friends from Johns Hopkins University, Thomas Dixon and D. W. Griffith. The film celebrated the Ku Klux Klan as the saviors of Aryan culture over what the film depicted as inferior blacks.

The conspiracy between Republicans and Democrats to maintain Jim Crow discrimination in the South continued through Wilson's presidency to that of Franklin D. Roosevelt's administrations. Andre Schiffrin explains this process in his book *Dr. Seuss & Co. Go to War*:

> Because of the stranglehold of Southern Democrats in the Senate, legislation abolishing the poll tax, or even lynching, was blocked by the threat, and reality, of the filibuster. Roosevelt, for the most part, went along with this Southern veto, depending as he did on the electoral votes of the Southern Democrats, who were kept in power by a tiny fraction of the voters because of the very racist laws they were able to maintain. The poll tax, which Seuss and *PM* [New York City political tabloid] opposed continuously, completely distorted the American political scene. Not only were black voters in the South completely excluded, but so were a large number of the poorer whites. When the tax was finally abolished in Florida in the 1940s, Democrats calculated that 70 percent of white voters had also been excluded. …Others in Congress who actually represented the vast majority of Americans were thus stymied by a small number of racists, who, benefitted from seniority as well as the threat of the filibuster…[30]

Other cases in the 1960s, set the stage for improving the quality of justice afforded indigent or poorly educated suspects and defendants. In *Gideon v. Wainwright* (372 U.S. 436, 1963), the U.S. Supreme Court ruled that indigent defendants have the rights to Sixth Amendment protection, that is to counsel, especially when charged with major crimes that may result in the deprivation of one's life, liberty, or property. Three years later, in 1966, the Supreme Court, in *Miranda v. Arizona* (384 U.S. 436, 1966), forced the issue of police first notifying suspects of their rights against incrimination (being Mirandized) as well as the availability to counsel prior to making any disclosures to the police that may be incriminating. A year later, in 1967, the issue of due process for juveniles was addressed by the U.S. Supreme Court case *In re Gualt* (387 U.S. 1, 87 S.Ct., 1428, 18 L.Ed.2d 527). In it, the Supreme Court strongly suggested that due process provisions be extended to the juvenile justice system. The Court reached this decision because of the failure of the rehabilitation philosophy surrounding these proceedings up to that time within the closed juvenile courts and by juvenile judges. Accordingly, three due process procedural requirements now became standards within the federal and state judiciaries: (1) parents needed to be notified of the nature and terms of any juvenile adjudication, (2) sufficient notice needed to be provided to counsel with counsel provided for the indigent, and (3) the courts needed to maintain a written record adequate to allow for review for appeal purposes. These requirements now provided Fourteenth Amendment rights to juveniles, sans the right to a petit (jury) trial.[31]

Two other cases addressed the issue of capital punishment in the United States. In 1972, the U.S. Supreme Court, in *Furman v. Georgia* (408 U.S. 238, 345, 1972), in a five-to-four decision, held that the imposition of the death penalty constituted cruel and unusual punishment in violation of the Eighth and Fourteenth Amendments of the U.S. Constitution. The death penalty, up to that point in American society, was disproportionately used against minorities and the poor for a number of offenses other than homicide, especially in the South. Here, the U.S. Supreme Court allowed the reinstatement of capital punishment as long as it was restricted to serious offenses, notably first-degree murder, and consisted of a two-phase process with the first stage addressing the petit trial process and the second phase requiring a separate review of the relationship of mitigating versus aggravating circumstances prior to the administration of the death sentence. Nonetheless, public sentiment for the death penalty prevailed at this time and three companion cases were again brought before the U.S. Supreme Court attempting to reinstate capital punishment: *Gregg v. Georgia* (428 U.S. 153, 96 S.Ct. 2902, 49 L.Ed.2d 859, 1976), *Jurek v. Texas* (428. U.S. 262, 96 S.Ct. 2950, 1976), and *Proffit v. Florida* (428 U.S. 242, 96 S.Ct. 2960, 1976). The U.S. Supreme Court felt that these three cases met the required standards set forth following their Furman Decision, thus setting the stage for the reinstatement of capital punishment. The federal death penalty was reinstated under the administration of President Ronald Reagan in November 1988 when he signed the Anti-Drug Abuse Act, which included the Drug Kingpin Act (DKA) allowing the death penalty for certain drug-related offenses. Ironically, Canada did away with the death sentence in 1976.[32]

Clearly, the new Federal death penalty is directed toward minorities, notably blacks, Hispanics, and American Indians (it is now the law in Indian Country). Hispanics, notably those of Mexican heritage, the group with the largest proportion of Indian heritage (Mestizos), have long suffered within U.S. society with a more subtle form of discrimination following the harsh backlash to the *Plan de San Diego* fiasco during the early part of the 20th century. In one regard, Hispanics were denied the end of segregation even following the U.S. Supreme Court 1954 decision, *Brown v. Board of Education*.

Mexican Americans suffered under the same Jim Crow segregation as black Americans but without the protection of law because their segregation was of a de facto nature due to their *other white* status. Even then, both Hispanics and blacks were affected by the Supreme Court decision in *Brown v. Board of Education*. Part of the problem was the intent of the League of United Latin American Citizens (LULAC) to Americanize Mexican Americans as part of the larger dominant society. Shortly following LULAC's establishment in 1929, and as a reaction to the reemergence of white supremacist groups, such as the Ku Klux Klan, the 1930 *Del Rio ISD v. Salvatierra* decision labeling Mexican Americans as the "other white race" was initially welcomed by LULAC, given that this classification separated them from African Americans. However, with the creation of the American GI Forum (AGIF) in 1948, educational inadequacies were again brought to the forefront. Southern border states systemically segregated Mexican Americans and whites within their public school systems. The de facto segregation in Texas public schools led to both LULAC and AGIF challenges before the courts resulting in

Delgado v. Bastrop ISD. Similarly, another case was working its way through the California courts. At this time (1948), it was estimated that in Texas more than one-fourth of children of Mexican heritage received no schooling at all and that separate schools were provided for Spanish-surname children with minimal facilities and poor curriculum restricted to domestic and vocational training.

The circumstances surrounding *Mendez v. Westminster School District* began in March 1945 when a number of Mexican American families filed suit in U.S. District Court in Los Angeles, claiming that thousands of children of Mexican heritage were segregated into inferior schools within Orange County. The district court ruled in favor of the plaintiffs, rendering its decision on February 18, 1946. The school district appealed the decision to the Ninth Circuit Court of Appeals in San Francisco, which ultimately upheld the lower court decision. Yet, this ruling did not settle the "separate-but-equal" issue addressed in the 1896 *Plessy v. Ferguson* case due to the "other white" status of Mexican Americans. Noted black lawyers Thurgood Marshall and Robert L. Carter joined *Mendez v. Westminster* as *amicus curiae* (friends of the Court). They are the black attorneys who successfully argued the 1954 *Brown v. Board of Education* case before the U.S. Supreme Court.[33]

Unfortunately, neither the *Delgado* nor *Brown v. Board of Education* case immediately resolved the de facto segregation issues in Texas public schools. Again, the major issue here was the argument that Mexicans were not a colored minority, and as "other whites," they did not benefit from the *de jure* ruling of the U.S. Supreme Court in the 1954 *Brown* decision. The rationale for the separate, and grossly unequal, education offered to those of Mexican ancestry was due to the language barrier. Indeed, following the *Brown* decision, Texas school districts transferred black students into the inferior Mexican schools under the pretense that they were in compliance by integrating white, albeit "other white," schools. The issue of desegregation of Mexican schools was not resolved until 1957 with the *Herminca Hernandez et al. v. Driscoll Consolidated ISD* case, which for all intents and purposes ended pedagogical and *de jure* segregation in the Texas public schools.[34]

These cases reflect the intragroup conflicts facing Mexican Americans in the mid 20th century. The descendents of the Criollos (Mexican/Spanish heritage), those who considered themselves to be phenotypically Caucasoid ("other whites"), pitted themselves against the larger mixed-blooded brown Mestizos. The issue facing Mexican American communities during the turbulent 1960s was which of these groups should provide the identity and leadership for Hispanics. During the turbulent civil rights and antiwar era of the 1960s and 1970s, Cesar Chavez became the most prominent of these Brown Power Mexican Americans, much like Benito Juárez, the first Mexican president of pure Indian descent, in Mexico a century earlier. Chavez got his start within the Mexican American middle class–oriented Community

Service Organization (CSO), which supported LULAC principles of getting Hispanics involved in language and citizenship classes and registered to vote in local and state elections.

Together these efforts were termed "La Causa" during the 1950s, ostensibly sharing the same mandate of electing Hispanics in Texas, New Mexico, Arizona, and California. Chavez's affiliation with farm workers began in 1965 when he became the strike leader for both striking Filipino Americans and Mexican Americans working in the vineyards of California. The prolonged strike gave Chavez and the National Farm Workers Organization international attention and support. Finally, in the fall of 1970, the last holdout agreed to the farm workers' demands for a minimum wage. This attention also happened while numerous other groups were demonstrating across the country for civil rights for minorities and against the Vietnam War. The groups that came to rally with the Mexican American farm workers included college students, blacks, and young men of draft age. With this support and notoriety, Chavez and his Mexican American United Farm Workers took their battle to the fruit and vegetable fields and orchards throughout California. The attention of Chavez's group spread to the barrios where many other Mexican Americans lived in substandard, ghetto-like conditions.

The riots of the 1960s and early 1970s, drew attention to urban poverty especially among minorities of color. Los Angeles, originally a Mexican outpost prior to the 1848 treaty giving it to the United States, played a significant role in this unrest. Wheeler and Becker describe the effects of the LA riots on the American conscience in their book *Discovering the American Past*:

> The Watts riot of 1965 in Los Angeles shocked many Americans with its violence and revealed poverty and despair in the midst of what had appeared to be prosperity and optimism... During the six days that the Watts riot lasted, it spread to adjoining areas, and the National Guard was called out to help contain it. Thirty-four people were killed, more than a thousand were injured, and $40 million worth of property was damaged or destroyed. In 1970, and again in 1992, more riots broke out in Los Angeles.[35]

Wheeler and Becker eluded to yet another factor that impacted urban dissent among Latinos. During the Vietnam conflict and following the end of the Bracero Program, the United States began to loosen its immigration restrictions, resulting in a new wave (fourth wave) of immigration with many coming from Latin America, especially Mexico, in addition to those migrating from Asia (the target of the original immigration laws in 1917) and the Pacific Islands. Wheeler and Becker claim that this opened the floodgate of immigration to Southern California with over one million new immigrants, mostly Hispanic and Asian, arriving in the Los Angeles area. With the crowding of the poorer inner-city areas already occupied by

African Americans, interracial tensions heightened, forcing each subgroup to take action to assert its cultural identity within this conflicting ecosystem. Hence, the emergence of the Brown Power movement.[36]

It took a professional boxer from the barrios of Denver, Colorado, to ignite and activate the bronze element of the Mexican American community. Rodolfo "Corky" Gonzales was a fighter well known in the Hispanic community, and he was the catalyst that inspired the more radical elements of the Brown Power movement of the 1960s and 1970s. Gonzales broke away from his role with the Crusade for Justice Organization in Denver in 1965. His stance was not integration, such as that espoused by LULAC. Instead, he advocated for a separate Chicano movement. In 1968, he advocated for a Brown Power orientation for Chicanos in the larger dominant white society. The vehicle for the separatist-oriented Brown Power movement was the La Raza Unida Party (LRUP), which aligned itself with the more radical elements of social discontent at the time, including the Black Panthers.

The short fall of the LRUP was its failure to align with either Gutierrez's or Chavez's organizations. This weakness came to light at the 4-day conference Gonzales called for in September 1972 at the El Paso del Norte Hotel. During this time, a campus-based movement was underway that was much like the Anglo students' counterpart: the Students for a Democratic Society (SDS). The Hispanic student movement was MECHA: *El Movimiento Estudiantil Chicano de Aztlan*. It was an outgrowth of the Chicano Youth Liberation Conference held in Denver in March 1969 with the movement now designated the Plan de Aztlan. MECHA originally was an ally of the more radical views held by Corky Gonzales but moderated by the early 1970s. Even the Brown Berets, originally patterned after the Black Berets and Black Panther groups, began to lose their radical edge by the early 1970s. The cathartic event for the collective expression of Brown Power, collectively known as the La Raza Unida Party, was the National Chicano Moratorium March of August 29, 1970, held at Laguna Park in Los Angeles with representation from Mexican American organizations across the Southwest. Police reaction to the Moratorium March led to three people being killed, including *Los Angeles Times* columnist Ruben Salazar. Corky Gonzales was among the 70 arrested and jailed by the Los Angeles Police Department (LAPD). Sixty-four policemen were injured in the ensuing riot that they clearly aggravated.

It is with this history of the Chicano movement that Corky Gonzales called for a national convention of the La Raza Unida Party in 1972. But at this juncture, Corky Gonzales's dream of a strong separatist movement was waning. Nonetheless, this was to be a test of who would direct the Mexican American Political Association (MAPA) within the larger Chicano movement. Three thousand delegates met in El Paso, Texas, to determine the direction of the national La Raza Unida Party. Hispanics from the entire Southwest as well as the Midwest were represented, and in the end, the moderates, those advocating peaceful change via the ballot box like that demonstrated earlier in Crystal City, Texas, prevailed. Jose Angel Gutierrez, of the Mexican American Youth Organization (MAYO), with the support of Cesar Chavez and his United Farm Workers (UFW), beat out Corky Gonzales for the position of party chairman. Gonzales was given the largely ceremonial position of the presiding officer of the national convention, Congreso de Aztlan, as a token for his role in organizing the convention. The major outcomes of the La Raza Unida Convention were support for a guaranteed annual income for Latino workers, national health insurance, no land taxation, bilingual education, parity in employment, increase in admissions to medical schools, parity in jury selection, support for organizing farmworkers, and enforcement of the land grant conditions of the 1848 Treaty of Guadalupe Hidalgo. Essentially, this outcome represented the synthesis of the "other white" thesis and the reactive antithesis Brown Power separatists.[37]

American Indians, blacks, and Hispanics battled the white status quo during the turbulent 1960s and 1970s with the hopes of making positive changes in American society only to continue to be demonized under a new form of discrimination termed "The War on Drugs." Drug laws can be traced to the Harrison Narcotic Act of 1914, which targeted Asians residing on the West Coast. It was Harry J. Anslinger, along with his colleague, J. Edgar Hoover, who set the stage for class and race discrimination relevant to the War on Drugs. The enforcement agencies began in 1920 with Prohibition and the creation of the Bureau of Prohibition in 1927. The Federal Bureau of Narcotics (FBN) emerged in 1930, providing Harry Anslinger his "reefer madness" pulpit, culminating in passage of the 1937 Marijuana Transfer Tax Act. Anslinger, who directed the Federal Bureau of Narcotics for 31 years, was seen as the front man for U.S. capitalists, notably Randolph Hearst, Andrew Mellon, and the DuPont family, who viewed marijuana, notably hemp, as a threat to their interests in synthetic fibers. Indeed, Anslinger was related to Andrew Mellon through marriage.

Clearly, the reefer madness movement was directly linked to the *hemp conspiracy* given that the advent of the decorticator machine made hemp a more economical alternative to paper pulp used in the newspaper industry. Hearst felt his large timber holdings were threatened, and the DuPont industries had just come out with a new synthetic fiber, nylon. Mellon, the richest banker in America at this time, felt compelled to support his captains of industry's investments. This capitalist's propaganda effort then linked racial fears to fuel Hearst's *yellow journalism* with his national circulation of newspapers spreading stories of rape, murder, and violence by "Negroes, Mexicans, and Orientals," all under the influence of the evil drug marijuana. J. Edgar Hoover, the director of the Federal Bureau of Investigation (FBI), played into this scenario with his racist slant of criminal justice and questionable statistics used to promote racial unrest and fears throughout America using the FBI annual publication, *Uniform Crime Report*.[38]

This link between illicit drugs and minorities continued until the 21st century with the marked differential in incarceration rated for minority cocaine use (crack cocaine) versus that of the more affluent whites in American society who use powder cocaine. Anslinger was eventually forced to resign in 1962, but his influence continued with the creation of the Bureau of Narcotics and Dangerous Drugs in 1968 and eventually the current Drug Enforcement Agency (DEA) under President Richard Nixon. It was President Ronald Reagan, however, who militarized the drug enforcement agencies by involving the FBI, CIA, and U.S. military in international anti-drug operations, providing the excuse for massive intrusions into Panama, Colombia, and eventually, Mexico. Indeed, the War on Drugs became the paramount vehicle for enforcing the Monroe Doctrine following the end of the Cold War in the Americas, only supplanted with the terrorist attacks of September 11, 2001, and the beginning of the War on Terrorism.[39]

Canada Comes of Age and the Perils of Quebec Separatism

Influence of French Leaders in Canada

Canada's parliamentary form of government produced five distinguished francophone/French Canadian Prime Ministers out of a total of 18 to date: Sir Wilfrid Laurier (seventh PM: 1896–1911), Louis St. Laurent (12th PM: 1948–1957), Pierre Trudeau (15th PM: 1968–1979, 1980–1984), Jean Chretien (20th PM: 1993–2003), and Paul Martin (21st PM: 2003–2006). Martin, like St. Laurent, was of Irish Catholic and French Catholic descent. Canada also had its first Catholic Prime Minister, Sir John Thompson, who was the fourth PM (1892–1894) elected 68 years before President John F. Kennedy of the United States. Canada was also far ahead of the United States when it elected Kim Campbell as the first female Prime Minister (1993). Although Laurier was the fourth longest serving Prime Minister behind W. L. Mackenzie King, John A. Macdonald, and Pierre Trudeau, his 15-year tenure remains the longest unbroken term of office for Canadian Prime Ministers. He was also the Prime Minister that took Canada into the 20th century. His popularity was primarily due to his secularism, notably his belief in the separation of church and state—a position that did not endear him to the Catholic bishops in Quebec. He also strengthened Canadian and U.S. relations with his support of reciprocal trade between the neighboring countries. And he played a significant role in the Conscription Crisis of 1917 in his capacity as opposition leader. Trudeau is the father of the 1982 Canadian Constitution, the main instrument welding Canada together as a nation, keeping it from the fate of the former Yugoslavia and the dissolution of states following the breakup of the Soviet Union.[40]

Thus, the 20th century witnessed both the threads of solidarity and separation with ethnic strife between the Anglo Protestant and French Catholics in Canada again heightened during the First World War with military conscription for Canadian men to serve on the side of Great Britain in the war. The problem arose when an anti-Catholic Ulsterman was appointed as Minister of Militia, and Protestant clergymen were assigned as recruiting officers in Quebec, leading to riots in Quebec in 1916. J. M. S. Careless notes, "The bitterness and suspicion produced on both sides would take a long time to live down. And politics and governments would long be affected by the memories of the conscription crises."[41] Nonetheless, Canada's involvement in the First World War provided incentives toward greater autonomy within the British Empire when Sir Robert Borden's administration (eighth Prime Minister) demanded that Canadian troops serve within their own unit and not be scattered throughout the British military. Hence, the Canadian Corps was formed, setting the stage for national recognition, including the right of signing and approving the peace treaty ending the war.

William Lyon Mackenzie King, Canada's longest serving Prime Minister (10th Prime Minister: 12/1921–6/1926, 9/1926–8/1930, 10/1935–11/1948), took the nationalism issue further during this reign. This time the draft (conscription) actually aided in bringing French and Anglo service personnel closer in that it was the first opportunity for either group to meaningfully interact with each other. Colonel C. P. Stacey, in his chapter in Careless and Brown's 1968 book, notes, "Within the armed forces themselves 'French' and 'English' got on rather better than their civilian compatriots did. ... The comradeship of the battlefield was an admirable solvent of traditional prejudices."[42]

Following the war, in the mid-1920s, Canada joined other members of the British Empire in forging a Commonwealth out of the previous British Empire in which the respective nations would be *equal in status* with the United Kingdom, hence being unified under the British Crown but not necessarily with the British government. Although Canada traces its national origin to July 1, 1867, when it established its union of British North American colonies (Confederation/Constitution Act), its membership in the British Commonwealth of Nations on January 11, 1931, marked its international representation as a semiautonomous nation throughout the world. The road to nationalism began with the Imperial Conference of 1926 and the Dominion-Provincial Conference of 1927. The Balfour Declaration of 1926 declared equality in status of the Dominions within the United Kingdom, setting the stage for the formal transformation of the British Empire into the British Commonwealth. The transformation was official with the 1931 Statute of Westminster. Under this arrangement, Canada's governor general, like that of the other dominions within the United Kingdom, would only represent the symbol of the British Crown and not necessarily the interests of the British Government. However, changes to the Canadian constitution still needed to be brought before the Parliament of the United Kingdom. The League of Nations (forerunner of the United Nations), through the "Canadian Resolution," also granted an exception to Article X of the covenant, requiring it to come to the defense of other nations within the League.[43]

This change from Great Britain to the United Kingdom (UK) marked not only a diminishing British influence in Canada but also the beginning of a greater U.S. influence, for better or worse, in the areas of national or regional defense and economics. This new era began in 1926 when Canada established its first diplomatic office in the United States. Nationhood within the British Commonwealth came under W. L. Mackenzie King's term with the long road toward this end clearly paved by the Laurier and Borden administrations. Thus, although Canada's march toward nationhood began under the direction of its first French Canadian Prime Minister (Laurier), it was completed following the Second World War, in 1949, during the tenure of its second French Canadian Prime Minister, Louis S. St. Laurent, King's French Canadian External Affairs Minister.

During this transition period, Newfoundland finally joined the Canadian Union, completing the Confederation, making it the second largest country in landmass. Again, this process began under the long tenure of Mackenzie King and had much to do with the presence of U.S. armed forces stationed on Newfoundland during and following the Second World War. In a deal with British Prime Minister Winston Churchill, President Roosevelt gained permission to have U.S. military bases on Newfoundland in early 1941 even before the United States formally entered the war. Mackenzie King countered by petitioning the United Kingdom to have his own Canadian forces stationed on the last British colonial holdout within the former British North America domain. So, for the duration of the Second World War and until Newfoundland joined the Union, two separate military defense forces, one Canadian and the other American, occupied Newfoundland. The Union of Newfoundland with the rest of Canada was effective at midnight March 31/April 1, 1949.[44]

Canada grew in international stature during the St. Laurent administration, joining the North Atlantic Treaty Organization (NATO) in 1949, having a seat on the National Security Council at the United Nations (UN), and being one of 16 UN members contributing military forces to the Korean Conflict from 1950–1955. Indeed, Canada provided the third largest military contingent to the Korean Conflict. St. Laurent and his Secretary of State for External Affairs, Lester B. Pearson, took the lead in resolving the 1956 Suez Canal crisis, providing the prototype for the United Nations Emergency Force (UNEF), the UN peacekeeping force. Pearson won the 1957 Nobel Peace Prize for this effort and went on to become Canada's 14th Prime Minister (1963–1968). Canada at this time also allowed the positioning of U.S. radar stations across the Canadian Arctic as part of the Distant Early Warning

Line (DEW Line), leading to his successor, Prime Minister John Diefenbaker (13th PM: 1957–1963), signing the North American Air Defense (NORAD) agreement with the United States in 1958. Postwar Canada also saw the completion of the St. Lawrence Seaway, a major endeavor that benefitted both Canada and the United States, and the completion of the Trans-Canada gas and oil pipeline—events that greatly enhanced domestic and international commerce in the newly emerging independent Canada.[45]

J. M. S. Careless and R. Craig Brown, in their 1968 history of Canada, note that the increased influence of U.S. capitalism in Canada would lead to the end of Canada's unique and independent character, making it yet another component of America, which was adding Alaska and Hawaii to statehood status: "Many people regarded the growing integration of the Canadian and American economies in the post-war period as a big step towards the inevitable disappearance of Canadian independence."[44] Clearly, Canada was caught in the U.S.–Soviet nuclear buildup during the Cold War era that emerged following the Second World War, but even then it was able to keep its independence by not agreeing with all U.S. policies and actions, including not joining the Southeast Asia Treaty Organization (SEATO) and maintaining healthy trade and international relations with both Cuba and China during the strong anti-Communist McCarthy era in America. Even then, the audacity of America's Monroe Doctrine was still being felt in Canada during this time when the U.S. Senate vilified one of Canada's most respected public servants, Herbert Norman, for an incident involving a Russian spy, contributing to Norman's suicide in 1957. Canada differed from both Britain and the United States in regards to the growing colonial independence movement through Asia and Africa, usually siding with the anti-colonialists. This was a time when the United States and Britain were shoring up proxy anti-independence governments under the guise of anti-Communism. President Eisenhower took over the role of the defeated French in Indochina, and Britain fought rebels in Kenya and other colonial strongholds. Thus, Canada walked a tightrope between its NATO and UN obligations and its anti-colonial sentiments during the two decades following the Second World War. Indeed, Canada, under Prime Minister Lester Pearson, rejected the deployment of Canadian Forces to Vietnam, and later, Prime Minister Paul Martin (2003–2006) rejected the U.S. Missile Treaty.[46]

Quebec Separatism and the "Quiet Revolution"

But Canada had its own internal disputes and had to fight a long battle to keep the country from falling apart during the 1970s. Part of this problem stemmed from John Diefenbaker's One Canada policy in which he was unwilling to make special concessions to Quebec's francophones. On the other hand, this policy reversed Laurier's policy of disenfranchising status Indians from voting.

Nonetheless, Diefenbaker's successor, Lester Pearson, kept the French versus Anglo issue alive by establishing the Royal Commission on Bilingualism and Biculturalism. This was the period of both the "Quiet Revolution" and the Separatist Movement, which were transforming Quebec. These events would play out in a more dynamic fashion during Pierre Trudeau's administration. Canada, especially Quebec Province, was caught up in the turbulent 1960s that caused considerable social turmoil in the United States. Antiwar, antidraft, anti-ROTC (Reserve Officers Training Corps), antiestablishment, and anti-segregation protests manifested themselves in riots in the ghettoes of major U.S. cities, on Indian reservations, and on college campuses. Prime Minister Pearson's rejection of the Vietnam War meant Canada became involved in the U.S. protests by becoming the designated safe haven for draft dodgers from the United States. The events in the United States were played out in the worldwide media, often overshadowing Quebec's own Quiet Revolution: the Province's transformation from a Catholic-run theocracy to a secular society. This internal dispute led to the infamous October Crisis of 1980, an event that not only shook Canadian society, but brought notoriety and worldwide attention to Quebec and the separatists movement.

The Quiet Revolution pitted the Vatican-sponsored French Canadian Catholic Bishops and the ruling elite attempting to maintain the status quo against the secular nationalists, who drew their inspiration from secular France. Fueling this dispute, in part, was the Canadian (federal) Bill of Rights enacted by Prime Minister John Diefenbaker on August 8, 1960. Starting with Diefenbaker, Prime Minister Lester Pearson's administration continued to expand social programs at the federal level with universal health care, a pension plan, and student loans setting the stage for cultural preservation with the Royal Commission on Bilingualism and Biculturalism. Even a new Canadian flag was introduced during Pearson's (1963–1968) tenure. With these changes at the federal level, the provincial government in Quebec took over health care and education from the Roman Catholic Church, creating ministries of education and health and, at the same time, allowing the unionization of civil services. Quebec's government also took steps to gain control over its natural resources, most of which were being exploited by foreign investors, mostly U.S. capitalist firms.

The Quiet Revolution began with the death of Premier Maurice Duplessis in 1959, an event ending his conservative regime and leading to the election of Jean Lesage and the Liberals in June 1960. By most accounts, the Quiet Revolution lasted 10 years until just prior to the October Crisis of 1970. Up to that time, both the Conservative government and the Catholic Church backed the foreign investors who were not only exploiting the rich resources of Quebec, but providing them with a cheap workforce as well. The impact of the Catholic Church in provincial matters dates back to the establishment of the Canadian Constitution creating the Confederation in 1867. Under the original Constitution, education was designated as a provincial responsibility and, in accordance with this decree, Quebec established a Ministry of Public Instruction the following year, only to have it abolished in 1875 under pressure from the Catholic Church, which wanted to continue its control over this important aspect of community socialization.

At the time of the Quiet Revolution in 1960, there were some 1,500 different school boards in Quebec Province, each with their own curricula and standards. And like their counterparts in the Franco-American communities in the United States, education for the average person was not highly valued under this system with a dismal proportion of students completing high school in comparison to English-speaking students in Canada. Thus, a major change brought about by the Quiet Revolution was the reestablishment of a Ministry of Education in 1964. The schools became secular in the province, and although the schools were still segregated by languages, a standardized curriculum was adopted, and the age for compulsory education was raised to age 16, like that in the United States.[47]

Another important element of the Quiet Revolution was the nationalization of the Province's natural resources, an action taken by Rene Levesque in 1962, when he was the Province's Minister of Natural Resources; this set in place his plans for Hydro-Quebec. The Province set up a parallel investment scheme in 1962, the General Financing Corporation, so that Quebec citizens could invest in the emerging public companies (iron, mining, forestry, petroleum, hydropower). The Province also created its own pension plan in 1965. The Quiet Revolution provided Quebec Province with the opportunity to catch up with the rest of Canada and the region regarding social, educational, and economic progress that emerged through the various social upheavals dominating the 1960s worldwide.

The Quiet Revolution also sparked the fires of nationalism within French Canada, a phenomenon that challenged Pierre Trudeau early in his administration. The separatist issue was fought by two capable adversaries, Rene Lévesque, leader of the *Parti Quebecois*, and Pierre Trudeau, Canadian Prime Minister. In Quebec the *Front de Liberation du Quebec* (FLQ) initiated a not-so-quiet revolution, one patterned after those occurring in Cuba and Algeria at the time, and the more violent Weathermen, American Indian Movement, and Black Panther movements in the United States during the turbulent 1960s and 1970s.[48]

The FLQ reigned from 1963 until the early 1970s with sporadic episodes thereafter. Initially, the FLQ was more a nuisance group than a real threat to the government of either Canada or Quebec Province. It consisted of loosely connected cells that acted mostly independent of each other, robbing banks and placing bombs in the mailboxes of prominent Anglo-Quebecers. Their more notorious actions included the bombing of a railway in 1963 in an attempt to assassinate then Canadian Prime Minister John Diefenbaker as well as placing bombs at an Army Recruitment Center and at McGill University and Loyola College. In 1964, some FLQ cells calling themselves the Quebec Liberation Army increased their funding efforts through bank robberies. In 1965, Charles Gagnon and Pierre Vallieres (authors of *White Niggers of America*) combined their Popular Liberation Movement with the FLQ, adding to the growing prosovereignty movement. The FLQ then started its own publication, *La Cognee* ("The Hit"). In 1969, a powerful bomb at the Montreal Stock Exchange caused massive damage and seriously injured 27 people, and later that year, the FLQ bombed the home of Montreal Mayor Jean Drapeau. Overall, the various cells of the FLQ were responsible for more than 160 violent incidents, which killed eight people and injured dozens of others in their war against Anglo-Saxon imperialism, the overthrow of the Quebec government, and the establishment of socialist French-only Quebec.[49]

Although these activities were well documented throughout Canada, the FLQ captured worldwide attention in 1970 during the October Crisis with the kidnapping of the British Trade Commissioner, James Cross; the kidnapping and murder of Quebec Labor Minister and Vice Premier, Pierre Laporte; and the discovery of plans for the kidnapping of the Israeli and United States Consuls. This incident propelled Prime Minister Trudeau to the world stage as well as his main adversary, Rene Levesque, leader of the emerging *Parti Quebecois* and a provincial leader during the two votes for Quebec independence. In reaction to the October Crisis and at the request of both Robert Bourassa, Premier of Quebec, and Jean Drapeau, Mayor of Montreal, Prime Minister Trudeau requested the Governor General of Canada to ask the Queen to invoke the War Measures Act. This marked the first peacetime use of this measure allowing the deployment of the military under the direction of the Quebec Provincial Police (*Surete du Quebec*) and granted the Royal Canadian Mounted Police (RCMP) and the Quebec Police sweeping powers of arrest and detention. In their sweep of potential FLQ members, the police arrested 497 individuals with all but 62 eventually released. This action was popular with both Anglos and French Canadians with the overwhelming majority of both groups supporting Trudeau's actions. This marked the end of a violent attempt toward separatism in Quebec Province and the realization that a political solution was the only viable avenue toward Quebec independence.

Rene Levesque led the political movement toward a separate French Quebec in 1968 with the creation of *Parti Quebecois* (PQ) and became the Premier of Quebec in 1976 (23rd Premier of Quebec; November 1976–October 1985). The first vote for Quebec independence was in 1980 while he was Premier of Quebec. Setting the stage for these votes, Levesque and the PQ enacted the Charter of the French Language (Bill 101) in 1977, making French the official language of business in Quebec as well as restricting the use of English on signs. This bill also compelled French Canadians residing in

Quebec Province to attend French elementary and high schools. Under this law, only Anglos residing in Quebec Province could attend English schools. Bill 101 appeared to be a challenge to Prime Minister Trudeau's Official Languages Act of 1969 that stated that all federal government services were to be available in both of Canada's official languages: English and French. The economic development of Quebec Province's natural resources, including Hydro-Quebec, continued under Levesque's leadership, a factor shoring up his argument for economic and political independence for the Province. These efforts led to the creation of Nunavut Territory for Canada's Inuit, a process started in the 1970s, and finally completed under Prime Minister Chretien's administration. Here, Inuit claims regarding lands needed for Hydro-Quebec were traded for a massive, semiautonomous Native homeland. Ironically, Nunavik, the Inuit homeland in Quebec, came to mirror the conditions that the first Quebec separatist referendum wanted for itself within the federal confederation.

Premier Levesque then began promoting his "sovereignty-association" plan, calling for a partially sovereign Quebec Province but with continued economic ties to the rest of Canada. The first Quebec referendum was held May 20, 1980, with "yes" or "no" responses to the following question:

> The Government of Quebec has made public its proposal to negotiate a new agreement with the rest of Canada, based on the equality of nations; this agreement would enable Quebec to acquire the exclusive power to make its laws, levy its taxes and establish relations abroad—in other words, sovereignty—and at the same time to maintain with Canada an economic association including a common currency; no change in political status resulting from these negotiations will be effective without the approval by the people through another referendum; on these terms, do you give the Government of Quebec the mandate to negotiate the proposed agreement between Quebec and Canada?[50]

In the end, the "No" vote won out with about 60% of the vote. To counter the PQ separatism, Prime Minister Trudeau promised a new constitution (Canada Act/Constitution Act, 1982) with a Charter of Rights as an incentive for continued unity within Canada. The 1982 Constitution Act provided Canada with full and final independence from the United Kingdom, essentially, full sovereignty, and was endorsed by all provinces except Quebec. Attempts were then made to appease the Quebec government via the Meech Lake Accord, beginning in 1987 under Prime Minister Brian Mulroney, getting it to endorse the 1982 Constitution. The Accord provided for recognition of Quebec as a "distinct society," increasing its provincial powers regarding immigration and providing the provinces with veto powers. Initially, the other 10 provincial premiers and the public at large agreed with the provisions of the accord, but by June 1990, the deadline for acceptance, attitudes changed and the accord failed. Part of this is due to former Prime Minister Pierre Trudeau's opposition to the accord, citing that it would weaken federal powers and leave the door open for the dissolution of Canada itself. On the other hand, the *Bloc Quebecois* (BQ) party, formed by Lucien Bouchard in June 1991, was seen as the federal vehicle for setting the separation agenda for those supporting the annexation of Quebec Province. Adding to this public sentiment was the breakup of the former Soviet Union and the unraveling of the former Yugoslavia. Trudeau did not want Canada to become North America's Yugoslavia.[51]

The failure of the Meech Lake Accord led to the second Quebec referendum in 1995, which asked the provincial voters for a "yes" or "no" vote on this question:

> Do you agree that Quebec should become sovereign after having made a formal offer to Canada for a new economic and political partnership within the scope of the bill respecting the future of Quebec and of the agreement signed on June 12, 1995? (Again the sovereignty question failed.)

Another referendum in 1995 was based on the Charlottetown Accord initiated in 1992, and supported by all 10 provincial ministers, calling for amending the 1982 Constitution in such a manner that it would weaken the federal government and strengthen provincial authority. This referendum called for full sovereignty for Quebec. Jean Chretien, a Trudeau colleague and proponent of a strong Canada, as Prime Minister (1993–2003) supported the referendum. However, the referendum was strongly opposed by former Prime Minister Pierre Trudeau. This coupled with the unpopularity of the current Prime Minister, Brian Mulroney, led to the defeat of the Charlottetown Accord in 1992 with 54.3% voting "no/*non*" and 45.7% "yes/*oui*."

In order to curtail continued chaos and endless referendums, the federal government passed the Clarity Act (Bill C-20), which raised the bar for these votes, stipulating the need for a "clear majority" in support of a "clear question" before future referendums could be entertained and, at the same time, authorizing the government to determine the definition of these terms. Bill C-20 established conditions for Provinces to separate from Canada, and it passed in June 2000. The Parliament of Canada has the power to determine whether or not a referendum question is stated in clear enough wording so it holds the same meaning in French, English, and Aboriginal languages. This was a problem with the 1995 referendum with wording leading to confusion as to what the voters thought they were voting for. The Canadian Supreme Court sided with the Canadian government, stating that no province has the right to unilaterally secede under Canadian or international law.[52] The issue of Kosovo complicated matters when the International Court of Justice delivered its advisory opinion in July 2010 regarding the unilateral declaration of independence of Kosovo from Serbia. As it stands now, provincial votes aside, separation issues can only be valid following successful negotiations between the federal government and the provincial government. Only then can the Constitution be amended.

Jean Chretien was Prime Minister when the terrorist attacks of September 11, 2001, occurred south of the border in the United States. During his tenure, Canadian forces were deployed as part of the peacekeeping forces in Bosnia and Herzegovina, and they participated in the NATO attacks on Serbia during the Kosovo War. And although Canada opposed the invasion of Iraq, Canadian Forces, including many French Canadians, participated in the War in Afghanistan.[53] From 1992 to 1995, Canadian Forces were part of the UN peacekeeping force (UN Protection Force or UNPROFOR) and were involved in Operation Medak Pocket against Croatian militants. In 2002, Canadian forces that participated in this operation were awarded the Commander-in-Chief Unit Commendation—the first military decoration since the Korean War. In 1999, the Canadian Air Force was deployed during the Kosovo War (March 14–June 11) in which they delivered 10% of the air attacks against Serbian forces. For this, additional military commendations were awarded: the General Campaign Star (GCS), and the 441st and 425th Tactical Fighter Squadrons were awarded the Battle Honor "KOSOVO."

The involvement of Canadian forces in the Balkan Wars was a stark reminder for many Canadians that these same horrors could be inflicted on Canadians if another FLQ-type uprising occurred, promoting the breakup of Canada. The unraveling of the former Yugoslavia from 1991 to 2002 resulted in more than 100,000 deaths, mostly civilians, and millions displaced due to ethnic cleansing. In L. A. French's public forum in the fall of 2010, as visiting endowed chair of criminology and criminal justice at St. Thomas University in Fredericton, New Brunswick, he noticed that the current Anglo and French ethnic strife in Canada could prove to be as deadly as that in Yugoslavia—the worst in Europe since the Second World War. The speech was on the heels of the 2010 close vote of Canadian Parliament's to retain gun control. French pointed out that this is a critical deterrence given the ready availability of assault weapons and ammo from the United States. These weapons have already increased the lethality of the drug wars in Mexico and could easily do the same for Canada.[54]

This brief overview of comparative events during the 20th century shows that both the French Canadians and their Franco-American counterparts were greatly affected by the dictates of the Second Vatican Council of the early 1960s, contributing to both the Quiet Revolution and the not-so-quiet FLQ separatist movements and referendums and leading to the end of the French Catholic ethnic parochial school system and ethnic dioceses in New England. The unique French Canadian culture, although transformed by events since the 1960s, has survived and still retains its unique attributes in French communities throughout Canada, despite no longer being dominated by the Roman Catholic Church.

Mexico in the 20th Century: Growth, Corruption, and U.S. Interventions

Implementing the New Constitution of 1917 with Interference from the United States

Mexico in the 20th century emerged from the revolution and the ensuing Constitution of 1917. Even then wide differences continued to exist between those favoring nationalism and those favoring agrarian demands. Article 27 granted Mexico the ownership of subsoil wealth taking this valuable resource from outsiders who had long exploited Mexico's riches. Article 27 was based on colonial legal foundations in which mining was an activity reserved for the crown because the wealth laid in the subsoil. This article also authorized the creation of *ejidos* based on family or communal arrangements; hence Zapata's followers' demands for the redistribution of land from the wealthy few to the common folks: peasants, American Indians, Mestizos. Now, subsoil ownership meant that foreign and national companies would fall under the new law. A major effect of the law was the 1938 nationalization of Mexico's substantial oil reserves. This was a blow to U.S. oil companies who were promised leases in perpetuity under the prerevolution *porfiriato* regime.

Initially, the Obregon administration promised the U.S. Government, in 1923, that existing oil deals would not be affected by the new law in exchange for U.S. recognition of his presidency. However, this changed with the presidential administration of Plutarco Elias Calles (1924–1928) under which a new law called for modification of the oil leasing policy. The new law was postponed due to the outcry from U.S. oil companies. Calles was also a strong opponent of the influence of the Catholic Church in Mexico. This transition period of attempting to secularize education and other public institutions long dominated by the Catholic Church led to a 3-year (1926–1929) internal conflict known as the Cristero Rebellion in Central Mexico, resulting in nearly 90,000 deaths.

Consequently, the decision to delay implementation of oil legislation saw the heavy hand of the U.S. business interests and the fear of yet another intrusion under the pretext of the Monroe Doctrine. Interestingly, in this scenario, the U.S. oil giants were willing to arm those affiliated with the Catholic Church in an effort to maintain the status quo regarding the continued exploitation of Mexico's oil reserves. Complicating matters, Mexico in 1924 recognized the Soviet Union, further aggravating the United States, resulting in a strong rebuke from U.S. Secretary of State Frank Kellogg. Adding fuel to the fear of U.S. intrusion, Calles again delayed the nationalization of oil resources and other far-reaching reforms stipulated under Article 27 (land ownership, secular education, and labor policies) for another decade.

Revolutionary Changes Finally Enacted

In 1934, Lazaro Cardenas was elected president. He is regarded as the most revolutionary of all modern Mexican leaders. He is credited with the distribution of more land to *campesinos* (peasants) than any other leader since the revolution. Indeed, during his 6-year presidency, he distributed more land than all his predecessors together. Cardenas also did much to expand public education, building thousands of schools in rural areas and providing training for teachers in order to educate the mestizo, Indians, and other peasants. His administration also reformed labor laws and promoted labor organization leading to the 8-hour workday and the right to strike. He is credited with consolidating the National Revolutionary Party (PNR) into the Party of the Mexican Revolution (PRI), the party that dominated Mexican politics until 2000 and is again in power in 2016.[55]

The PRI, under Cardenas, put together a coalition of peasants through the National Peasant Confederation (CNC), labor organizations via the Mexican Confederation of Workers (CTM), government workers with the National Confederation of Popular Organization (CNOP), and the military. Business and corporate interests were kept out of the government but encouraged to form their own affiliations, such as the National Confederation of Chambers of Commerce and the National Chamber of Manufacturing Industry. Now the interests of urban workers and peasants were met under the government and in compliance with the Constitution. Obviously, the big British and U.S. oil companies operating in Mexico were not pleased with this nationalistic trend. Neither were the large landowners, the *hacendados*, which also included foreign companies, many American owned. Cardenas also challenged the delay in the implementation of the 1925 oil legislation leading to the Expropriation Law, again with concessions made to outside oil interests. However, a dispute over wages led to a decision by the Mexican Supreme Court in 1938 favoring the workers. The oil companies ignored the Supreme Court's decision forcing Cardenas to nationalize Mexico's oil resources.

The extensive land expropriations as well as the oil nationalization provided the Mexican public with a sense of renewed nationalism. The lower urban and rural classes finally felt that the revolution was working for them. This euphoria ended after the Cardenas administration in 1940 and the advent of the Second World War. The war effectively ended Mexico's ability to conduct foreign policy free from the influence of the United States.

U.S. foreign policy under Franklin D. Roosevelt forced a shift to the right in Mexico away from the left-leaning programs instituted under the Cardenas administration. The Monroe Doctrine was now termed the "Good Neighbor Policy" whereby Mexico and all of Latin America was under scrutiny for any pro-Nazi or pro-Communist leanings. The United States was most concerned with its southern neighbor, Mexico, especially the guarantee of access to its oil resources.[56]

U.S. Cold War Interventions

This recognition of an independent Mexican state, free to exercise its own internal affairs, was shrouded within the realities of the newly polarized international scheme, meaning that any major decisions needed to follow the mandate of the dominant nations emerging from the Second World War. For Mexico, the room for maneuvering in foreign policy was determined in large part by the priorities of the United States. After the war, the composition of the international community shifted, and consequently, so did the role of Mexico as a world player. The Cold War now dictated the new realities in which countries such as Mexico had to choose between subscribing to the dictates of the United States or to those of the Soviet Union. This was not really a choice for Mexico given the numerous military incursions by the United States during its history as an independent nation. And by acquiescing to the United States, Mexico delayed the intrusion of the CIA and the conflicts forced upon its southern neighbors in Central and South America.[57]

In compliance with U.S. influence, the Mexican Communist Party was declared illegal in 1946. This alliance with the United States also served to dispel the notion that the PRI revolutionary regime was Marxist oriented as many in the United States contended during the pre-World War II years. Moreover, this alignment in the new world order was not based solely on external factors. Internal political considerations also played a role in forcing change within the Mexican political and economic system. For instance, those who felt that they were left out of the "revolutionary family" and those who opposed the official PRI party mandate established in 1929 felt left out even though they were enfranchised. Change was taking place in all areas of social development. Yet, the PRI still held its status within the populace. The generals who finally got the upper hand in the internal struggle and later influenced the voters became the trustees of the revolution and its authority until 1960.

Nonetheless, opposition electoral forces began to emerge. The generals who claimed the mantle of the revolution were met with challenges from the onset. During the 1920s, the historical record accounts for scores of high-ranking military officers being killed in power struggles in order to depose Alvaro Obregon, the general who defeated Francisco Villa and who ultimately outfoxed the father of the 1917 Constitution, Vanustiano Carranza. The emergence of the PRI was an effort to replace the bullets with ballots, thus ending the postrevolution conflicts. Even then, election fraud persisted albeit without the killings. In 1939, conservatives outside the revolutionary PRI clique founded the National Action Party (PAN), and it took them 50 years to win their first gubernatorial election. In 2000, PAN was finally able to defeat the PRI in a presidential election.

The key operating concept for the postrevolutionary government was political stability even if it meant fraudulent elections. Mexico's stability became an important component of the Cold War divisions, a factor made clear by its more powerful neighbor to the north. It fared better initially than its Latin American neighbors, which were universally governed by a parade of military dictators during the Cold War era. Although Mexico escaped that form of government, it did so by establishing a de facto single-party system. In fact, part of the saving grace for the PRI in the eyes of the United States was the prolonged political stability it provided Mexico and, in turn, the U.S. tendency to ignore government corruption, much like it did during the tenure of Porfirio Díaz during the 19th century. In its overwhelming fear of Communism within the hemisphere, the United States was willing to turn a blind eye to the democratic ideals it so strongly espoused, notably the rule of law, respect for human dignity, and other tenets of democracy.[58]

Oppression and Change: Transitioning to Globalization

The PRI offered a symbiotic relationship between the military, government offices, the private sector, and the Catholic Church, each allowed its turf with minimum interference as long as they did not challenge the party or its operations. Those who dared to challenge the system or who did not partake in the co-opting enticement offered by the government were dealt with harshly as was the case with the railroad union in the late 1950s. The railroad was nationalized in the 1930s with the support of the National Railroad Union. But its leadership was corrupt, and a group of dissident workers organized several work stoppages and called for a general strike only to be met with force and its leaders sent to prison. A serious blow came to the PRI in 1968 with the increase in labor and peasant organizations, ostensibly influenced by the Cuban Revolution and guerrilla movements emerging in southern Mexico, notably among its indigenous peoples. Clearly, the student movement of the late 1960s revealed the cracks in the system more than any other previous social movement or unrest outside the revolution. This involved students demonstrating against what they perceived as a harshly repressive political system, much like what was occurring in the United States at the time. Toward this end, college and university students organized a demonstration in Mexico City on October 2, 1968, just days before the start of the

Summer Olympic Games. Ironically, the Summer Olympics were designed to showcase Mexico's recent advances. Unfortunately, like the fate of their counterparts in the United States, this demonstration was met with force. In the end, hundreds of students disappeared with the death toll believed to be in the thousands in what is known as the Tlatelodo Massacre.

The repression of students did not stop there. In 1971, alleged government special forces once again massacred students. Luis Echeverria was the president (1970–1976), and his strategy was to use a nationalistic theme, siding Mexico with the nonaligned countries comprising the Third World Nations. He also espoused anti-imperialist rhetoric. This action was seen in part to appease opposition forces in Mexico. His populist message was designed to favor the masses while, at the same time, bring opposing political forces into the fold. President Echeverria was instrumental in having the voting age lowered from 21 to 18 in order to placate the disgruntled urban middle class youth, that is, students. At the same time, the government was engaged in fighting urban and rural insurrection. The urgency to placate these activities spawned widespread violations of human rights, not unlike in other Latin American countries or the United States.[59]

The changing of administrations in 1976 coincided with Mexico suffering the first of a series of horrendous peso devaluations, plunging the country into desperate straits not seen since the debt crisis of the mid-1800s that led to the Tripartite Convention and armed intervention by European powers. This latest crisis was predicated by obtaining loans on the basis of newly discovered oil reserves. In what had become the norm, the Portillo (1976–1982) administration raised the hopes of the Mexican people with the promise of this new wealth. The subsoil wealth was going to lift up the Mexican people out of their abject poverty with the rural sector and its Indian population to be among the main beneficiaries. With this promising wealth, President Jose Lopez Portillo floated loans in advance of any actual oil production. This increase in borrowed income allowed the government to make promises to disgruntled groups and political opponents alike. Essentially, the PRI could return to its practice of "greasing the wheel" now that new monies were available. Foreign borrowing was based on the then-current prices of oil, which had been escalating as a consequence of the early 1970s Oil Petroleum Exporting Countries (OPEC) oil embargo. Although not a member of OPEC, Mexico nonetheless pegged its oil prices at parity with those of the cartel. Unfortunately, the early 1980s resulted in an oil glut and a marked decrease in oil revenues. Given that oil was Mexico's chief export in the 1980s, it marked a decade that placed Mexico in considerable debt. Its foreign debt was at the point that Mexico had to be bailed out by the United States and the International Monetary Fund (IMF) in 1986. Mexico was at the mercy of not only U.S. capitalists but the IMF as well. The IMF called for a curtailment of social expenditures and for Mexico to begin free market reforms, resulting in the state selling back to the private sector many government-run companies, some 1,500 enterprises, and Mexico applied for admission to the General Agreement on Trade and Tariffs (GATT) consortium. This entailed relaxing Mexico's cumbersome laws regulating foreign investments leading up to U.S. President William Clinton being able to entice Mexico to join the United States and Canada in forging the North American Free Trade Agreement (NAFTA).[60]

From NAFTA to the 21st Century

5

Introduction

Although the North American Free Trade Agreement (NAFTA) is credited with greatly improving Mexico's emergent middle class, this was not the case with the indigenous peoples, such as peasants and Mestizos. On the other hand, the economic benefit to all three trading partners was considerable, sufficient to buffer the impact of the 2008 worldwide Great Recession. Moreover, the September 11, 2001 (9/11), terrorist attacks on the United States resulted in greater border security between Mexico and the United States and Canada and the United States, resulting in innovative solutions that benefitted the licit trade between these partners but at the expense of the free movement of the indigenous peoples who once had free access across these now militarized borders. Data from the Border Policy Research Institute indicates the proportion of total U.S. foreign trade associated with major trade partners (1990–2013). During this time frame, the United States imported less from Canada in 2013 (14.6%) than in 1990 (18.4%) while importing more from Mexico in 2013 (12.4%) than in 1990 (6.1%). U.S. exports to Canada also declined from 1990 (21.1%) to 2013 (19.0%), and Mexico again saw a gain from 1990 (7.2%) to 2013 (14.3%).[1]

NAFTA seems to have benefited Mexico economically, more so than Canada, despite the increased border barriers as a consequence of the terrorist attacks on the United States in 2001. Until the 9/11 terrorist attacks, the Canada–U.S. border was a 5,525-mile porous and poorly policed barrier between two friendly, developed nations. This was in marked contrast with the 1,933-mile U.S.–Mexico border, which had a long tradition of increased border patrols. Prior to the terrorist attacks of 9/11/01, a July 2000 federal report but the U.S. Department of Justice Inspector General noted that fewer than 4% of the total Border Patrol agents were assigned to the Canada–U.S. border; hence, 300 agents were assigned to protect this 5,525-mile border, and nearly 8,000 agents were assigned to the shorter border with Mexico. The U.S.–Mexico border has been fortified to some degree since the War with Mexico (1846–1848) with the capacity to hold those suspected of illegal entry. Along the U.S.–Canada border, on the other hand, there has never been sufficient federal detainment facilities to house those attempting illegal entry; hence, most have been merely released and allowed to retreat back to Canada.

Border Perspective Since 9/11

The terrorist attacks of September 11, 2001, caught the United States and Canada off guard, forcing the North Atlantic Treaty Organization (NATO) partners to take a new look at border protection. At the time of 9/11, the United States saw Mexico as the major contributor to both the illegal immigration (human trafficking) and the illegal drug trades. This was not an unreasonable focus given that it was estimated that the illegal immigrant count in the United States at the time of 9/11 was five million, about 2% of the total U.S. population with the vast majority of these illegal persons being of Hispanic heritage, the majority being Mexican. Most of the Hispanics came through Mexico with the exception of Haitians and Cubans, and East Europeans and Asians mainly came through the U.S.–Canada border along with nearly 100,000 illegal Canadians.

The group not being scrutinized carefully was Middle Eastern Muslims who entered the United States mainly from Canada. Even following the terrorist attacks, increased border scrutiny was focused on the U.S.–Mexico border and not the more likely terrorist entry point of Canada. Nonetheless, North American border security was dominated by the United States with Canada and Mexico compelled to comply. The terrorist attacks led to the creation of a new non-cabinet level administrative position, that of Homeland Security Director and the Department of Homeland Security (DHS). With the creation of the Department of Homeland Security, the Wars on Drugs and Terrorism were blended. Given that most of the drug trade came from the southern border, post–9/11 security measures focused mainly on the Mexican border, the region known as "the Borderlands." Since its creation in March 2003, Homeland Security has oversight over: (1) U.S. Customs and Border Enforcement (CBE), (2) U.S. Citizenship and Immigration Services (USCIS), and (3) U.S. Immigration and Customs Enforcement (ICE). Under this arrangement, the U.S. Border Patrol falls under the CBE, and ICE is in charge of deportation. Since the establishment of DHS, more than 95% of those arrested entering the United States illegally are arrested coming from Mexico: the Borderlands. Given the economic success of NAFTA, a dual system emerged, a "Fast Track" system for NAFTA business and a militarized zone in order to combat illicit business, such as drugs and human trafficking, and to filter out potential terrorists. The major impact of these efforts to better secure borders while not hindering legitimate NAFTA trade was established in January 2009 under the Western Hemisphere Travel Initiative

(WHTI). WHTI was intended to maintain the smooth flow of trade under NAFTA while, at the same time, increasing security for others attempting transborder entry into the United States. Now, approved NAFTA groups have access to Free and Secure Trade Express (FAST) passage, but official passports are required for all others.

Impact of the Militarization of the U.S. Borders

Of the two U.S. borders, the one with Mexico (the Borderlands) has historically been the one most fortified. Not only do military installations dot the 1,933-mile border, the first federalization of the National Guard (by President Woodrow Wilson) was used during Mexico's revolution. The federalized National Guard also participated in the 1917 Punitive Expedition into Mexico in pursuit of General Pancho Villa. Indeed, this military intrusion into Mexico, led by Brigadier General John J. "Black Jack" Pershing, is credited with preparing the United States for its entry into the First World War when the National Guard troops became the U.S. Expeditionary Force. A major issue with using the U.S. military, including federalizing the National Guard, is the 1878 Posse Comitatus Act, which specifically prohibits the use of soldiers or marines as a domestic security force other than during a declaration of martial law. Exceptions included the mustering of National Guard units along the U.S.–Mexico border during the Mexican Revolution. Another notable exception was the federalization of the National Guard for the purpose of protecting black students following the U.S. Supreme Court's 1954 school desegregation order during the Eisenhower administration. The National Guard was also employed during the turbulent riots of the 1960s, climaxing with the killing of students at Kent State University and Jackson State University in 1970. And, as stated earlier, the U.S. military was actively involved in the Wounded Knee II crisis later in the 1970s.

The plan for increased border security was part of President Clinton's NAFTA proposal. Calling this the Southwest Border Strategy, the Clinton administration's plan was to shore up the most porous sections of the Borderlands. These designated Borderland sites included the areas adjacent to San Diego, California; Tucson, Arizona; and El Paso, Texas. In addition to the creation of DHS in 2003, the George W. Bush administration put forth a plan in 2006 known as Operation Jump Start, which used the National Guard from Borderland states (California, Arizona, New Mexico, and Texas), thus avoiding the prohibition of the use of federal troops within the United States for domestic purposes (although President D. Eisenhower did so in 1958 to enforce school integration in the South). Under the Bush plan, the governors of the Borderland states would receive federal monetary incentives for them to call up their respective National Guard units, avoiding a federal call-up like that under President Wilson. Operation Hold the Line was initiated at the Juárez, Mexico–El Paso, Texas, entryway, and Operation Gatekeeper addressed the main California entry from Tijuana, Mexico, into the Imperial Beach/San Diego region. Operation Safeguard was designed to reinforce the Nogales, Mexico–Douglas, Arizona, entryway to Tucson. These border operations resulted in increased Border Patrol officers in addition to the introduction of military personnel.

Canada's post–9/11 efforts at increased militarization of its borders was met with widespread public outcry. Although the United States increased its security along its borders with Canada (lower 48 states and Alaska), Canada's attempt to create military security zones in order to thwart potential terrorist attacks on its country fell short of U.S. expectations. Drafted as Public Security Act C-42, it was withdrawn on April 25, 2002, due to mounting criticism from civil libertarians who felt this would provide secret powers to politicians. As written, Bill C-42 gave cabinet ministers broad powers in issuing emergency decrees, tantamount to martial law, especially when the defense minister declared a domestic area a "military security zone." In response to the public outcry, the Canadian government introduced a modified antiterrorism bill, C-55, gutting the martial law component of the designated security zones. Indeed, C-55 does not allow the military to be involved in quelling civil disobedience, such as that long associated with World Trade Organization meetings. Instead of the military, C-55 allows the Royal Canadian Mounted Police (RCMP) to scan air passenger manifests for possible terrorists or for anyone with a serious felony warrant. Canada has also allocated a billion Canadian dollars toward national security, immigration control, customs, and the military since 9/11.

Although Canada toned down its reaction to the War on Terrorism, despite the efforts of the United States to do otherwise, unauthorized vigilante militias proliferated along the U.S. borders with most of them focusing on the U.S.–Mexico border. The construction of a border fence in 2007 along the Mexican, and not Canadian, border helped fuel this controversy. White supremacists, including neo-Nazi and other militia groups and border state extremists, are at the center of the anti-immigration hate mongering, a phenomenon now echoed by President-elect Donald Trump. Further fueling these hate groups are ultraconservative religious groups and others supporting the white supremacy mantra. The marked increase in racist-bent hate groups in the United States followed the election of Barack Obama, the first black to be elected President of the United States. The combination of increased military (National Guard) and paramilitary (militias) presence has effectively created death corridors, crossing from Mexico to the United States. The increasingly deadly passage has fostered a human trafficking subculture of *coyotes*, agents who smuggle people across the border.

From NAFTA to the 21st Century

On the Mexican side of the Borderlands, there has been increased U.S. involvement in the training of Mexico's police. This effort was initiated as a post-NAFTA joint effort to fight the War on Drugs as well as to curtail undocumented entries into southern Mexico from Central and South America and to reinforce the Mexican frontier with the United States. This joint law-enforcement effort, known as the Mexico–U.S. Plenary Group on Law Enforcement, was created in 1995 and involves coordination between the U.S. and Mexican attorney general's offices. In order to coordinate these efforts, Mexico's past president, Vicente Fox, initiated the Mexican Federal Agency of Investigation (AFI) as an independent police agency modeled after the U.S. Federal Bureau of Investigation (FBI). Since then, thousands of AFI agents have received training by the U.S. Drug Enforcement Administration (DEA) as well as from the French National Police.

Prior to 9/11, Mexico trained its own law enforcement officers for participation in the joint Border Patrol Search, Trauma, and Rescue (BORSTAR) teams. President George W. Bush built on these joint activities, incorporating them into his administration's Homeland Security Presidential Directive to Help Combat Terrorism. Part of this plan was to create a North American secure perimeter around the entire NAFTA zone despite Canada's reluctance to cooperate in this endeavor. It is important to note that both Canada and Mexico, both of which have done away with capital punishment, are reluctant to extradite their citizens to the United States if they are to face capital offenses. President-elect Donald Trump's vitriolic anti-Mexican rhetoric and plans for a wall along the entire 1,933-mile border with Mexico, with Mexico paying for it, has stirred latent racism within the United States to levels not seen since the Civil Rights era of the mid-1960s and early 1970s. President-elect Trump often cites the high drug cartel-related homicide rate in Mexico, a problem fueled, in part, by the U.S. Bureau of Alcohol, Tobacco, Firearms and Explosives, commonly known as the ATF. In 2006, the ATF initiated a 5-year (2006–2011) secret sting operation, Project Gunrunner. The idea behind this program was to sell assault weapons to Mexican gang members from U.S. gun dealers so that these weapons then could be traced to those using them in Mexico. These weapons included AK-47 assault rifles as well as .50-caliber rifles and ammunition. Some 2,000 weapons found their way from Arizona to Mexican gangs and cartels. The gun-running project began in Tucson, Arizona (2006–2008) as Operation Wide Receiver and as Fast and Furious in Phoenix from 2009–2011.

Things went wrong when the ATF and Mexican officials could only account for 710 of the 2,000 weapons that investigators were monitoring. The clandestine operation drew public and Congressional attention when two of the weapons were linked to the murder of U.S. Border Patrol Agent Brian Terry on December 14, 2010. On May 29, 2011, Mexican Federal Police helicopters came under fire from .50-caliber weapons while attacking a cartel compound. Clearly, the introduction of these military assault weapons greatly increased the firepower of the drug cartel gangs. It is estimated that more than 200 Mexican citizens died due to the availability of these illicit weapons. The secret gun-running operation strained U.S.–Mexican relations, resulting in former U.S. Attorney General Eric Holder being held in Criminal Contempt of Congress for his refusal to disclose internal U.S. Department of Justice documents to Congress.[2]

Border Security's Impact on North American Indians

Transnational tribes are supposedly allowed intratribal movement to traditional tribal lands between the United States and Canada as a condition of the 1794 Treaty of London (the Jay Treaty). These rights were extended to those tribes transcending the U.S.–Mexico border as conditions of both the 1848 Treaty of Guadalupe Hidalgo and the 1854 Gadsden Purchase. Border restrictions implemented by the United States following the terrorist attacks of September 11, 2001, have further complicated these treaty agreements. Hence, geopolitical differences between the United States and Canada extend beyond their differences in identifying native lands as either reservations or reserves. The 565 "recognized" Indian groups in the United States ultimately fall under federal supervision and collectively comprise Indian Country. The inhabitants of Indian Country are known as American Indians or Alaska Natives (AI/AN). American Indians and Alaska Natives are recognized by their official tribal enrollment, usually based on some historic record compiled by U.S. Census takers and by blood degree. Cross-border tribes along the U.S.–Canada border include the Assiniboine and Ojibwe of North Dakota; Iroquois of New York; Maliseet, Passamaquoddy, and Mi'kmaq of Maine; the Athabaskan (including the Dine) tribes and Siouan tribes of the western United States; and the Aleut (Eskimo), Tlingit, Haida, and northern Athabaskan and others from the 227 federally recognized Indian tribes in Alaska. Along the U.S.–Mexico border, transborder tribes include the tribes of southern Arizona: the largest reservation, the Tohono O'odham (Papago) tribe, and the Yuma, Yaqui, and Athabaskan (Apache) that have traditionally transcended the border region. New Mexico's Pueblo and Athabaskan tribes (Apache, Navajo) are not located close to the international border although there is a noticeable presence of Tarahumara along the Mexican side of the Borderland region of New Mexico. Texas had a strong Indian presence prior to its independence and subsequent entry as part of the United States. However, the genocidal practices of the Texas Rangers decimated the Comanche, Kiowa, Apache, Wichita, Cherokee, and other indigenous peoples who once populated the Borderland region. California, like New Mexico, has a presence of Mexican Indians along the Mexican side of the Borderlands. Mestizos (mixed bloods) are common along the entire Mexican side of the Borderland region.

Status of Canada's Indigenous People

Canada's aboriginal people, on the other hand, are divided into three basic categories: Indians (First Nation), Inuit, and Métis. Another determination is made as to whether they are status Indians, treaty Indians, or nonstatus Indians. A Canadian status Indian is similar to their U.S. counterparts in that they are registered, which is similar to being enrolled. Status Indians reside among 633 bands located on 2,281 reserves. Most status Indians are also treaty Indians with the exception of those residing in British Columbia. Nonstatus Indians are usually Indian women who married non-Indians and to Indians serving in the Canadian military. These exclusions of Indian women and veterans from status recognition changed in 1985, adding some 92,000 Indians to the registry. Métis, on the other hand, are people of mixed Indian and non-Indian (mostly French Canadian), accounting for another 400,000 Canadians. The Inuit is the term Canada uses for what the United States calls Alaska natives (some still refer to this population as Eskimos). There are about 35,000 registered Inuit in Canada.[3]

Unlike the United States and its varied policy changes regarding American Indians, Canada has used the Royal Proclamation as the foundation of Canadian–aboriginal relations based on basic Indian civil rights. These rights have been incorporated into the Constitutional Act of 1982. Nonetheless, by 1830, British North America, like the United States, came to view the American Indians as economic liabilities and an impediment to white expansionism. Here, peace and friendship treaties were replaced with land cession and surrender treaties in which First Nation traditional territories and hunting grounds were taken in exchange for reserves and trust relationships. With conditional tribal sovereignty came inferior social status. This process began in 1850 in Ontario Province and continued as the westward movement progressed, continuing until 1921.

The Constitutional Act of 1867 and Confederation spelled out Canada's federal relationship with American Indians. This relationship was made into law in 1876 with the first consolidated Indian Act. With this codification came the legal definition of "Indian." Indian is the term used to denote all aboriginal people of Canada who are not Inuit or Métis. All three groups are recognized as aboriginal in the Constitutional Act of 1982. Canada did a far better job in allowing its aboriginals to continue the practice of their traditional ways as is evident in Treaty No. 11, verified on July 17, 1922, whereby the King allowed Indians the right to pursue their usual vocations of hunting, trapping, and fishing throughout Canada. Article 25 of the Constitutional Act of 1982 recognized aboriginal rights and freedoms stipulated by the Royal Proclamation of October 7, 1763, as well as any rights of freedoms that now exist by way of present or future land claim agreements. Additionally, the Supreme Court of Canada affirmed that section 35 of the Constitutional Act of 1982 reinforces the existing aboriginal and treaty rights. Section 35 of the Rights of Aboriginal Peoples of Canada addresses (1) a recognition of existing aboriginal and treaty rights, (2) definitions of aboriginal peoples of Canada, (3) land claim agreements, (4) aboriginal and treaty rights gender guarantees, and (5) aboriginal participation in provincial constitutional conferences. Canada has recently extended the rights and benefits for Métis and nonstatus Indians (those left off registers and hence excluded from residence on reserves). On April 14, 2016, Canada's Supreme Court added Métis and nonstatus Indians to the rights for Indians under the Constitution Act of 1867—provisions long denied them by the conservative administration of Prime Minister Harper. The current Prime Minister, Justin Trudeau, supports the Supreme Court's decision.[4]

Post–9/11 Border Requirements and Their Impact on Border Tribes

The terrorist attacks of 9/11 changed border regulations for non-NAFTA activities, resulting in identification requirements that many North American Indians do not possess or have the requisite documentation of birth in order to obtain, such as a passport. This challenge to Indians attempting to either enter or leave the U.S. border regions within North America began with the establishment of the Department of Homeland Security. Not only are North American Indians and Native Alaskans/Inuits now greatly restricted in their travels to relatives residing outside the U.S. border, the United States now has free access to militarize Indian Country in the name of homeland security: There is now a Director of Tribal Government Homeland Security appointed by the U.S. Government. The director's role is to ensure Indian tribes with jurisdiction over lands adjacent to the Canadian and Mexican borders are adequately prepared to help protect U.S. borders. This includes cross-border Indian Trives as appropriate in the coordination of the Homeland Security Department's immigration and nationality functions in the same manner as state and local law enforcement. At the same time, those tribal members born in the traditional fashion without an official birth certificate or a state-appointed driver's license cannot obtain a U.S. passport and, hence, are now restricted from crossing the border. Clearly, these post–9/11 tribal restrictions, including those for freely crossing the border, not only violate treaty obligations, but impact tribal justice issues, including those of a cultural, social, and criminal nature.

From NAFTA to the 21st Century

House Resolution 5490 (107th Congress, 2nd Session)
September 26, 2002

(A)(1) To ensure the coordination and integration of Indian tribes in the National Homeland Security strategy and to establish an Office of Tribal Government Homeland Security within the Department of Homeland Security and for other purposes.

> (2) Based on Article I, Section 8 of the United States Constitution, treaties, Federal statutes, and court decisions, the United States has a unique historical and legal relationship with American Indian and Alaska Native people, which serves as the basis for the Federal Government's trust responsibility and obligations. There are currently 558 federally-recognized Indian tribes in the United States, with some 40 percent of Indian tribes located in the State of Alaska. Indian tribes have principle responsibility for lands and people within their jurisdiction.
>
> (3) Despite the government-to-government relationship between Indian tribes and the United States, the United States has failed to include and consult with Indian tribes with regard to homeland security prevention, protection, and response activities planning…
>
> (4) Throughout many areas of the United States, facilities operated, and services, activities and government functions carried out, by Indian tribes, the BIA and Indian Health Service are the only sources available to provide emergency health services, disaster response, and law enforcement to the tribal and non-tribal community, thus serving the role of "first responders" in the event of a terrorist attack.

Section 4. Office of Tribal Government Homeland Security.

> (1) Establishment. There is hereby established within the Department of Homeland Security an office to be known as the "Office of Tribal Government Homeland Security."
>
> (2) Director: The Office shall be headed by a Director, appointed by the Secretary in consultation with Indian tribes, whose title shall be the Director of Tribal Government Homeland Security. The Director shall be equal in pay and authority of an Assistant Secretary.
>
> (B) ensure Indian tribes are included in the coordination activities of the Homeland Security Department's Border and Transportation functions in the same manner as State and local law enforcement entities;
>
> (C) ensure Indian tribes with jurisdiction over lands adjacent to the Canadian and Mexican borders are adequately prepared to help protect United States borders, territorial waters, waterways, and other transportation systems;

(E) ensure that Indian tribes are properly equipped to prepare for, prevent, and respond to terrorist activities in the same manner as State and local governments;

(I) include Indian tribes, as appropriate in the coordination of the Homeland Security Department's Immigration and Nationality functions in the same manner as State and local law enforcement entities.[5]

Mexico's Daunting Role as a Filter for Drug and Human Trafficking

In the summer of 2014, the migration of unaccompanied children crossing the U.S.–Mexico border became the focus of news headlines. The ensuing debate became a hot political topic among differing groups. As normally happens, when the public is caught by "surprise," scapegoating becomes the order of the day. The immediate reactions do not wait for any thoughtful analysis of possible cause-and-effect factors. And so the finger-pointing continues unabated. Two years later, the debate continues, and positions on the matter have hardened by, among other factors, sheer ideological and political positioning fed by the long presidential campaign whose start coincided with the upsurge in unaccompanied minors illegally crossing the U.S.–Mexico border.

This section examines a human tragedy by looking at geopolitical explanations for the migratory phenomenon that is taking place. Although there is much to be said about the vestiges of the Cold War in Central America and its ligatures to high crime indexes in the Northern Triangle region, which encompasses El Salvador, Honduras, and Guatemala, more immediate geopolitical considerations weigh heavily on public policy choices for both the United States and Mexico. Both countries are becoming increasingly unified due precisely to this Central American socioeconomic reality. The crisis is but one of the catalysts for the increased attention the United States is paying to the region. Consequently, Mexico's concerns have shaped its policies toward Central America with the apparent adoption of the American geopolitical objectives as part of Mexico's foreign policy.

Meanwhile, the debate about immigration has turned into how to tighten border security on the one hand and calls for humanitarian approaches to this debacle on the other hand. When the upsurge in crossings of unaccompanied children became a news item, it also became a crisis in the eyes of many. And as with anything dealing with crises, what seems to merit attention is what is apparent—what is in front of us; therefore, the discussion about illegal immigration of children and women focused on the immediate reasons and consequences of this human tragedy.

Moreover, examining this problem requires at minimum an understanding of the geopolitical context that originated this massive immigration wave. The current crisis was long in the making, and it was not until the summer of 2014 that the American public was exposed to the outcomes the U.S. policies implemented in Central America a few decades ago. This immigration phenomenon also converges with the dynamics of the Mexican state of affairs of the last few years, namely the war on drugs. Thus, the Central American context and its linkages to the waves of killings in Mexico are examined here. In this broad examination of policies, the U.S. approach to immigration and drug trafficking put in perspective the plight of thousands of children and mothers who venture into crossing the U.S.–Mexico border. The convergence of illegal immigration, drug trafficking, national security priorities, and a long presidential campaign in the United States have turned the debate on immigration into a matter of geopolitical urgency.

Central America and the Cold War

It would be disingenuous to suggest that Central America's current problems, as they relate to the exodus of children, are solely a consequence of historical involvement by the United States in the region. However, it would be equally erroneous to ignore the geopolitical significance that the United States has traditionally placed on these countries, particularly during the Cold War era. In general, U.S. interventions in Latin America were an ongoing occurrence throughout the 20th century. Although the United States issued the Monroe Doctrine in December 1823, seeking to reshape international relations in the western hemisphere, it remained an empty threat to European powers for most of the 19th century. However, the intent of such foreign policy orientation was clear, and it became the modus operandi in the following century.

> We owe it…to the amicable relations existing between the United States and those powers, to declare, that we should consider any attempt on their part to extend their system to any portion of this hemisphere, as dangerous to our peace and safety…[the U.S. asserts] as a principle in which the rights and interests of the United States are involved, that the American continents, by the free and independent condition which they have assumed and maintain, are henceforth not to be considered as subjects for future colonization by any European powers…[6]

European powers continued their military interventions in Latin America without regard for any serious danger coming from the United States; Mexico, for instance, was invaded by the United States, Spain, Great Britain, and France. The latter imposed an emperor, Maximilian of Hapsburg, between 1862 and 1867.[7]

As power relationships began to shift at the outset of the 20th century from the European to the American hegemonic dominance in the world, the United States issued the Roosevelt Corollary to the Monroe Doctrine. In 1898, the United States went to war against Spain. At the end of the conflict, the American hegemony in the western hemisphere became an indisputable reality as Cuba and Puerto Rico became territories of the United States; in 1903, President Roosevelt supported a rebellion to have Panama secede from Colombia, thus removing an obstacle for the construction of the Panama Canal. Among the heroes of the Spanish-American War was Theodore Roosevelt who became president and in whose name the corollary to the Monroe Doctrine is named. The corollary purportedly created the framework "…for the United States to prevent European intervention in the New World, Roosevelt argued, the United States had to assist the nations under threat of intervention, so as to eliminate the conditions for intervention and to promote governments of political stability and financial responsibility."[8] The Roosevelt corollary expanded the Monroe Doctrine's scope by granting the United States the framework to justify its meddling in the internal affairs of Latin American countries in the name of political stability. LaFeber wrote more than three decades ago:

> …this compact region has been the target of highly disproportionate amount of North American investment and—especially—military intervention. Every twentieth-century intervention by the U.S. troops in the hemisphere has occurred in the Central American-Caribbean region.[5]

The U.S. presence, especially a military one, spread throughout the whole region for the greater part of the 20th century, leaving these countries in a rather trying state of affairs. Nicaragua and El Salvador, for instance, saw devastation as part of the armed conflicts in the late part of the last century. The Sandinista National Liberation Front in Nicaragua and the Farabundo Marti National Liberation Front in El Salvador embarked on long wars against regimes that were supported by the United States and, as in the case of Nicaragua, by internal factions opposed to those liberation movements. All this happened in the last quarter of the 20th century. Guatemala experienced similar violence from 1960 to 1996 as the various governments, many times supported by the United States, engaged in armed confrontations with mostly left-leaning groups. And as if this were not a sufficient condition that has driven these countries to their current socioeconomic state, nature has not helped either. This geographical area has been ravaged by natural disasters in the form of earthquakes and hurricanes with an ensuing lack of resources by these governments to assist their citizens. In short, Guatemala, Honduras, Nicaragua, and El Salvador have gone through wars, revolutions, coup d'états, earthquakes, and hurricanes—problems that, instead of being resolved, have gotten worse. The protracted armed conflicts in the region along with natural disasters and weak government institutions contributed to the current state of affairs, which led to the massive migration of nearly 60,000 unaccompanied children to the U.S.–Mexico border in 2014 alone.[6]

Mexican War on Drugs

Until recently, Mexico was considered a nearly ineffective buffer zone as Central American immigrants continued to pour over the U.S.–Mexico border. Compounding this perception was Mexico's internal security quagmire as Mexico took the drug cartels head on. The newly inaugurated President Felipe Calderón (2006–2012) made a point of fighting drug lords by extensive use of military forces. The results of the implementation of such a policy have been abysmal in terms of human lives: "The war on drugs has taken a brutal toll on Mexico in the past decade." As of 2015, there have been more than 120,000 people killed since 2006 and nearly 27,000 reported as missing.[9]

Although in previous decades this country's approach to fighting drug cultivation and trafficking was comparatively lukewarm, the new impetus was initially seen by many as a welcomed policy, albeit with a degree of skepticism. However, the unintended consequences of this frontal approach against the drug cartels soon began to show. Apprehensions and killings of cartel leaders brought about a brutal war among the different crime organizations; some to exert revenge, others to take control of drug trafficking routes. The crime rates increased throughout the country—and in some regions more than in others. For example, although the annual national rate in 2015 was 12.85 homicides per 100,000 inhabitants, in the State of Guerrero, the rate was 51.12 per 100,000 (see Figure 5.1).[10-12]

Although faced with these internal challenges, Mexico has also had to contend with the migratory stream from Central America. Even though the destination for most of these immigrants is not Mexico, the events on September 11, 2001, reconfigured Mexico's—and U.S.—policies toward these migratory patterns. It was at this juncture that both immigration and the war on drugs converged with the war on terrorism, thus posing new challenges to both countries. The war on drugs itself is not a new phenomenon for Mexico, which began its antinarcotics policy in the 1920s and officially in 1948 started working with the United States to combat production of illegal drugs.[13] However, the pressure to end drug cultivation and trafficking became apparent in the 1960s. The development of such policies are illustrated in Table 5.1.[14-16] The cultivation and rerouting of South American drugs through Mexico altered the ways both countries began to address these problems, leading to the current state of affairs.

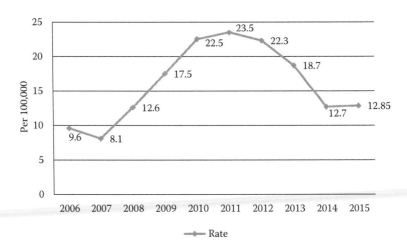

Figure 5.1 Homicide rates in Mexico, 2006–2015. (From Heinle, Molzahn, and Shirk 2015; Angel 2015; Gagne 2015.)

U.S. Drug, Security, and Immigration Concerns

As noted, the events of September 11 dramatically modified some approaches to U.S. foreign policies with direct impact on U.S.–Mexico relations. In this regard, American policy proposes a series of measures in order to control its borders. In pursuing this goal, the U.S. Government attempts to address two other issues that have been on the table for a while. One is the war on drugs, an unfinished business that restarted with such fanfare in the 1980s under President Ronald Reagan. The other is the more elusive problem of illegal immigration, particularly migration from Mexico and now Central America. Together these U.S. concerns are viewed in contemporary policy discussions as a single issue at least for the purposes of persuading the American public of the urgency to focus on them. In the best of cases, this troika is framed as a crisis, but it is not unusual for these problems to be framed as "wars." The fight against drug contraband has been called the War on Drugs since its beginning. For reasons of diplomatic sensitivity, the immigration debacle could not (and has not) been tagged as a "war"—at least not officially. However, there is ample evidence in media reports that segments of the American public do think of this problem as a war. Moreover, such distinctions are no longer necessary. The war against terrorism in the post–9/11 world has blurred these distinctions in the public discourse. The catchall labels for addressing the problems of drug trafficking, illegal immigration, and terrorism are synthesized by phrases such as "securing our borders" or "gain control of our borders." But it seems that the clear reference to "borders" indicates one border in particular: the U.S.–Mexico border. The focus on immigration reform and the increasing drug-related problems widely publicized in the American

From NAFTA to the 21st Century

Table 5.1 Major Events in U.S.–Mexico Efforts to Fight the War on Drugs

Year	Event	Purpose
1961	Single Convention on Narcotic Drugs	Under pressure from the United States, Mexico signs this agreement between the two countries.
1969	Operation Intercept	Vehicular inspection along the U.S.–Mexico border was intended to force Mexico to do more about fighting drug production.
1970–1975		After Turkey engages in a crackdown on heroin production, Mexico becomes a significant producer. By 1975, it produces about 70% to 80% of the drug consumed in the United States.
1975	Operation Condor	The United States and Mexico hold secret meetings, and Operation Condor is launched (the Drug Enforcement Agency [DEA] was created a year earlier). Mexico doubles the size of its federal police, and military personnel are added to the antidrug efforts. Spraying of the highly toxic herbicide paraquat was introduced, and the spraying campaign was finally stopped in the mid-1980s.
Mid-1980s		The DEA and the U.S. Coast Guard and other law enforcement agencies were successful in closing Florida as a main port of entry for illicit drugs. Drug traffickers from South America began to use Central America and Mexico as their new routes.
1985	Second Operation Intercept	DEA Special Agent Enrique Camarena was abducted, tortured, and murdered. The United States initiated a second Operation Intercept. Traffic jams at the border disrupted commerce and created a partial closing of the border.
1986		President Ronald Reagan formally starts U.S. counter-narcotics efforts as a matter of national security. The U.S. military and the Central Intelligence Agency were called to play a greater role than before.
2001		The United States began strict narcotics certification for western hemisphere countries.
2008	Merida Initiative	This is launched by President Bush to combat narcotics traffic but also to counter terrorism.

Source: (Osorno 2009; Andreas, Smuggler Nation: How Illicit Trade Made America 2013; Andreas, Border Games 2009.)

media leave very little doubt about what the general notion is when talking about "border security." Thus, in light of this association of problems, immigration, drug trafficking, and terrorism are viewed as a war for the protection of U.S. national security.

After the terrorist attacks of September 11, the opportunity to fight a frontal war against drugs and illegal immigration became more plausible than before from the perspective of a twin law enforcement problem. In this context, the war on terrorism is indeed for many in the United States and in Mexico a reactivation of the war on drugs and the war on illegal immigration. Moreover, the fight against terrorism has provided fuel for groups in the United States who have opposed Mexican and, recently, Central American immigration. Sprouting along the border, several anti-immigrant groups have taken the form of vigilante cliques whose sole goal is to intimidate, harass, and generally threaten immigrants with jail and death if necessary to stop them from crossing the border. Such were the vehement pronouncements made during the summer of 2014 when the Central American unaccompanied children made headlines. Political leaders and commentators were among those leading the rhetorical charge clamoring for the "sealing" of the border or for a speedy deportation of children and mothers who were fleeing El Salvador, Honduras, and Guatemala.[17]

Children who were escaping poverty and violence were seen as a threat to national security. Those who opposed any leniency were clamoring for quick deportation proceedings even if proper legal advice was not afforded to these children. The thinking is not uncommon among these groups: Because the children entered the country illegally, other standards of law apparently apply to them. Such illogical construction could only be justified by arguing that minors posed a serious threat to American national security. In the 2015 National Security Strategy plan sent by President Obama to the U.S. Congress, the administration contends that organized crime and immigration, among other matters, are the main national security concerns of the United States. In this context, Latin American immigration, especially of underage kids, is considered an example of how these countries' weak institutions and economies have a push effect on the human migration to the north.[18]

To understand the massive migration of children from Central America to the United States, one has to take into account the geopolitical dynamics that have kept this region in conditions of poverty and violence.

Figure 5.2 illustrates poverty levels in the region. The unintended consequences of U.S. foreign policies and of domestic inequalities became the catalyst for the massive migration of children from Central America. But this is not something that came to life in the last couple of years. Soon after the United States suffered the terrorist attacks of September 11, 2001, Mexico began developing policies aimed at controlling the immigration flows from Central and South America. From that date on, all three Mexican presidential administrations have engaged in one way or another in turning Mexico into a de facto buffer zone between the United States and Central America. Moreover, since 2001, the impetus has been driven by U.S. security priorities; in that sense, the role Mexico plays is directly related to

From NAFTA to the 21st Century

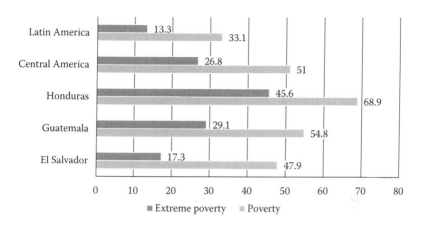

Figure 5.2 Percentage of people living in poverty. (Adapted from Villalobos, 2014.)

security concerns. However, with the rise in the number of immigrants crossing into the United States from Mexico, the immigration debate in the United States became even more pronounced than before. The coupling of immigration—a century-old point of contention between the United States and Mexico—with national security, as a consequence of the war on terrorism, required new approaches.

The new security scenario intensified the discussion about immigration. But the public discourse expanded the old tug-of-war between the two nations to include any and all types of undocumented immigrants coming from the rest of the continent. Of particular relevance were the concerns about potential terrorists sneaking through the U.S.–Mexico border—never mind the lack of historical or contemporary proof that could attest to any such incursions. Nonetheless, the security perimeter was for all intents and purposes created to address U.S. geopolitical interests. Immigration as such was couched in terms of the potential for terrorists to cross illegally into American Territory using Mexico as a springboard. In this view, immigration was no longer thought to be a purely domestic issue that had to be continuously addressed between two neighboring nations. It became a bona fide interhemispheric affair in which public policies had to be expanded beyond the traditional scope of the southern border. It now included Central America.

As the economies of the region worsened, spikes in crime rates also increased. One logical consequence of such state of affairs was the expulsion of an increasingly high number of people from such places as El Salvador, Honduras, and Guatemala. Presidents Vicente Fox (2000–2006) and Felipe Calderón (2006–2012) governed Mexico during the initial stages of the war on terrorism and the financial meltdown that gripped the world starting 2008. Fox's and Calderón's *Plan Sur* (Southern Plan) and Program *Frontera*

Sur Segura (Southern Border Security Program), respectively, sought to address the Central American immigration flow.[19] Coincidently, these policies were created at the time when the U.S. security priorities were heightened as consequence of the 9/11 terrorist attacks on American soil. The Mexican programs under previous administrations and now under President Enrique Peña Nieto's *Programa Frontera Sur* (Southern Border Program) were officially conceived to protect immigrants' human rights for those traveling through Mexico, to upgrade crossing border facilities, and to create a system of identity for immigrants.[20]

However, the Advocacy for Human Rights in the Americas and other human rights organizations have complained about the ongoing abuses by Mexican government officials and other criminal organizations against these immigrants.[21] And with the closing of some border crossing points, Central American immigrants are forced to take more dangerous routes than before. In 2007, Mexican President Calderón and U.S. President Bush joined to create the Merida Initiative to combat crime. It allocated $400 million to Mexico and Central American countries participating in this program. The initiative provided military and police equipment to help the region to fight drug organizations. Little in the way of human rights advocacy was proposed by the Merida Plan. It was designed to provide security instead of economic development.[22]

The most recent Mexican southern border strategy was adopted in July 2014 at the height of the unaccompanied Central American children crisis. The data in Figure 5.3 shows clearly the upward trend since 2009 reaching its highest point in 2014. From a total of 19,418 apprehensions in 2009 to 67,339 in 2014, this is an increase of 247%. After 2014, we begin to observe a

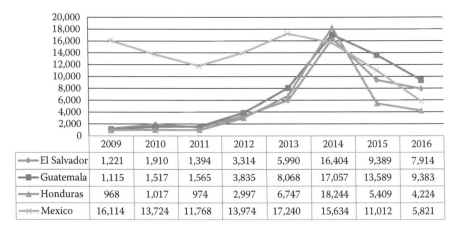

Figure 5.3 Apprehensions of unaccompanied children, FY 09–FY16. Numbers reflect data from October 15, 2015–March 3, 2016. (From U.S. Customs and Border Protection 2016; Krogstad 2016.)

From NAFTA to the 21st Century

downward trend in apprehensions of all unaccompanied children, including those from Mexico.

What accounts for this dramatic change? In the case of the Northern Triangle countries, crime rates continue to be alarmingly high. Economic conditions have not adequately improved either. What is left to ponder is whether the current U.S. and Mexican policies to deal with this flow of immigrants have a direct relationship to the decrease in apprehensions by the U.S. Border Patrol. When the data is disaggregated to examine only apprehensions of unaccompanied children from El Salvador, Guatemala, and Honduras, the trend continues to be in a downward direction after 2014. The graph shows this phenomenon very clearly. Overall, we see a decrease in apprehensions by the U.S. Border Patrol after 2014 (see Figure 5.4).[23,24]

Mexico's role in adopting an anti-immigration enforcement posture is clear. The Central American immigration debate has been couched as a U.S. national security issue. The framework continues to be the war on terrorism, but the immediate preoccupation is with American domestic politics. Among the prevailing views, immigration from the Northern Triangle countries, as exemplified by the thousands of unaccompanied children, has to be stopped by any means necessary, including a speedy process to deport these minors. The most effective method of stopping these migrants is by using Mexico as an effective buffer zone.

The thousands of children who made the trek from the Northern Triangle through Mexico en route to the United States did not embark on this odyssey of nearly 1,500 miles for fun. Poverty, crime, and other social and natural factors contributed to the expulsion of these and other immigrants (see Figure 5.5).[25]

As Villalobos contends, "paradoxically, peace and democracy in Central America accelerated migration to the North"—a phenomenon that is not abating. The north in this context means both Mexico and the United States.

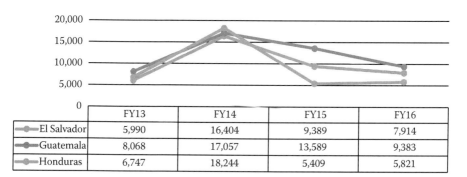

Figure 5.4 Apprehensions of unaccompanied Central American children, 2013–2016. FY16 numbers reflect data from October 15, 2015–March 3, 2016. (From U.S. Customs and Border Protection 2016; Krogstad 2016.)

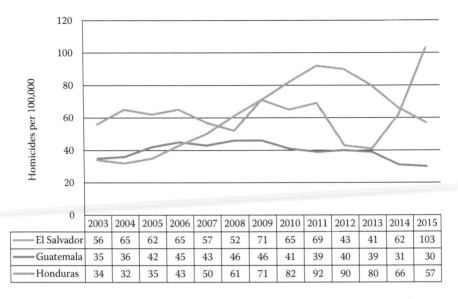

Figure 5.5 Rate of homicides in the Northern Triangle, 2003–2015. (From Villalobos 2014; Cagne 2016.)

For Mexico, it has become a security problem for its southern *and* northern borders.[26]

Crime in the region is a function of several broad political and social changes. In the political realm, as noted above, the insistence of the United States to keep leftist factions—often labeled as communists—from taking power led to policies that kept in power repressive, antidemocratic regimes. Consequently, in most countries of the region, armed rebellions ensued, bringing with them economic and social devastation. Paradoxically, the end of hostilities did not coincide with economic prosperity, thus forcing people to flee up north. Among those migrating to the United States were ex-military elements who brought with them the learned techniques for torturing and killing. These techniques were introduced, according to Villalobos, in Mexico and in the United States.[27] In the case of El Salvador, the deportation from the United States of members of the *maras*, street gangs, back to the Central American nation increased violent crime rates. The convergence of factors noted in this chapter illustrates rather unsurprisingly why the rate of violent crimes has been between 32 in Honduras to 103 homicides per 100,000 in El Salvador for more than a decade. Consequently, push factors have led to thousands upon thousands of children and mothers fleeing the Northern Triangle.

From NAFTA to the 21st Century

The overall U.S. security concerns have driven the formulation of policies that now include Mexico in a more prominent role than before, both in terms of national security and immigration concerns. Under the premise of protecting its southern border, the United States is using Mexico as a buffer to slow down the migration of Central American unaccompanied children.

It is important to note that in 2015, there were more Central Americans apprehended and deported by Mexican authorities than by American officials (see Figure 5.6).[28] The decline in border apprehensions of Northern Triangle children can be attributed in great measure to the direct impact of the joint policies undertaken by the United States and Mexico. Whether this law enforcement approach will succeed by itself remains unclear. The fundamental push–pull effect has its roots in both economic underdevelopment and domestic insecurity in the sending region, and the United States offers relative safety and potentially a good chance for economic prosperity for those immigrants. The intervening variable represented by Mexico can arguably continue to be significant if Mexico embraces the notion that these transient migrants represent a serious threat to its national security. Second, and whether or not the previous assumption is adopted, is the willingness of the United States to continue offering its neighbor military and other types of assistance and Mexico's disposition to receive such assistance. Granted, international geopolitics will also influence future efforts regarding the worldwide Wars on Drugs and Terrorism, including Britain's leaving the EU and the U.S. presidential election.

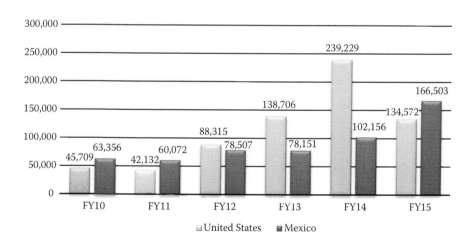

Figure 5.6 Total apprehension of Northern Triangle nationals by the United States and Mexico. (From the Migrant Policy Institute 2016.)

Appendix I: Chronology of Major Events

1492–1493	Christopher Columbus discovers the Americas; first to term inhabitants "Indians."
1521	Spain claims the Philippine Islands in the Pacific.
c.1540	Horses are introduced to the Americas by the Spanish.
1562	Edict of Saint-Germain leads to rights for Huguenots in France.
c.1600	Sheep are brought to the Americas by the Spanish.
1603	James I unites Scotland and England, creating Great Britain.
1603–1615	Samuel de Champlain establishes the fur trade in New France.
1607	John Smith establishes the first English settlement, Jamestown, Virginia.
1608	Champlain establishes the first permanent French settlement, Quebec City.
1608	The Spanish establish Santa Fe, New Mexico. Henry Hudson trades alcohol for Indian goods.
1611	Jesuit missionaries arrive in New France.
1613	The French introduce the policy of scalp bounties to Indians.
1619	The First Anglican missionaries arrive in Virginia.
1620	Pilgrims land at Plymouth Bay, Massachusetts.
1619–1633	The Spanish establish missions among Pueblo tribes.
1621	The Pilgrims and Wampanoag Indians share "Thanksgiving."
1624	The Dutch claim New Amsterdam (Manhattan) and Fort Orange (Albany), New York.
1641	The Dutch offer scalp bounties on Indians.
1653–1658	Oliver Cromwell's Rebellion against the Church of England occurs.
1659	The Navajo carry out their first raid on horseback.
1661	The Spanish raid Pueblo tribes, destroying Kivas and Kachinas.
1670	The Hudson Bay Company is chartered by Britain.

1682	Rene Cavalier de la Salle claims the Mississippi Valley and the Gulf of Mexico for France.
1685	King Louis XIV revokes Huguenots' rights in France.
1691	Virginia banishes Anglos who marry Indians, blacks, or those of mixed ancestry.
1755–1756	The Acadian Expulsion occurs.
1763	The Treaty of Paris cedes New France to Great Britain.
	The English introduce biological warfare to the Americas with smallpox-infected blankets in Pontiac's Rebellion.
1776	The U.S. Declaration of Independence from Britain is signed.
	The Spanish found San Francisco, California.
1783	The Treaty of Paris ends the U.S. Revolutionary War.
1789	The French Revolution happens.
1792–1795	George Vancouver claims the Pacific Coast for England.
1802	The French Republic is established beginning Napoleon's Reign (1802–1814).
	President Jefferson doubles the size of the United States with the Louisiana Purchase from France. The treaty is ratified by the U.S. Senate on October 20, 1803.
1809–1821	Sequoyah creates the Cherokee syllabary, creating written native language.
1810	Mexico begins revolts against Spanish rule.
1812	The United States initiates the War of 1812 with Britain in an attempt to gain territory in Canada.
1817	General Andrew Jackson starts war with Spain over Florida—the First Seminole War—resulting in the United States acquiring Florida in 1819.
1819	The Adams-Onís Treaty ends the Seminole Wars, not only ceding Florida to the United States, but also establishing the Mexico–U.S. border at the Sabine River (ratified in 1821).
1820	The Mexican Constitution outlaws slavery and enfranchises all adult males regardless of race or social status.
1821	Mexico gains independence from Spain. Republic of Mexico established September 21, 1821.
	Americans seek land grants (*empresarios*) in northern Mexico (eastern interior provinces). Conditions include converting to Catholicism.
	Texas Rangers begin as "rangers" for policing the Austin *empresario* in Mexico.
1823	Monroe Doctrine: The United States proclaims itself as the premier colonial authority in the Americas.

Appendix I

1824	Mexico emperor Augustín de Iturbride's reign is short-lived and replaced with a federalist system, which evolves into a centralized government in 1830.
1826	The Fredonian Rebellion: The Edward brothers lead rebellion among Anglo *empresarios* and declare independence from Mexico, calling the new nation Fredonia. The rebellion ended in 1827 with the rebels escaping back to the United States.
1828	*Cherokee Phoenix* published using Sequoyah's syllabary.
1830	The U.S. Congress passes the Indian Removal Act to allow whites to take Indian lands east of the Mississippi (Indian Territory established in lands acquired under the Louisiana Purchase). The U.S. Supreme Court challenges the law, but President Jackson overrides Justice Marshall.
1833	Antonio López de Santa Anna's first term as president of Mexico begins.
1836	Texas declares independence, stating opposition to Catholicism and Mexico's antislavery stance.
	Santa Anna's forces defeat the rebels at the Alamo (San Antonio).
	U.S. forces defeat Santa Anna's forces at San Jacinto.
	Sam Houston becomes president of the Republic of Texas.
1838	The Cherokee Nation is forcefully removed to Indian Territory (Oklahoma) in a drama termed the "Trail of Tears."
1839	Santa Anna's second term as president of Mexico begins.
1840	The Union Bill establishes the Province of Canada.
1841	Santa Anna's third term as president of Mexico begins.
1842	The Webster–Ashburton Treaty ends the Aroostook War and establishes the eastern border between the United States and Canada, dividing the Algonquin tribes (Maliseet and Mi'kmaq) between the Maritime Provinces of Canada and the U.S. State of Maine.
	The Union between Upper and Lower (Quebec) Canada occurs.
1843	The Russian–Greek Orthodox Church establishes an Indian mission school in Alaska.
1844	Santa Anna is again elected president but is replaced by José Joaquin de Herrera.
1845	Texas is annexed by the United States as a slave state.
1846	The United States declares war on Mexico.
	Santa Anna's fourth term as president of Mexico begins.

	Sam Houston becomes the U.S. senator from the State of Texas.
1847	Brigham Young brings the Mormons (LDS) to Salt Lake, Utah.
1848	The Treaty of Guadalupe Hidalgo ends the Mexican War with the United States gaining half of Mexico.
1850	The U.S. Compromise of 1850 and the Fugitive Slave Act are enacted.
1853	Santa Anna returns from exile in Venezuela and assumes presidency of Mexico for the fifth time.
	The Ostend Manifesto is an ill-fated attempt to force Spain to sell Cuba to the United States to be added as a slave state.
	U.S. President Franklin Pierce gets Santa Anna to relinquish more Mexican Territory with the Gadsden Purchase.
1855	Santa Anna is again exiled; he returns in 1874 and dies in 1876.
1857	The Gradual Civilization Act is passed in Upper Canada, disenfranchising all Indian and Métis peoples, classifying them as an inferior category to Canadian citizens.
1859	Sam Houston becomes governor of Texas (he loses his second term and dies in 1863).
1861	Benito Juárez becomes the first full-blooded Indian president of Mexico.
	The Tripartite Convention in London initiates armed intervention in Mexico with forces from Britain, France, and Spain arriving in Veracruz due to the default of 82 million pesos in loans.
	The U.S. Civil War begins; it ends in 1865.
1862	Cinco de Mayo: General Díaz defeats Napoleon III's forces at Puebla on May 5, 1862—an important anniversary celebrated to the present.
	Spanish and British forces withdraw, leaving only French forces.
	The largest mass execution in the United States—38 Santee Sioux warriors publically hanged on a single platform—happens on December 26.
	U.S. President Lincoln enacts the Emancipation Proclamation on September 22, 1862, and January 1, 1863.
1864	Archduke Maximilian accepts the Mexican Crown as European dictator.
1865–1890	The longest U.S. official war is the Indian campaign.

Appendix I

1866	Napoleon III withdraws French troops from Mexico. Fenian crisis occurs in Canada.
1867	Maximilian is defeated and executed (on orders of General Porfirio Díaz). The United States purchases Alaska from Russia. The British North American Act creates the Dominion of Canada.
1869–1885	Louis Riel leads the Red River Rebellion in Manitoba, Canada.
1872	Benito Juárez dies.
1874	The Indian Act is passed in Canada, making its indigenous peoples legal wards of the state who are compelled to be imprisoned on set-aside reserve lands.
1877	Porfirio Díaz is elected president of Mexico and remains either president (six terms overall) or de facto leader until his resignation and exile to Paris in 1911; he dies in 1915.
1878	The Posse Comitatus Act (*18 U.S.C.: 1385*) restricts the use of federal troops in the South during the Reconstruction era.
1882	Mexico and the United States sign a treaty allowing reciprocal border crossings.
1884	State-funded, church-administered Indian Residential Schools are established in Canada.
1885	Louis Riel is hanged for treason in Canada.
1885	The U.S. Congress passes the Major Crimes Act, imposing federal laws throughout Indian Country.
1887	The U.S. Congress passes the General Allotment Act, ending federal treaty protection for Indian Country and opening up reservations to white settlers.
1888	Mexico and the United States form the International Boundary Commission along with extradition provision.
1896	Sir Wilfred Laurier becomes Canada's first French Canadian Prime Minister (1896–1911).
1898	The Spanish-American War: The United States declares war on Spain over Cuba and Puerto Rico.
1899	A peace treaty is signed with Spain; the United States acquires Puerto Rico and Spanish colonial holdings in the Pacific: the Philippine Islands; Guam; and the Mariana, Carolina, and Marshall Islands. Spain relinquishes control over Cuba. The United States begins war in the Philippines.
1890	The Wounded Knee massacre occurs on December 29.
1901	Rebellion in the Philippines ends.
1904	President Theodore Roosevelt issues his Roosevelt Corollary, establishing the right of the United States to

	unilaterally intervene in the Caribbean and Central America to protect them from foreign interventions. The U.S. Marines become the international police force for this policy.
1907	The medical inspector for the Canadian Department of Indian Affairs reports on poor conditions in the compulsory church-run Indian residential schools.
1908	Duncan Campbell Scott, notorious Canadian Superintendent of Indian Affairs, suppresses the medical inspector's report.
1910	D. Campbell Scott forges his "final solution to the Indian Problem" by contracting churches to run the harsh Indian residential schools.
1911	The Mexican Revolution begins. Ciudad Juárez falls, and 20,000 U.S. troops muster along the Mexican–U.S. border.
1914	U.S. troops occupy Veracruz just as the First World War begins in Europe. Civil War begins in Mexico with Generals Carranza and Obregón fighting Generals Villa and Zapata. Canada joins British forces during WWI.
1915	The Plan de San Diego is exposed as an unlikely revolution to regain Mexican Territory lost to the United States. It was initiated by a small radical element of Hispanic revolutionaries. Overreaction by the Texas Rangers leads to excessive force and terror among Mexican Americans living in Texas. Wilson's critique: President Wilson sides with the Carranza forces (Carranzitas), believing they would better protect U.S. oil interests in Mexico.
1916	General Villa attacks a U.S. military facility (Camp Furlong) in Columbus, New Mexico. The Zimmerman communiqué exposes German attempts to involve Mexico in World War I.
1917	The U.S. Immigration Act of February 5, 1917 (*39 Statutes-at-Large 874*) states Mexican laborers are exempt due to the manpower shortage during World War I. Mexico establishes a new Revolutionary Constitution, restricting presidents to one 6-year term and also allowing for a free secular primary education. The constitution has a de facto prohibition of the death penalty for civilian offenses. The new constitution greatly restricts the role of the Catholic Church in public matters.

Appendix I

	The United States begins an 11-month Punitive Expedition into Mexico under General John "Black Jack" Pershing without finding General Villa.
	The United States enters World War I with Pershing as commander of U.S. Expeditionary Forces.
1918	World War I ends.
1919	D. Campbell Scott abolishes the post of medical inspector for Indian residential schools in Canada, resulting in a marked rate of tuberculosis deaths among the Indian children (some as high as 75%).
1920	Canada makes it mandatory for every Indian child, seven or older, to be interned at a residential school.
1921	The U.S. Quota Law of May 19, 1921 (*42 Statutes-at-Large 5*) is passed.
	William Lyon Mackenzie King, Canada's longest serving Prime Minister (1921–1926, 1926–1930, 1935–1948) begins serving.
1922	The U.S. Immigration Act of May 26, 1924 (*43 Statutes-at-Large 153*) is passed.
	The Act of May 28, 1924 (*43 Statutes-at-Large 240*) establishes the U.S. Border Patrol.
1924	The U.S. Indian Citizenship Act enfranchises all American Indians and Alaska Natives at the federal level as citizens; Idaho, Maine, Mississippi, New Mexico, and Washington continue to exclude enrolled tribal members from voting until prohibited by the passage of the Indian Civil Rights Act in 1968.
1929	The Act of March 4, 1929 (*45 Statutes-at-Large 1551*) articulates deportable classes convicted of felonies.
	The League of United Latin American Citizens (LULAC) emerges as a political front for Hispanics, notably Mexican Americans.
1931	The Act of February 18, 1931 (*46 Statutes-at-Large 1171*) expands deportation for illicit drugs: heroin, opium, or coca leaves.
1933	Canada makes residential school officials legal guardians of all Indian students at their facility. Parents are compelled to do so or face imprisonment.
1934	The U.S. Congress passes the Indian Reorganization Act and the Johnson-O'Malley Act, both pertaining to governmental and educational standards within Indian Country.

1935	The Texas Rangers are brought under the authority of the Texas Department of Public Services instead of acting as the governor's private police force.
1935	The Philippines are made a U.S. Commonwealth Territory.
1939	Canada joins British forces during WWII.
1940	The Act of June 14, 1940 (*54 Statutes-at-Large 230*) transfers INS from the Department of Labor to the Department of Justice. The Alien Registration Act of June 28, 1940 (*54 Statutes-at-Large 670*) requires fingerprinting of all aliens over age 14.
1941	The United States enters World War II on the side of the Allies. The conflict ends in 1945.
1941–1945	The Philippines is occupied by Japan, ousting the United States.
1942	The Bracero Agreement is established between Mexico and the United States allowing Mexican migrants to work as seasonal agriculture laborers. The program ends in 1964.
1945	World War II ends.
1946	The Philippines gains independence from the United States. The U.S. CIA enters into a secret agreement with Canada to use Indian children as involuntary test subjects for medical, biological warfare, and mind control experiments. This practice continues until the 1970s.
1948	The American G.I. Forum (AGIF) is formed by Hispanic veterans of World War II.
1949	Newfoundland leaves Great Britain, joining the Canadian Confederation.
1950–1953	The United States and Canada become part of UN forces during the Korean War.
1951	The United States is involved in the Korean Conflict as a primary UN force. Conflict ends in 1953. More Hispanics join the AGIF.
1954	Operation Wetback begins under the direction of General Joseph "Jumping Joe" Swing in an attempt to entice illegal Mexican workers to return to Mexico.
1958	The United States takes over France's role in Southeast Asia, leading to the Vietnam conflict, which extends until 1975.
1959–1975	The long involvement of the United States in Vietnam begins. Canada opposes the Vietnam War.
1962–1965	The Second Vatican (Ecumenical) Council under Pope John XXIII occurs.

Appendix I

1964–1966	The United States enacts Civil Rights Acts that prohibit discrimination based on race, color, religion, sex, or national origin.
1965	Cesar Chavez begins to organize Mexican and Filipino farm workers into the United Farm Workers union.
1968	A prodemocracy demonstration results in the massacre of student protestors in Mexico City.
	The Indian Civil Rights Act is passed in the United States.
	Pierre Trudeau becomes Prime Minister of Canada (1968–1979, 1980–1984).
1969	MECHA (*El Movimiento Estudiantil Chicano de Aztlan*) begins at the Chicano Youth Liberation Conference held in Denver.
	Canada passes the Official Language Act, making both English and French the official languages.
1970	La Raza Unida Party (LRUP) and Bronze/Brown Power movements bring nonwhite Hispanics together as a political force.
	The Racketeer Influence and Corrupt Organization Act (RICO) is established in the United States.
1972	The U.S. Supreme Court finds the death penalty unconstitutional.
1973	Wounded Knee II occurs at Pine Ridge Oglala Indian Reservation.
1975	The U.S. Congress passes the Indian Self-Determination and Education Assistance Act.
	Wounded Knee II, Part 2, FBI agents are killed in a firefight.
1976	The U.S. Supreme Court reinstates the death penalty with conditions for its application.
	Canada outlaws the death penalty.
1978	The U.S. Congress passes the Indian Child Welfare Act.
1982	The Canadian Constitution (Charter of Rights) is established under PM Trudeau.
1984	Canada's last Indian residential school closes.
1988	President Reagan signs the Anti-Drug Abuse Act, which includes the Drug Kingpin Act (DKA) allowing the reinstatement of the federal death penalty.
1989	President George H. W. Bush establishes the Joint Task Force-6 (JTF-6) as part of the U.S. war on drugs.
1994	The North American Free Trade Agreement (NAFTA) goes into effect on January 1.

	On the same day, the Zapatista Army of National Liberation (EZLN) declares war on Mexico to protest NAFTA's opposition to land reform and the *ejido* system.
1998	The First Independent Tribunal, the UN International Human Rights Association of American Minorities (IHRAAM), is convened in Vancouver, Canada, finding the Catholic, United, and Anglican Churches guilty of complicity in genocide regarding its formal Indian residential school programs.
1999	NATO forces (including U.S. and Canadian military) unilaterally attack Serbia in response to events in Kosovo.
2000	Vicente Fox becomes the first Mexican leader to break the Institutional Revolutionary Party's (PRI) monopoly on the presidency. He was a member of the conservative National Action Party (PAN).
2001	Terrorist attacks on the United States on September 11 initiate the war on terror, which, combined with the existing war on drugs, leads to the increased militarization of the U.S.–Mexico border.
2006	President George W. Bush initiates Operation Jump Start, allowing border state governors to deploy the National Guard along their section of the U.S.–Mexico border. Felipe Calderon succeeds Fox as president of Mexico. He also belongs to the conservative PAN Party and, like Fox, has welcomed U.S. aid for the war on drugs.
2009	The Obama administration begins in the United States. Obama is the first post-Columbian North American leader of black African descent.
2015	Justin Trudeau, son of Pierre, becomes Canada's Prime Minister.
2016	Billionaire Donald Trump is elected as the 45th President of the United States. Canada's Supreme Court extends "Indian aboriginal status" to Métis and nonstatus Indians.

Appendix II: Maps

Early map of British North America.

Appendix II

Appendix II

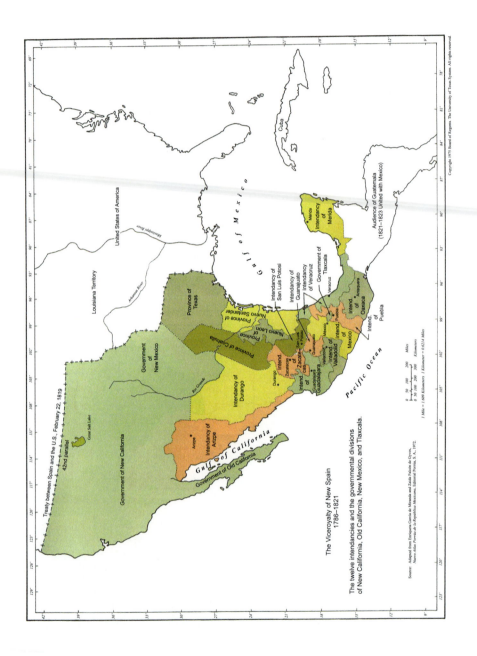

Appendix II

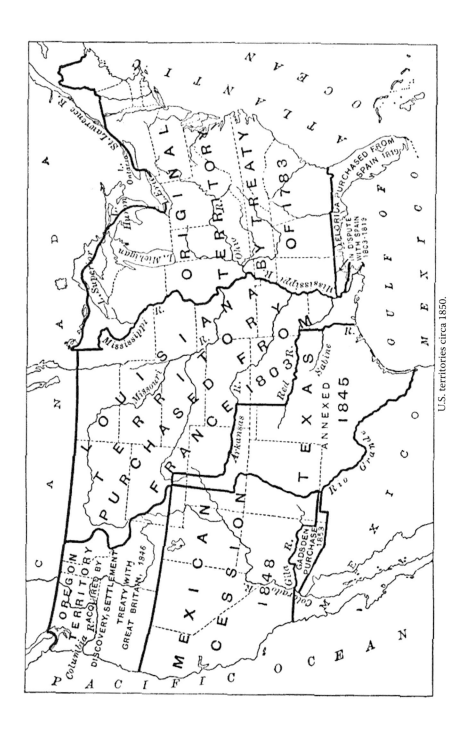

U.S. territories circa 1850.

Appendix II

Mexico at the Time of the Conquest (1519), Showing the Extent of the Culhua Mexica (Aztec Empire) and of the Maya Holdings

Provinces of the Empire of the Culhua Mexica

1. Cihuatlan
2. Tepequaculco
3. Tlachco
4. Ocuilan
5. Tuluca
6. Malinalco
7. Quahuacan
8. Xocotitlan
9. Atotonilco de Pedraza
10. Quauhtitlan
11. Xilotepec
12. Axocopan
13. Hueypuchtla
14. Oxitipan
15. Cihuatlan
16. Tuchpa
17. Atlan
18. Tlapacoyan
19. Atotonilco el Grande
20. Acolhuacan
21. Chalco
22. Quauhnahuac
23. Huaxtepec
24. Tlalcocauhtitlan
25. Quiauhteopan
26. Tlatlauhquitepec
27. Quauhtochco
28. Cuetlaxtlan
29. Tochtepec
30. Xoconochco
31. Tepeacac
32. Yoaltepec
33. Tlapan
34. Tlachquiauco
35. Coayxtlahuacan
36. Coyolapan
37. Citlaltepec and Tlatelolco
38. Petlacalco

Source: Robert Stoner Chamberlain, *The Conquest and Colonization of Yucatan, 1517–1550*, 1948
Robert Hayward Barlow, *The Extent of the Culhua Mexica*, 1949

- - - Individual provinces of the empire of the Culhua Mexica
- - - State of territorial boundaries
——— International boundaries

Copyright 1975
Board of Regents, The University of Texas System

Appendix II

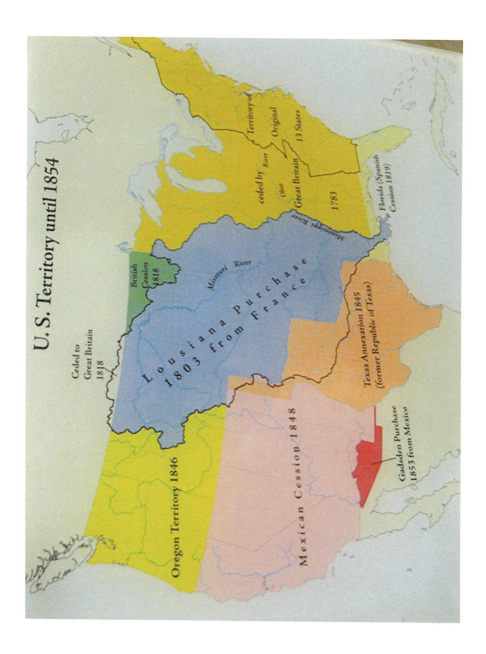

Appendix II

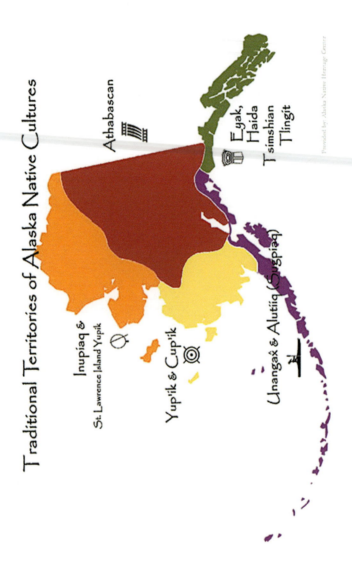

Appendix II

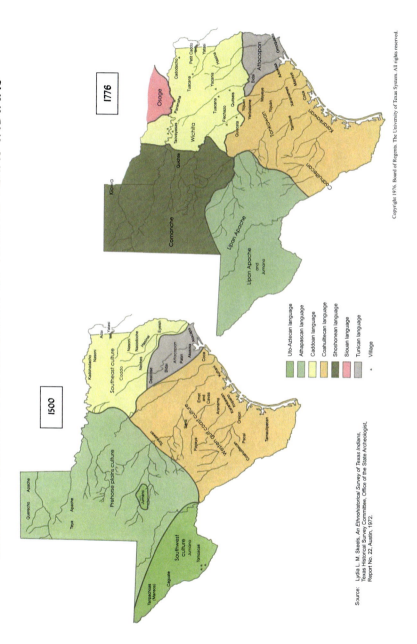

Appendix II

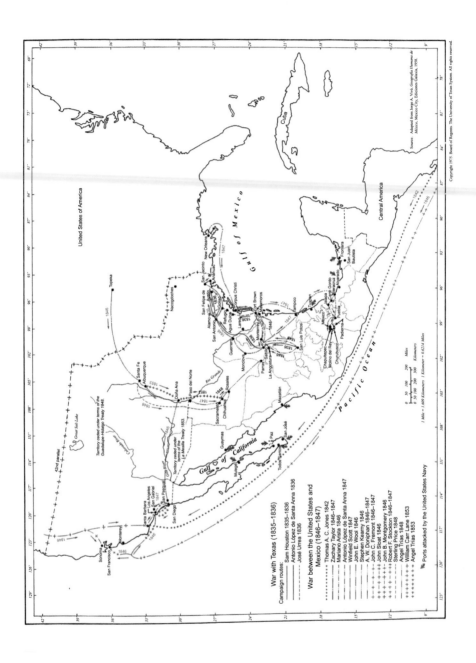

Appendix II

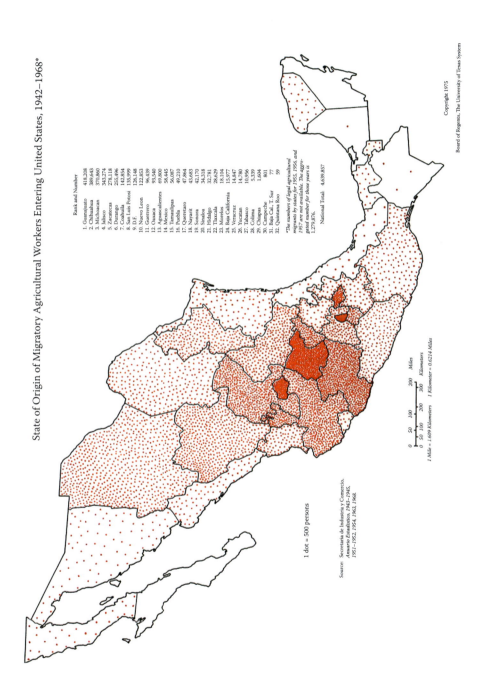

State of Origin of Migratory Agricultural Workers Entering United States, 1942–1968*

Rank and Number	
1. Guanajuato	418,208
2. Chihuahua	389,643
3. Michoacan	370,860
4. Jalisco	343,274
5. Zacatecas	278,118
6. Durango	255,496
7. Coahuila	142,854
8. San Luis Potosi	135,999
9. D.F.	126,148
10. Nuevo Leon	122,853
11. Guerrero	96,439
12. Oaxaca	93,540
13. Aguascalientes	69,800
14. Mexico	58,445
15. Tamaulipas	56,087
16. Puebla	49,310
17. Queretaro	47,864
18. Nayarit	43,683
19. Sonora	42,170
20. Sinaloa	34,318
21. Hidalgo	32,781
22. Tlaxcala	28,629
23. Morelos	18,104
24. Baja California	15,977
25. Veracruz	14,847
26. Yucatan	14,780
27. Tabasco	10,956
28. Colima	5,339
29. Chiapas	1,604
30. Campeche	801
31. Baja Cal. T. Sur	77
32. Quintana Roo	59

*The numbers of legal agricultural migrants by states for 1955, 1956, and 1957 are not available. The aggregated number for those years is 1,279,876.

National Total: 4,639,857

1 dot = 500 persons

Source: Secretaria de Industria y Comercio, *Anuario Estadistico, 1943–1945, 1951–1952, 1954, 1963, 1968*.

Copyright 1975
Board of Regents, The University of Texas System

188 Appendix II

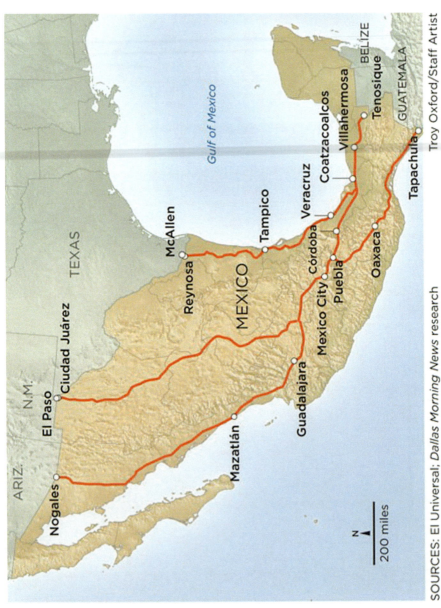

Appendix II

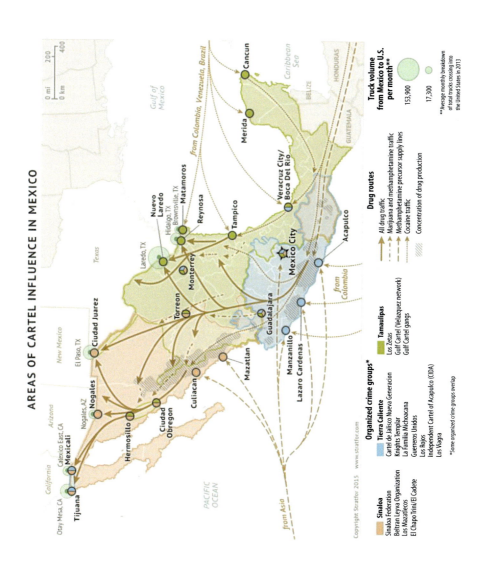

Endnotes

Chapter 1

1. P. Holder. *The Hoe and the Horse on the Plain.* Lincoln, NE: University of Nebraska Press, 1970; C. Martinez Novo. *Who Defines Indigenous? Identities, Development, Intellectuals and the State in Northern Mexico.* New Brunswick, NJ: Rutgers University Press, 2006; CIA. *Mexico: The 2012 World Factbook* (online). Washington, DC: Central Intelligence Agency, 2012.
2. J. Mooney. The Aboriginal Population of America North of Mexico, *Smithsonian Miscellaneous Collections,* vol. 80 (J. R. Swanton, ed.). Washington, DC: Smithsonian Institution, 1928: pp. 1–40.
3. D. H. Ubelaker. Prehistoric New World Population Size: Historical Review and Current Appraisal of North American Estimates, *Journal of Physical Anthropology,* Vol. 45, 1976: pp. 661–666.
4. F. Fernandez-Armesto. *The Americas: A Hemispheric History.* New York: Random House (Modern Library Edition), 2005: p. 88.
5. G. Nash. *Red, White, and Black: The Peoples of Early America.* Englewood Cliffs, NJ: Prentice Hall, 1974; W. I. Katz. *Black Indians.* New York: Atheneum Books, 1986.
6. F. Fernandez-Armesto, *op cited #4:* pp. 57–66.
7. F. Fernandez-Armesto, *op cited #4:* pp. 141–146.
8. P. Holder. *The Hoe and the Horse on the Plains.* Lincoln, *op cited #1.*
9. J. Adair. *History of the American Indians* (S. Williams, ed.). Johnson City, TN: East Tennessee University Press, 1930.
10. L. A. French. *Legislating Indian Country: Significant Milestones in Transforming Tribalism.* New York: Peter Land Publishing, 2007.
11. M. Weber. *The Protestant Ethic and the Spirit of Capitalism* (T. Parsons, Translator). New York: Charles Scribner's Sons, 1958.
12. *Standing Bear v. Crook,* 25 Federal Cases, 695, 697, 700-01 (May 12, 1879).
13. W. S. Churchill. *History of the English-Speaking People.* New York: Barnes & Noble, 1955.
14. K. T. Erikson. *Wayward Puritans: A Study in the Sociology of Deviance.* New York: John Wiley & Sons, 1966.
15. H. H. Bancroft. *History of Mexico,* Vol. 15. San Francisco: The Bancroft Library, The History Company Publishers, 1886.
16. A. De Leon. *Mexican Americans in Texas: A Brief History.* Arlington Heights, IL: Harland Davidson, 1993.

17. J. Butler. *The Huguenots in America: A Refugee People in the New World Society.* Cambridge, MA: Harvard University Press, 1992; C. M. Gilman. *The Huguenot Migration in Europe and America, its Cause and Effect.* Colts Neck, NJ: Arlington Laboratory for Clinical and Historical Research, 1962.
18. J. Abbott. *Life of Napoleon Bonaparte.* Whitefield, MT: Kessinger Publishing, 2005; S. Englund. *Napoleon: A Political Life.* Cambridge, MA: Harvard University Press, 2005.
19. L. A. Coser. *The Functions of Social Conflict* (1956); *Continuities in the Study of Social Conflict* (1962), both published by The Free Press, New York; G. Simmel. *Conflict* (K. A. Wolff, translator). New York: The Free Press, 1955.
20. K. C. Davis, God and Country, *Smithsonian* (October, 2010): pp. 86–96.

Chapter 2

1. F. F. Fernandez-Armesto. *The Americas: A Hemispheric History.* New York: Modern Library, Random House, 2005.
2. A Declaration of the State of the Colony and Affairs in Virginia, *Chronicles of American Indian Protest.* Greenwich, CT: A Fawcett Premier Book, 1971: pp. 1–6.
3. T. Pinto, All of us know about slavery, in R. Costo & J. Henry-Costo (eds.) *The Missions of California.* San Francisco: Indian Historian Press, 1987: pp. 139–140.
4. T. Pinto. *Missions of California, op cited* above.
5. F. Folsom. *Indian Uprising on the Rio Grande: The Pueblo Revolt of 1680.* Albuquerque, NM: University of New Mexico Press, 1973; H. C. James. Attempts at reconquest, *Pages from Hopi History.* Tucson, AZ: University of Arizona Press, 1974.
6. E. Speare. King Philip's War, *Stories of New Hampshire: A Living History of the Granite State.* Chelsea, MI: Sheridan Books, 2000.
7. F. Anderson. *The War that Made America: A Short History of the French and Indian War.* New York: Viking, 2005; F. Jennings. *Empire of Fortune: Crowns, Colonies and Tribes in the Seven Years in America.* New York: Norton, 1990.
8. G. G. Campbell. *A History of Nova Scotia.* Toronto, Canada: The Ryerson Press, 1948; J. Reid et al. *The Conquest of Acadia, 1710: Imperial, Colonial, and Aboriginal Constructions.* Toronto, Canada: University of Toronto Press, 2004; G. F. G. Stanley. *New France: The Last Phase, 1744–1760.* Toronto, Canada: McClelland and Stewart, 1968.
9. F. Anderson, *op cited* #7.
10. G. G. Campbell, *op cited* #8.
11. *Ibid.*
12. M. Beschloss. *The Presidents: Every Leader from Washington to Bush.* New York: American Heritage/Simon & Schuster, Inc., 2003.
13. L. A. French. *Frog Town: Portrait of a French Canadian Parish in New England.* Lanham, MD: University Press of America, 2014.
14. J. M. Faragher. Preface, *A Great and Nobel Scheme: The Tragic Story of the Expulsion of the French Acadians from their American Homeland.* New York: W. W. Norton, 2005.

Endnotes

15. G. G. Campbell, *op cited #8*: p. 127.
16. H. Bruce. *An Illustrated History of Nova Scotia*. Nova Scotia. Canada: Nimbus Publishing Limited & Province of Nova Scotia, 1997: p. 113.
17. R. A. LeBlanc. The Acadian Migrations, *Cahiers de Geographie de Quebec*, Vol. 11, 1967: pp. 523–541.
18. J. S. Martell. The second expulsion of the Acadians, *Dalhouise Review*, Vol. 13, 1933: pp. 359–371.
19. M. Leon-Portilla. La vision de los vencidos, *Broken Spears: The Aztec Account of the Conquest of Mexico*. Mexico City, Mexico: Universidad Nacional Automoma de Mexico Press, 1992: p. 165.
20. O. Paz. *El Laberinto de la Soledad (the Laberynth of Solitude)*. Mexico City, Mexico: Fondo de Cultura Economica, pp. 200–205; S. Ramos. *El perfil del hombre y la cultura en Mexico (Profile of Man and Culture in Mexico)*. Mexico City, Mexico, Espasa-Calpe Mexicana, 1976; R. E. Ruiz. *Triumphs and Tragedy: A History of Mexican People*. New York: W. W. Norton & Company, 1992; B. Diaz del Castillo. *History of the Conquest of New Spain*. New York: Penguin Books, 1963; L. A. French & M. Manzanarez. *NAFTA & Neocolonialism*. Lanham, MD: University Press of America, 2004.
21. F. Fernandez-Armesto. *The Americas: A Hemispheric History*. New York: Modern Library/Random House, 2005: p. 58.
22. M. Manzanarez, The Genesis of Neocolonialism, *NAFTA & Neocolonialism: Comparative Criminal, Human & Social Justice*. (L. A. French & M. Manzanarez). Lanham, MD: University Press of America, 2004: pp. 13–41.
23. G. Friederici. Scalping in America, in W. G. Spitall (ed.), *Irografts Indian Reprints: Scalping and Torture*. Ontario, Canada, 1985: pp. 423–438. Originally published in 1906 in the *Annual Report of the Smithsonian Institution*.
24. F. Jennings. *Empire of Fortune: Crowns, Colonies and Tribes in the Seven Years in America*. New York: Norton, 1990.
25. J. M. S. Careless. *Canada: A Story of Challenges*. Toronto, Canada: Macmillan of Canada. 1970.
26. *Ibid*.
27. M. Wade (ed.). *Canadian Dualism: Studies of French-English Relations*. Toronto, Canada: University of Toronto Press, 1960.

Chapter 3

1. C. G. Calloway. *The American Revolution in Indian Country*. New York: Cambridge University Press, 1995: p. xiii.
2. M. Beschloss. *The Presidents: Every Leader from Washington to Bush*. New York: American Heritage/Simon & Schuster, 2003.
3. M. Beschloss. Thomas Jefferson ibid: pp. 49–64.
4. A. A. Lipscomb. To Governor William H. Harrison, February 29, 1803, *The Writings of Thomas Jefferson*, Vol. 10. Washington, DC: The Thomas Jefferson Memorial Association, 1903: pp. 294–298.
5. B. Sheehan. *Seeds of Extinction*. New York: Norton, 1974; A. Stephanson. *Manifest Destiny: American Expansion and the Empire of Right*. New York: Hill & Wang, 1995.

6. *Indian Removal Act*, U.S. Statutes at Large, 4: 411–12, May 28, 1830.
7. *Cherokee Nation v. Georgia*, 5 Peters, 15–20, 1831.
8. *Worcester v. Georgia*. 6 Peters, 534–36, 558–63, 1832.
9. G. Jahoda. *The Trail of Tears: The Story of the American Indian Removals 1813–1855*. New York: Wings Books, 1975.
10. L. A. French. *Legislating Indian Country: Significant Milestones in Transforming Tribalism*. New York: Peter Land, 2007.
11. S. B. Ryerson. *Unequal Union: Confederation and the Roots of Conflict in the Canadas, 1815–1873*. New York: International Publishers, 1968.
12. *Ibid*.
13. W. L. McKeehan. *Adam-Onís Treaty of 1819*. New Spain Index, Sons of Dewitt Colony Texas (on-line site), 2001.
14. M. V. Henderson. Minor Empresario Contracts for the Colonization of Texas, 1825–1834, *Southwest Historical Quarterly*, Vol. 31 (4), 1928: pp. 295–324.
15. J. Holt. *The Edwards Empresarial Grant and the Fredonia Rebellion*. Masters of Arts Thesis, Stephen F. Austin State University, 1977; E. C. Baker. *Mexico and Texas, 1811–1835*. Dallas: Turner Publishing.
16. F. Merk. *Slavery and the Annexation of Texas*. New York: Knopf, 1972.
17. Barker, *op cited #15*.
18. *Ibid*.: p. 85.
19. J. M. Nance. *After San Jacinto: The Texas-Mexican Frontier, 1836–1841*. Austin, TX: University of Texas Press, 1963; D. J. Weber. *The Mexican Frontier, 1821–1846*. Albuquerque, NM: University of New Mexico Press, 1982.
20. R. B. Campbell. *An Empire for Slavery: The Peculiar Institution in Texas, 1821–1865*. Baton Rouge, LA: Louisiana University Press, 1989.
21. C. L. Dufour. *The Mexican War: A Compact History, 1846–1848*. New York: Hawthorn Books, 1968.
22. D. M. Potter. *The Impending Crisis, 1848–1861*. New York: Harper & Row, 1976.
23. J. H. Schroeder. *Mr. Polk's War: American Opposition and Dissent, 1846–1848*. Madison, WI: University of Wisconsin Press, 1973.
24. *J. P. Hale, of New Hampshire, on the Increase of the Army in Mexico* (speech). Delivered in the Senate of the United States, January 6, 1848: U.S. Senate Records.
25. *Treaty of Peace, Friendship, Limits, and Settlement between the United States of America, Concluded at Guadalupe Hidalgo, February 2, 1848; Ratified by President* [James K. Polk], *March 16, 1848*; Ratifications Exchanged at Queretaro, May 30, 1848; Proclaimed July 4, 1848.
26. H. H. Bancroft. *History of Arizona and New Mexico, 1530–1888*. San Francisco: The History Company Publishers, 1889.
27. L. E. Gomez. Off-White in an Age of White Supremacy: Mexican Elites and Rights of Indians and Blacks in Nineteenth-Century New Mexico. *Chicano-Latino Law Review*, Vol. 25 (Spring), 2005: pp. 9–59.
28. E. C. Rozwenc (ed.). *The Compromise of 1850: Problems in American Civilization*. Boston: Heath and Company, 1957.
29. A. Z. Carr. *The World and William Walker*. New York: Harper & Row, 1963; R. E. May. *Manifest Destiny's Underworld: Filibustering in Antebellum in America*. Chapel Hill, NC: University of North Carolina Press, 2002.

Endnotes

30. *Ostend Manifesto:* The Columbia Electronic Encyclopedia, 6th Edition. New York: Columbia University Press, 2005.
31. R. V. Hine. *Bartlett's West: Drawing the Mexican Boundary.* New Haven, CT: Yale University Press, 1968.
32. *Gadsden Purchase Treaty, December 30, 1853. Articles 1-9.* The Avalon Project at Yale Law School.
33. J. A. Michener. *The Eagle and the Raven.* New York: Tom Doherty Associates, 1990; L. A. French, *Running the Border Gauntlet: The Mexican Migrant Controversy.* Santa Barbara, CA: Praeger/ABC-CLIO, 2010.
34. J. Mora-Torres. *Mexican Border: The State, Capitalism, and Society in Nuevo Leon, 1848-1910.* Austin, TX: University of Texas Press, 2001; M. C. Myer et al. *The Course of Mexican History.* New York: Oxford University Press, 1999.
35. M. Beschloss. Abraham Lincoln: The Great Emancipator. *The Presidents: Every Leader from Washington to Bush,* op cited #2: pp. 189-208.
36. R. Ginsburg. *100 Years of Lynching.* New York: Lancer Books, 1962.
37. S. B. Ryerson. *Unequal Union: Confederation and the Roots of Conflict in the Canadas, 1815-1873,* op cited #11.
38. J. Fitzmaurice. *Quebec and Canada: Past, Present, Future.* London, England: Hurst, 1985.
39. J. A. Dallison. *Turning Back the Fenian: New Brunswick's Last Colonial Campaign.* Fredericton, New Brunswick, Canada: Goose Land Press, 2006.
40. Sir R. Coupland. *The Quebec Act: A Study in Statesmanship.* Oxford, England, Clarendon Press, 1968; G. Woodstock. *The Century that Made Us Canada, 1814-1914.* Toronto, Canada: Oxford University Press, 1989.
41. T. Flanagan. *Louis 'David' Riel, Prophet of the New World.* Toronto, Canada: University of Toronto Press, 1979.
42. J. Reid. *Louis Riel and the Creation of Modern Canada.* Albuquerque, NM: University of New Mexico Press, 2008; P. Charlebois. *The Life of Louis Riel.* Toronto, Canada: NC Press, 1975.
43. M. Manzanarez. The Genesis of Neocolonialism, *NAFTA & Neocolonialism: Comparative Criminal, Human & Social Justice.* (L. A. French & M. Manzanarez). Lanham, MD: University Press of America, 2004, pp. 13-41.
44. L. Harris. *Strong Man of the Revolution.* Silver City, NM: High Lonesome Press, 1995.
45. G. A. Cosman. *An Army for Empire: The United States Army in the Spanish American War.* Columbia, MO: University of Missouri Press, 1971; T. Roosevelt. *The Rough Riders.* New York: Charles Scribner's Sons, 1899; D. Smythe. *Guerilla Warrior: The Early Life of John J. Pershing.* New York: Charles Scribner's Sons, 1973; W. Manchester. *American Caesar: Douglas MacArthur 1880-1964.* Boston: Little, Brown and Company, 1978.
46. R. Ai Camp. *Politics in Mexico.* New York: Oxford University Press, 1993.
47. B. II. Johnson. *Revolution in Texas: How a Forgotten Rebellion and Its Bloody Suppression turned Mexicans into Americans.* New Haven, CT: Yale University Press, 2003: p. 113.
48. *Ibid:* p. 120.
49. F. Tompkins. *Chasing Villas: The Last Campaign of the U.S. Cavalry.* Harrisburg, PA: Military Service Publishing Company, 1934.

50. W. J. Hurst. *The Villista Prisoners of 1916-1917.* Las Cruces, NM: Yucca Tree Press.
51. R. W. Stewart. *Winning the West: The Army in the Indian Wars, 1865-1890.* Vol. 1 (Army Historical Series). Washington, DC: U.S. Government Printing Office, 2001.
52. J. D. McDermott. *A Guide to the Indian Wars of the West.* Lincoln, NE: University of Nebraska Press, 1998.
53. D. Brown. *The Galvanized Yankees.* Lincoln, NE: University of Nebraska Press, 1963, 1985; F. N. Schubert. *Black Valor: Buffalo Soldiers and Medal of Honor, 1870-1898.* Wilmington, DE: Scholarly Resources, 1997.
54. D. Smythe. *Pershing: General of the Armies.* Bloomington, IN: Indiana University Press, 1986.
55. J. G. Bourke. *On the Border with Crook.* Lincoln, NE: University of Nebraska Press, 1971.
56. R. Hassrick. *The Sioux.* Norman, OK: University of Oklahoma Press, 1967; I. V. D. Heard. *History of the Santee Sioux War.* New York: Harper Brothers, 1864; C. M. Oehler. *The Great Sioux Uprising.* New York: Oxford University Press, 1959; L. H. Roddis. *The Indian Wars of Minnesota.* Cedar Rapids, IA: Torch Press, 1956.
57. L. Standing Bear. *My People the Sioux.* Lincoln, NE: University of Nebraska Press, 1975; *Standing Bear v. Crook (Indians are People Declaration)*, 25 Federal Cases, 695, 697, 700-701, May 12, 1879.
58. W. T. Hagan. *Indian Police and Judges: Experiments in Acculturation and Control.* New Haven, CT: Yale University Press, 1966.
59. A. H. Kneale. *Indian Agent.* Caldwell, ID: Caxton Printers, 1950.
60. W. T. Hagan, *op cited #54.*
61. J. P. Clum. The San Carlos Apache Police, *New Mexico Historical Review,* July, 1929. pp. 203-219; E. Luna-Firebaugh. *Tribal Policing: Asserting Sovereignty, Seeking Justice.* Tucson, AZ: University of Arizona Press, 2007.
62. F. H. Harrison. *Hanging Judge.* Caldwell, ID: Caxton Printers, 1951; W. T. Hagan, *op cited #54.*
63. G. Shirely. *Law West of Fort Smith.* New York: Collier Books, 1961.
64. L. D. Ball. *The United States Marshalls of New Mexico and Arizona Territories, 1864-1912.* Albuquerque, NM: University of New Mexico Press, 1978.
65. S. J. Brakel. *American Indian Tribal Courts: The Costs of Separate Justice.* Chicago: American Bar Foundation, 1978.
66. S. L. Harring. *Crow Dog's Case: American Indian Sovereignty, Tribal Laws, and United States Law in the 19th Century.* New York: Cambridge University Press, 1994; *Ex Parte Crow Dog,* 109 U.S. Reports, 557, 571-72, December 17, 1883.
67. W. C. Canby, Jr. *American Indian Law in a Nutshell.* St. Paul, MN: West Publishing, 1998; *Major Crimes Act.* U.S. Statutes at Large, 23: 385, March 3, 1885; *United States v. Kagama,* 118 U.S. Reports, 375, 382-85, May 10, 1886.
68. *Public Law 280,* U.S. Statutes at Large, 67: 588-90, August 15, 1953.
69. L. A. French. *The Winds of Injustice: American Indians and the U.S. Government.* New York: Garland Reference Library of Social Science, Vol. 847, 1994; L. A. French. *Legislating Indian Country: Significant Milestones in Transforming Tribalism.* New York: Peter Lang, 2007.

Chapter 4

1. Section 185. Protection of Indians Desiring Civilized Life. *United States Code Annotated, Title 25—Indians*. St. Paul, MN: West Publishing Company, 1963, pp. 159-160.
2. W. E. Washburn. *The Assault on Indian Tribalism: The General Allotment Law (Dawes Act) of 1887*. (H. H. Hyman, ed.) Philadelphia, PA: J. B. Lippincott Company, 1975.
3. *General Allotment Act (Dawes Act)*. U.S. Statutes at Large, 24: 388-91 (February 8, 1887); *Curtis Act*. U.S. Statutes at Large, 30: 497-98, 502, 504-05 (June 28, 1898).
4. *Indian Citizenship Act*. U.S. Statutes at Large, 43: 253 (June 1, 1924).
5. L. Meriam et al. *The Problem of Indian Administration*. Baltimore: Johns Hopkins University Press, 1928; *Wheeler-Howard Act (Indian Reorganization Act)*, U.S. Statutes at Large, 48: 984-88 (June 18, 1934).
6. *Ibid*; *Johnson-O'Malley Act*. U.S. Statutes at Large, 48: 596. (April 16, 1934).
7. W. C. Canby. Indian Tribal Government (Ch. IV). *American Indian Law: In a Nutshell*. St. Paul, MN: West Group, 1998: pp. 59-95.
8. *House Concurrent Resolution 108*. U.S. Statutes at Large, 67: B132 (August 1, 1953).
9. D. L. Fixico. *Termination and Relocation: Federal Indian Policy, 1945-1960*. Albuquerque, NM: University of New Mexico Press, 1986/1992; *Indian Claims Commission Act*. U.S. Statutes at Large, 60: 1049-1056 (August 13, 1946).
10. *Public Law 280*. U.S. Statutes at Large, 67: 588-90 (August 15, 1953).
11. R. Costo, & J. Henry-Costo. The New War against the Indians, *Indian Treaties: Two Centuries of Dishonor*. San Francisco: Indian Historian Press, 1977: pp. 41-70.
12. C. F. Wilkinson, & E. R. Biggs. The Evolution of the Termination Policy, *American Indian Law Review*, Vol. 139, 1977: pp. 151-157; *Menominee Restoration Act*. U.S. Statutes at Large, 87: 700ff. (December 22, 1973).
13. Y. Bushyhead. In the Spirit of Crazy Horse: Leonard Peltier and the AIM Uprising. (Cp.5) *The Winds of Injustice: American Indians and the U.S. Government*. (L. A. French). New York: Garland Publishing, 1994, pp. 77-112.
14. *Congressional Joint Resolution Establishing the American Indian Policy Review Commission*. U.S. Statutes at Large, 88: 1910-1913 (January 2, 1975); *Final Report, Vol. 1. A Policy for the Future. American Indian Policy Review Commission*. Washington, DC: U.S. Government Printing Office, 1977, pp. 3-6.
15. Establishment of Assistant Secretary of Indian Affairs, U.S. Department of the Interior (September 26, 1977), *Federal Register*, Vol. 42: 53682, October 3, 1977.
16. *Indian Self-Determination and Education Assistance Act*. U.S. Statutes at Large, 88: 2203-2214 (January 4, 1975).
17. C. Wilkinson. *Blood Struggle: The Rise of the Modern Indian Nations*. New York: W. W. Norton, 2005: pp. 241-268.
18. *Indian Crimes Act of 1976*. U.S. Statutes at Large, 90: 585-586 (May 29, 1976); *United States v. Wheeler*. 435 U.S. 313, 98 S.Ct. 1079,55 L.Ed.2d 303 (1978); *Oliphant v. Suquamish Indian Tribe*. 435 U.S. 191 (1978); *Public La 102-37, Criminal Jurisdiction over Indians*, 105, U.S. Statutes at Large, 646, 25 U.S.C. 1301 (4), 1991; *Indian Tribal Justice Support;* Subchapter 1: "Tribal Justice System," Chapter 38, *United States Code—Title 25*, Sections 3611-3614.

19. L. A. French. Missionaries among the Eastern Cherokees: Religion as a Means of Interethnic Communication. *Interethnic Communication* (E. Lamar Ross, ed.). Athens. GA: University of Georgia Press, 1978: pp. 100–112.
20. Archeological Protection Act (October 31, 1979); Section 2 (a) (3): *U.S. Statutes at Large*, 93: 721–23.
21. L. A. French. Indian Self-Determination, *Legislating Indian Country: Significant Milestones in Transforming Tribalism*. Peter Lang, 2007: pp. 129–172.
22. *Public Law 103-344, American Indian Religious Freedom Act Amendments of 1994*. H.R. 4230, 103rd Congress, 2nd session, 1–3 (October 6, 1994).
23. *Indian Child Welfare Act*. U.S. Statutes at Large, 92: 3069, 3071–3076 (November 8, 1978).
24. U.S. Senate, *Part One—The Executive Summary: A New Federalism for American Indians, Final Report and Legislative Recommendations: A Report of the Special Committee on Investigations of the Select Committee on Indian Affairs*. 101st Congress, 1st Session, 101–639, 9–10 (November, 1989).
25. *Public Law 101-630, Indian Child Protection and Family Violence Prevention Act, Title IV*. 25 USC 3210 (November 28, 1990).
26. J. Archer. *The Plot to Seize the White House*. New York: Hawthorn Books, 1973, pp. 118–119.
27. R. S. McElvaine. *The Great Depression: America 1929-1941*. New York: Times Books, 1981.
28. J. Dinges. *The Condor Years: How Pinochet and his Allies Brought Terrorism in Three Continents*. New York: The New Press, 2004; J. P. McSherry. *Predatory States: Operation Condor and Covert War in Latin America*. Lanham, MD: Rowman & Littlefield, 2005.
29. L. A. French, & M. Manzanarez. Part III: Comparative Criminal & Human Justice, *NAFTA & Neocolonialism: Comparative Criminal, Human & Social Justice*. Lanham, MD: University Press of America, 2004: pp. 119–132.
30. A. Schiffrin. *Dr. Seuss & Co. Go to War*. New York: The New Press, 2009: p. 16.
31. W. F. Murphy, J. E. Fleming, & S. A. Barber. *American Constitutional Interpretation*. Westbury, NY: The Foundation Press, 1995.
32. E. R. Stoddard. The Period of Cultural Accommodation (1910–1941), *Mexican Americans*. New York: Random House, 1973: pp. 183–188.
33. J. Q. Quinones. *Chicano Politics: Reality & Promise 1940-1990*. Albuquerque, NM: University of New Mexico Press, 1990.
34. *Deogado v. Bastrop ISD*, Civ. No. 388 (W. D. Tex, June 15, 1948); *Hernandez v. Driscoll CISD*, 2 Race Rel. L. Rotr, 329, D. D. Tex., 1957; *Hernandez v. Driscoll CISD*, Civil Action (Civ.A.) 1384, U.S. District Court of the Southern District of Texas (S. D. Tex.), 1957; D. S. Ettinger. The History of School Desegregation in the Ninth Circuit, *Loyola of Los Angles Law Review*, Vol. 12 (481), pp. 484–487.
35. B. W. Wheeler, & S. D. Becker. *Discovering the American Past: A Look at the Evidence*, Vol. 2 (since 1885). Boston: Houghton Mifflin Company, 2002: pp. 209–307.
36. *Ibid*.
37. J. G. Quinones. *Chicano Politics: Reality & Promise 1940-1990*. Albuquerque, NM: University of New Mexico Press, 1990.
38. L. A. French & M. Manzanarez, *op cited #28*.
39. *Ibid*.

Endnotes

40. G. Donaldson. *Eighteen Men: The Prime Ministers of Canada.* Toronto, Canada: Doubleday Canada, 1985.
41. J. M. S. Careless. *Canada: A Story of Challenges* (revised edition). Toronto, Canada: Macmillan of Canada, 1970: p. 346.
42. C. P. Stacy. Through the Second World War (Cpt. 9), *Part One of the Canadians 1867–1967.* (J. M. S. Careless, & R. C. Brown, eds.). Toronto, Canada, Gage Publishing Limited, 1968: p. 301.
43. W. Kilbourn. *The Firebrand: William Lyon Mackenzie and the rebellion in Upper Canada.* Toronto, Canada: Clarke, Irwin, 1956; S. B. Ryerson. *Unequal Union: Confederation and the Roots of Conflict in the Canadas, 1815–1873.* New York: International Publishers, 1968.
44. *Ibid.*
45. R. Chodos, & F. Hamovitch. Textile Towns, Cultural Struggles, and an Industrial Quebec, 1850–1929, *Quebec and the American Dream.* Toronto, Canada: Between the Lines, 1991.
46. W. Kilbourn. The 1950s, Careless, & Brown, *op cited #41*: p. 232.
47. L. Dion. *Quebec: The Unfinished Revolution.* Montreal, Canada: McGill-Queen's University Press, 1992; C. Nish. *Quebec in the Duplessi Era, 1935–1959.* Toronto, Canada: Copp Clark Publishing Company, 1970.
48. P. Desbarats. *Rene: A Canadian in Search of a Country.* Toronto, Canada: McClelland and Stewart-Bantam United, 1977; M. Richler. *Oh Canada! Oh Quebec! Requiem for a Divided Country.* New York: Viking, 1992.
49. P. Vallieves. *White Niggers of America: The Precocious Autobiography of a "Terrorists."* (J. Pinklam, trans.). New York: Monthly Review Press, 1971.
50. See www.canadahistory.com/sections/eras/eras.html.
51. P. Trudeau. *Federation and the French Canadians.* New York: St. Martin's Press, 1968.
52. P. Fournier. *The Meech Lake Post-Mortem: Is Quebec Sovereignty Inevitable?* Montreal, Canada: McGill-Queen's Press, 1991.
53. R. Chodos, & E. Hamovitch, *op cited #44*; S. Clarkson. *Canada and the Reagan Challenge: Crisis in the Canadian-American Relationship.* Toronto, Canada: James Lorimer & Company and the Canadian Institute for Economic Policy, 1982.
54. L. A. French, & L. Nikolic-Novakovic. *War Trauma and its Aftermath: An International Perspective on the Balkan and Gulf Wars.* Lanham, MD: University Press of America, 2012.
55. H. Anquilar Carmen, & L. Meyer. *A la Sombra de la Revolucion Mexicana.* Mexico City, Mexico: Cal y Arena, 1990; E. Krauze. *Biografia del poder, Caudillos del al Revolucion Mexicans 1910–1940.* Mexico City, Mexico: TusQuets Editores, 1997.
56. D. Levy, & G. Szekely. *Mexico: Paradoxes of Stability and Change.* Boulder, CO: Westview Press, 1983.
57. S. Niblo. Allied Policy toward Axis interests in Mexico during World War II, *Mexican Studies/Estudios Mexicanos*, Vol. 17 (2), 2001: pp. 375–402.
58. L. Medina. *Evolucion electoral en Mexico contemporaneo.* Mexico City, Mexico: Gaceta Informativa de la Comision Federal Electoral, 1978.
59. M. Serrano. The Armed Branch of the State: Civil-Military relations in Mexico. *Journal of Latin American Studies*, Vol. 27 (2), 1995: pp. 423–448.

60. M. Manzanarez. The Genesis of Neocolonialism (Cpt.1) in L. A. French, & M. Manzanarez. NAFTA & Neocolonialism, *op cited #28*.

Chapter 5

1. S. Globerman & P. Stover. Implications of Trade Trends Upon Canada–U.S. Border Infrastructure, *Border Policy Research Institute*, (Western Washington University), Vol. 9 (4), Fall 2014, p. 1.
2. S. Horwitz. A gunrunning sting gone fatally wrong, *The Washington Post*, July 27, 2011: http://www.washingtonpost.com/investigations/us-anti-gun running-effort-turns-fatally-wrong/2011/07/14/glQAH5dbYI.story.
3. R. J. Terrill. Canada (Cpt. II) *World Criminal Justice Systems*. Cinncinnati, OH: Anderson Publishing Company, 2003: pp. 115–197.
4. J. Smith. Supreme Court recognizes rights of Métis and non-status Indians, *Toronto Star*, April 15, 2016: http://thestar.com/news.canada.2016/04/14/.com.
5. W. LaFeber. *Inevitable Revolution: The United States in Central America*. New York: W. W. Norton & Company, 1984: p. 8.
6. Gilder Lehman Institute. Hames Monroe, Message to Congress, December 2, 1923 See: http://www.digitalhistory.uh.edu/disp_textbook.cfm?smtID=3&psid=161.
7. N. E. Jaffary, E. W. Osowski, & S. S. Porter. Mexican History. Boulder: Westview Press, 2010.
8. H. Davis, J. J. Finan, & F. T. Peck. Latin American Diplomatic History: An Introduction. Louisiana: Louisiana State University, 1997.
9. J. Villalobos. El Infierno al sur de Mexico, *Nexos,* September 1, 2014. http://www.nexos.com.mx/?p=22331.
10. Heinle, K, C. Molzahn, & D. A. Shirk. 2015. *Justice in Mexico Project*. San Diego: Department of Political Science & International Relations, University of San Diego.
11. Angel, A. 2015. *Guerrero cierra 2015 a la cabeza en homicidios, Tamaulipas en plagios y Jalisco en extorsiones*. December 15. http://www.animalpolitico.com/2015/12/guerrero-cierra-2015-a-la-cabeza-en-homicidios-tamaulipas-en-plagios-y-jalisco-en-extorsiones/.
12. Gagne, D. 2015. *InSight Crime 2014 Homicide Round-up*. January 15. http://www.insightcrime.org/news-analysis/insight-crime-2014-homicide-round-up.
13. K. Watson. Families of Mexico's missing students refuse to give up, *BBC News-Latin America & the Caribbean,* February 4, 2015. http://www.bbc.com/news/world-latin-america-31126597.
14. Osorno, D. E. 2009. *El Cártel de Sinaloa, una historia del uso político del narco*. Mexico: Grijalbo.
15. Andreas, P. 2009. *Border Games*. Ithaca: Cornell University.
16. Andreas, P. 2013. *Smuggler Nation: How Illicit Trade Made America*. New York: Oxford University Press.
17. I. Campo. Degeneration and the Origin of Mexico's War on Drugs. *Mexican Studies/Estudio Mexicanos,* 2010: pp. 379–408.

18. A. M. Ryden. Immigration lawyer: Congressman's bill would speed up deportation of unaccompanied children. This is why it's wrong. *AZ Central*, July 15, 2014. http://www.azcentral.com/story/opinion/op-ed/2014/07/14/matt-salmon-depot-children/12708299.
19. J. J. Esquivel. El crimen organizado pone en riesgo la democracia en Mexico y A: Obama, *Proceso*, February 15, 2015: http://www.proceso.com.mx/?p=395-193; D. Gonzalez. Pipeline of children: A Border Crisis Gang Violence, Lack of opportunity and Misinformation Lead to a Mass Exodus North to the United States, *The Arizona Republic,* July 10, 2014: http://www.azcentral.com/story/news/politics/immigration/2014/07/10/immigrant-children-border-kids=pipeline/12410517.
20. R. Donnelly. *Transit Migration in Mexico: Domestic and International Policy Implications.* Houston, TX: James A. Baker III Institute for Public Policy, Rice University, December 2014.
21. C. W. Valenzuela. *Mexico's Southern Border Strategy: Programa Frontera Sur.* Wilson Center: Mexico Institute, 2014.
22. Assessing the Alarming Impact of Mexico's Southern Border Program, *Advocacy for Human Rights in Americas,* May 28, 2015.
23. U.S. Customs and Border Protection. Accessed May 6, 2016. https://www.cbp.gov/newsroom/stats/southwest-border-unaccompanied-children/fy-2016.
24. J. M. Krogstad. Pew Research Center. May 4. http://www.pewresearch.org/fact-tank/2016/05/04/u-s-border-apprehensions-of-families-and-unaccompanied-children-jump-dramatically/.
25. D. Cagne. 2016. InSight Crime's 2015 Latin America Homicide Round-up. January 14. Accessed May 5, 2016. http://www.insightcrime.org/news-analysis/insight-crime-homicide-round-up-2015-latin-america-caribbean.
26. R. H. Espach. *Border Insecurity in Central America's Northern Triangle.* Washington. DC: MPI Migration Policy Institute, May 2, 1016; C. Inkpen. *Security and Human Rights Issues on the Guatemalan/Mexican Border.* Washington, DC: Center for Strategic and International Studies. May 2, 2016.
27. J. Villalobos, *op cited #6.*
28. Migrant Policy Institute. 2016. *Increased Central American Migration to the United States May Prove an Enduring Phenomenon.* http://www.migrationpolicy.org/article/increased-central-american-migration-united-states-may-prove-enduring-phenomenon.

Index

A

Acadian Expulsion, 24–28
Adams, John, 40
Adams, John Quincy, 40, 56
Adams-Onís Treaty of 1819, 47–48
African slaves, 3
Agent provocateurs, 89
Alcohol, Tobacco, Firearms and Explosives (ATF), 149
Aleut (Eskimo), 150
American GI Forum (AGIF), 124
American Indian Movement (AIM), 98, 108
American Indian Religious Freedom Act (AIRFA), 113
American Indians, policing of, *see* United States (emerging) and its expansionist mandate
American Indians or Alaska Natives (AI/AN), 150
American Legion, 119
American Liberty League, 118
Anasazi tribe, 114
Apache, 18, 150
Arapaho, 18
Archaeological Resources Protection Act, 113
Aroostook War, 46, 72
Arthur, Chester A., 96
Assimilative Crimes Act of 1825, 93
Assiniboine of North Dakota, 150
Athabaskan tribes, 150
Attribution bias, 14
Austin, Stephen F., 48
Ayutla Revolution, 79
Aztec Indian empires (Mexico), 3

B

Balfour Declaration of 1926, 130
Baptist Sects, 8, 9
Battle of Bunker Hill, 28
BIA, *see* Bureau of Indian Affairs

Bidai, 18
Billy the Kid, 96
Blackfoot Indian tribe, 77
Black Indian, 3
Black Panthers, 127
Bloc Quebecois (BQ), 137
"Blue laws," 11
Bonaparte, Napoleon, 12
Border Patrol Search, Trauma, and Rescue (BORSTAR), 149
Border Policy Research Institute, 148
Braddock, Edward, 23
Brown, John, 69
Brown Power, 127
Brown v. Board of Education, 124, 125
Buchanan, James, 69
Buchanan-Pakenham Treaty of 1846, 57
Buffalo Soldiers, 91
Bureau of Indian Affairs (BIA), 105, 106, 111
Burke Act, 99
Burnside, Ambrose, 61
Bush, George W., 147
Bustamante Decree, 51

C

Caddo, 18
Calderón, Felipe, 157
Calhoun, John C., 45, 63
Calvinism, 8
Campbell, Kim, 129
Canada comes of age and the perils of Quebec separatism, 129–139
    Balfour Declaration of 1926, 130
    Bloc Quebecois, 137
    Charter of Rights, 136
    Commonwealth, forging of, 130
    ethnic strife, 130
    French Canadian Catholic Bishops, 133
    Front de liberation du Quebec, 134
    Hydro-Quebec, 134

influence of French leaders in Canada, 129–132
kidnapping of the British Trade Commissioner, 135
Meech Lake Accord, 137
names of prime ministers, 129
nations equal in status, 130
Newfoundland, 131
Nobel Peace Prize, 131
NORAD agreement, 132
October Crisis of 1980, 133
Parliament of Canada, 137
Parti Quebecois, 135
Quebec separatism and the Quiet Revolution, 132–139
"sovereignty-association" plan, 136
Suez Canal crisis, 131
Canadian challenges during the Monroe Doctrine era, 71–79
Aroostook War, 72
dominion of Canada, 75–76
Fenian challenge, 73–75
Cardenas, Lazaro, 140
Carrizo, 18
Carter, Jimmy, 111
Catholicism (Catholic), 8
Anglo-American immigrants in Texas, 52
in Mexico, 139
missions, 3, 48
parochial system, higher education within, 38
Chavez, Cesar, 125
Cherokee, 35, 42, 102, 150
Cherokee Nation v. the State of Georgia, 42, 43
Cheyenne, 17
Chickasaw, 17, 35, 102
Chinantec, 18
Chippewa Tribe of Turtle Mountain Reservation, 105
Choctaw, 17, 35, 102
Ch'ol, 18
Chretien, Jean, 129, 137
Chronology of major events, 167–176
Church of England, 8
Cinco de Mayo battle, 69
Citizenship, Indians granted, 103
Civilian Conservation Corps, 106
Clay, Henry, 45, 63
Clinton, William J., 114, 147
Coahuiltecan, 18

Cold War
in Central America, 154
fears, hemispheric exploitation and, *see* 20th century, neocolonial conflicts of
interventions (United States), 141–142
Colonial intrusion and border battles, 17–38
aboriginals and their pre-Columbian boundaries, 17–18
Acadian Expulsion, 24–28
adaptations to colonial intrusions, 34–38
Iroquois Confederation, 36
rangs, 37
scalping, 35
ultramontane citadel, 38
anti-Quaker laws, 24
changing Spanish America, 28–34
encomienda system, 33
genocide, 33
New Spain's adaptations to the New World, 33–34
repartimiento system, 34
slavery, 33
colonial encroachment and conflict, 19–24
ethnic cleansing, campaign of, 24
Jamestown settlement, 19
mound builders, 17
New England area, tribes inhabiting, 17
oath of allegiance, 22
Puritan concept, 24
Comanche, 18, 150
Communism, guise of fighting, 119
Community Service Organization (CSO), 126
Confederate prisoners of war, 91
Contravening worldviews, 1–15
aboriginal harmony ethos and restorative justice, 6–7
economic competition, 4
"harmony ethos," 4
Jim Crow laws, 5
Protestant ethic and new world conflicts (Protestants, aboriginals, Catholics), 8–15
ambiguous situations, 14
attribution bias, 14
"blue laws," 11
Calvinist conservative Protestant Revolt, 9
Covenant of Divine Providence (Manifest Destiny), 9
ethnic cleansing, 9

Index

feudal system, 11–12
Massachusetts Bay Colony, 10
predestination, 8
realistic conflict, 14
religious tolerance, myth of seeking, 9
slavery, interdependency of, 4
sociocultural superiority, concept of, 1
white supremacy, concept of, 4
Cortes, Hernan, 33
Covenant of Divine Providence (Manifest Destiny), 9
Coyotes, 148
Cree Indian tribe, 77
Creek, 17, 35, 102
Criollos (Creoles), 11
Cristero Rebellion in Central Mexico, 139
Crow, 17
Crow Dog incident, 96, 97
CSO, *see* Community Service Organization
Cuban Revolution, 142
Curtis Act (1898), 103
Cuyapaipe reservation, 19

D

Dakota, 17
Dalton gang, 94
Davis, Jefferson, 61
Dawes Act, 103
DEA, *see* Drug Enforcement Agency
Defense Act of 1916, 87
Department of Homeland Security (DHS), 146
Díaz, Porfirio, 79, 142
Dinwiddie, Robert, 23
Discrimination
de facto, 121–129
Jim Crow, 5, 34, 122
Distant Early Warning Line (DEW Line), 132
Douglas, Stephen, 63
Dred Scott decision, 69
Drug Enforcement Agency (DEA), 129
Drug Kingpin Act (DKA), 124
Drug trafficking (Mexico), *see* Mexico's daunting role as a filter for drug and human trafficking

E

Echeverria, Luis, 143
Economic competition, 4
Eisenhower, Dwight, 106, 121, 147

Emancipation Proclamation, 4, 71
Encomienda system, 33
Episcopal Church in the United States, 9
Ethnic cleansing, 40
campaign of, 24
Protestant ethic and, 9
U.S. experiment with, 41–45
European French and Indian Wars, 21
Ex-Quebec Act, 75

F

Fascism, concerns leading to big business's form of, 118
Fast and Furious gun-running project, 149
Father Sky, 4, 6
Federal Bureau of Investigation (FBI), 112
harassment of young Indians, 108
racist slant of J. Edgar Hoover, 128
Federal Bureau of Narcotics (FBN), 128
Federal Enclaves Act, 92
Feudal system, Protestant ethic and, 11–12
Fianna, 73
First Nation people (Canada), 77
First United States Voluntary Cavalry, 82
Five Civilized Tribes, 35, 42
exemption of, 102
report calling for destruction of, 103
Flathead Tribe of Montana, 105
Fort Duquesne, 23–24
Fox, Vicente, 149, 161
Fox tribe, 102
Franco, Francisco, 119
Fredonian Rebellion, 50
Freedmen's Bureau, 71
Free and Secure Trade Express (FAST) passage, 147
Free Soil Party, 63, 65
French Catholic Church, 38
French colonization, 12
French and Indian War (Seven Years War), 23
Front de liberation du Quebec (FLQ), 46, 72, 134
Fugitive Slave Act, 64
Furman v. Georgia, 123

G

Gadsden Purchase, 65–70, 150
Galvanized Yankees, 91
General Agreement on Trade and Tariffs (GATT) consortium, 144

General Allotment Act (Dawes Act), 98, 102
General Campaign Star (GCS), 138
General Crimes Act, 92
Genocide, 33
Ghost Dance movement, 108
Gideon v. Wainwright, 123
"Good Neighbor Policy," 141
GOON squad, *see* Guardians of the Oglala Nation squad
Gossens, Salvador Allende, 119
Grant, Ulysses S., 40, 61, 88
Great Depression programs, 106
Great Recession (2008), 145
Gregg v. Georgia, 124
Guardians of the Oglala Nation (GOON) squad, 108

H

Haitian national police, 117
"Hanging judge," 95
"Harmony ethos," 4
Harper, Prime Minister, 152
Harper's Ferry, attack on, 69
Harrison Narcotic Act of 1914, 128
Hayt, Ezra A., 93
HBC, *see* Hudson Bay Company
Hemp conspiracy, 128
Henry VIII of England, 8, 12
Herminca Hernandez et al. v. Driscoll Consolidated ISD, 125
Hitler, Adolph, 119
Holder, Eric, 150
Hoover Task Force Commission, 105
Hopi Indians, 20
Hot pursuit, 86
House Un-American Activities Committee, 119
Houston, Sam, 54, 56
Huastec, 18
Hudson Bay Company (HBC), 76
Huguenots, 13
Human trafficking (Mexico), *see* Mexico's daunting role as a filter for drug and human trafficking
Hydro-Quebec, 134

I

IIM trust, *see* Individual Indian Money trust
IMF, *see* International Monetary Fund

Imperial Colonization Law, 48
Indian Child Abuse Prevention and Treatment Act of 1990, 116
Indian Child Welfare Act of 1978, 114, 115
Indian Claims Commission, 105, 106
Indian land grab, 40
Indian/Métis rebellions, 76–78
Indian religious freedom, 113
Indian Reorganization Act (IRA), 104
Indian Self-Determination and Education Assistance Act, 111
Indian Tribal Act of 1993, 113
Indian Wars of 1865–1891, U.S. Army and, 89–92
Individual Indian Money (IIM) trust, 98
Inouye, Daniel K., 114
Institutionalized Revolutionary Party (PRI) (Mexico), 101
International Monetary Fund (IMF), 143
Inuit, 136, 151
IRA, *see* Indian Reorganization Act
Irish Republican Brotherhood, 73
Iroquois Confederation, 36
Iroquois of New York, 150

J

Jackson, Andrew, 42, 44
Jackson, Stonewall, 61
Jamestown settlement, 19
Jay Treaty, 150
Jefferson, Thomas, 40, 95
Jim Crow discrimination, 5, 34, 122
Johnson, Andrew, 121
Johnson-O'Malley Act, 104
Johnson v. McIntosh, 41
Juárez, Benito, 82, 83, 152
Jumping Bull Ranch on Pine Ridge, 109

K

Karankawa, 18
Kellogg, Frank, 140
King, W. L. Mackenzie, 129, 130
King George's War, 22
King Henry VIII, 8, 12
King Philip's War, 21
King Ranch, 85
King William's War, 21
Kiowa, 18, 150
Kitsai, 18
Know Nothing Party, 64

Index

Kosovo War, 138
Ku Klux Klan (KKK), 71, 118

L

Lacey Act, 99
La Raza Unida Party (LRUP), 127
Laurier, Wilfred, 129
League of United Latin American Citizens (LULAC), 85, 124
Lee, Robert E., 61, 90
Legislation
    American Indian Religious Freedom Act (AIRFA), 113
    Archaeological Resources Protection Act, 113
    Assimilative Crimes Act of 1825, 93
    Burke Act, 99
    Defense Act of 1916, 87
    Drug Kingpin Act, 124
    Federal Enclaves Act, 92
    Fugitive Slave Act, 64
    General Allotment Act (Dawes Act), 98
    General Crimes Act, 92
    Harrison Narcotic Act of 1914, 128
    Indian Child Abuse Prevention and Treatment Act of 1990, 116
    Indian Child Welfare Act of 1978, 114, 115
    Indian Reorganization Act, 104
    Indian Self-Determination and Education Assistance Act, 111
    Lacey Act, 99
    Major Crimes Act, 93, 97
    Posse Comitatus Act, 147
    Reconstruction Act, 121
    Religious Freedom Act, 114
    Trade and Intercourse Acts, 92
    Wheeler-Howard Act of 1934, 104
Lewis and Clark Expedition, 40
Liberal-Conservative Coalition, 75
Lightfoot, Thomas, 93
Lincoln, Abraham, 40, 121
Litigation
    Brown v. Board of Education, 124, 125
    Cherokee Nation v. the State of Georgia, 42, 43
    Furman v. Georgia, 123
    Gideon v. Wainwright, 123
    Gregg v. Georgia, 124
    Herminca Hernandez et al. v. Driscoll Consolidated ISD, 125

    Johnson v. McIntosh, 41
    Mendez v. Westminster School District, 125
    Merrion v. Jicarilla Apache, 112
    Miranda v. Arizona, 123
    Olipnant v. Suquamish Indian Tribe, 112
    Plessy v. Ferguson, 125
    Proffit v. Florida, 124
    Stephen v. Cherokee Nation, 103
    United States v. Kagama, 97
    United States v. Wheeler, 112
Lkamath Tribe of Oregon, 105
Longfellow, Henry Wadsworth, 27
Louisiana Purchase, 40, 47
LRUP, *see* La Raza Unida Party
LULAC, *see* League of United Latin American Citizens

M

Macdonald, John A., 77, 129
Maderista Revolt, 83
Major Crimes Act, 93, 97, 101
Major events, chronology of, 167–176
Maliseet Indians, 27
Maliseet Passamaquoddy, 150
Manifest Destiny
    main tenet of, 113
    roots of, 24
    white Protestant supremacy and, *see* United States (emerging) and its expansionist mandate
Manitoba Act, 77
MAPA, *see* Mexican American Political Association
Maps, 177–189
Marijuana Transfer Tax Act (1937), 127
Marshall, John, 41
Marshall, Thurgood, 112
Martin, Paul, 129
Mascarene, Paul, 26
Massachusetts Bay Colony, 10
Mather, Cotton, 26
Maximilian of Hapsburg, 79, 155
Mayan Indians, 18, 53
Mazahua, 18
Mazatec, 18
McCarthy era, 132
McClellan, George G., 91
McKinley, William, 82
Meade, George, 61
Meeds minority report, 111

Mendez v. Westminster School District, 125
Menominee Tribe of Wisconsin, 105
Mercier, Honore, 78
Merida Initiative, 162
Merrion v. Jicarilla Apache, 112
Mestizos, 20
Metacom, 21
Methodism, 8, 9
Mexican American Political Association (MAPA), 127
Mexico (road to revolution), 79–84
    Ayutla Revolution, 79
    caste-like system, 80
    government goon squads, 81
    Porfiriato setting the stage for the Mexican revolution, 79–83
    reign of Porfirio Díaz (America's favorite despot), 79–84
    Rough Riders, 82
    seeds of Mexican discontent, 83–84
    Teller Amendment, 83
Mexico's daunting role as a filter for drug and human trafficking, 154–165
    Central America and the Cold War, 155–157
    geopolitical context, 155
    homicide rates in Mexico, 158f
    major events in U.S.-Mexico efforts to fight the War on Drugs, 159t
    Merida Initiative, 162
    Mexican war on drugs, 157–165
    percentage of people living in poverty, 161f
    push–pull effect, 165
    Sandinista National Liberation Front, 156
    U.S. drug, security, and immigration concerns, 158–165
Mexico/Tenochtitlan, conquest of, 31
Mexico in the 20th century (growth, corruption, and U.S. interventions), 139–144
    coalition of peasants, 140
    Cristero Rebellion in Central Mexico, 139
    fraudulent elections, 142
    GATT consortium, 144
    hacendados, 140
    implementing the new constitution of 1917 with interference from the United States, 139–140
    land expropriations, 140
    Mexican Communist Party, 141
    National Action Party, 142
    National Revolutionary Party, 140
    Obregon administration, 139
    oil leasing policy, 139
    oppression and change (transitioning to globalization), 142–144
    revolutionary changes finally enacted, 140–141
    "revolutionary family," 141
    Summer Olympics, 143
    Tripartite Convention, 143
    U.S. Cold War interventions, 141–142
Mexico–U.S. Plenary Group on Law Enforcement, 149
Miami tribe, 102
Mi'kmaq, 24, 25, 150
Mimbres tribe, 114
Miranda v. Arizona, 123
Mixe, 18
Mixtec, 18
Monroe Doctrine
    audacity of, 132
    expansion of in 20th century, *see* 20th century, neocolonial conflicts of
    as "Good Neighbor Policy," 141
    imperial designs and, *see* United States (emerging) and its expansionist mandate
Mormons, 60, 107, 114
Mother Earth, 4, 6
Mound builders, 17
Mulroney, Brian, 136
Mussolini, Benito, 119

N

NAFTA, *see* North American Free Trade Agreement
Nahuati, 18
National Congress of American Indians (NCAI), 106, 108
National Democratic Fair Play Association, 122
National Guard, 147
National Railroad Union, 142
Native American Church (NAC), 114
Native American Rights Fund (NARF), 114
NATO, *see* North Atlantic Treaty Organization
Navajo, 93, 150

Index

Nazi propaganda activities, investigation of, 119
NCAI, see National Congress of American Indians
NCOs, see Noncommissioned officers
New Deal initiatives, 104, 118
New England
    area, tribes inhabiting, 17
    colonies, anti-Catholic sentiment in, 23
New Spain, feudal system of, 11
Nixon, Richard, 111
Nobel Peace Prize, 131
Noncommissioned officers (NCOs), 117
North American Air Defense (NORAD) agreement, 132
North American Free Trade Agreement (NAFTA), 116, 145
North Atlantic Treaty Organization (NATO), 131, 146
Nova Scotia, 24–28

O

Oath of allegiance, 22
Obama, Barack, 148, 160
October Crisis of 1980 (Canada), 133
Oil leasing policy, 139
Oil Petroleum Exporting Countries (OPEC), 143
Ojibwe of North Dakota, 150
Olipnant v. Suquamish Indian Tribe, 112
Omaha, 17
Operation Hold the Line, 148
Operation Jump Start, 147
Operation Wide Receiver gun-running project, 149
Orangemen of English Canada, 77
Osage, 102
Ostend Manifesto, 65–70
Otomi, 18

P

Panama Canal, 68, 120
Pancho Villa, Francisco, 84, 86–87
Pan-Indianism, 106
Parti Quebecois (PQ), 135
Peoria tribe, 102
Pershing, John "Black Jack," 83, 91, 147
Philippine-American War (1899–1900), 83
Pierce, Franklin, 59, 64, 69, 74
Pietism, 8

Pine Ridge Reservation occupation of Wounded Knee, 108
Pinochet, Augusto, 119, 120
Plessy v. Ferguson, 125
Polk, James K., 56, 57, 58
Polk's war and a divided nation, 57–61
Ponca, 17, 92
"Pony clubs," 44
Porfiriato, 79
"Pork and Beans War," 46, 72
Posse Comitatus Act, 147
Pottawatomie Tribe of Kansas and Nebraska, 105
Powhatan Confederacy of the Algonquian tribes, 19
Predestination, 8
Prisoners of war (POWs), 91
Proffit v. Florida, 124
Protestant ethic and new world conflicts, see Contravening worldviews
Protestant Huguenots, 13
Pueblo tribe, 20, 150
Purepecha, 18
Puritan(s)
    asceticism of, 10
    concept, 24
    direction by "finger of God," 41

Q

Quaker persecutions, 10
Quebec separatism, perils of, see Canada comes of age and the perils of Quebec separatism
Queen Anne's War, 36
Queen Mary (Bloody Mary), 9
Quiet Revolution, 132–139

R

Rail system, 80
Rangs, 37
RCMP, see Royal Canadian Mounted Police
Reagan, Ronald, 121, 158
Reconstruction Act, 121
Reconstruction policies, inconsistencies of, 4–5
"Reefer madness" pulpit, 128
Rehnquist, William, 112
Religious artifacts, 114
Religious Freedom Act, 114
Restorative justice, 6–7

Revere, Paul, 13
Riel, Louis, 77, 78
Roman Catholic Church, 8, 133
Roosevelt, Franklin D., 104, 118, 141
Roosevelt, Theodore, 82, 120
Rough Riders, 82, 87
Royal Canadian Mounted Police (RCMP), 135

S

Sac tribe, 102
Sanchez Navarro hacienda, 34
Sandinista National Liberation Front, 156
Santa Anna, Antonio López de, 52, 53, 79
Scalia, Antonin, 112
Scalping, 35
Scott, Winfield, 61, 91
Second Vatican Council, 138
Seminole Indians, 35, 66, 102
Seneca Nation of New York Indians, 102
September 11, 2001 terrorist attacks, 138
Seven index crimes, 97
Seven Year War (French and Indian War), 23
Sherman, William Tecumseh, 90, 91
Siouan tribes of the western United States, 150
Sioux Nation in Nebraska, 102
Sitting Bull, 96, 97
Slavery
  interdependency of, 4
  issue, Mexican constitution and, 51–53
  Spanish America 33
  Texas constitution and, 54–56
Sons of Liberty, 72
Southeast Asia Treaty Organization (SEATO), 132
Spanish America, 28–34
  encomienda system, 33
  genocide, 33
  New Spain's adaptations to the New World, 33–34
  repartimiento system, 34
  slavery, 33
Spanish Succession, 36
Spotted Tail, 96
Standing Bear, 92
Stephen v. Cherokee Nation, 103
St. Laurent, Louis, 129
Suez Canal crisis, 131
Summer Olympics, 143

T

Taft, William Howard, 122
Tarahumara, 18
Tawakoni, 18
Taylor, Zachary, 57, 59, 61, 63
Tejanos, 53
Teller Amendment, 82
Texas constitution, slavery and, 54–56
Texas Rangers, 150
  Frontier Battalion, 81
  reign of terror (prelude to Pancho Villa's U.S. raid), 84–88
Texas republic, emerging, 53–54
Thomas, Clarence, 112
Thompson, John, 129
Tiapanec, 18
Tlatelodo Massacre, 143
Tlingit, Haida, 150
Tohono O'odham (Papago) tribe, 150
Tonkawa, 18
Totonac, 18
Trade and Intercourse Acts, 92
Trail of Tears, 44
Treaty of Aix-la-Chapelle, 23
Treaty of Guadalupe Hidalgo, 66, 128, 150
Treaty of Hubertusburg, 24
Treaty of Ryswick, 21
Treaty of Utrecht, 36
Trickery by treaty government policy, 40, 44
Trudeau, Pierre, 129
Truman, Harry, 105, 120
Trump, Donald, 148, 149
"Tucson Ring," 94
20th century, neocolonial conflicts of, 101–144
  Canada comes of age and the perils of Quebec separatism, 129–139
  Balfour Declaration of 1926, 130
  Bloc Quebecois, 137
  Charter of Rights, 136
  Commonwealth, forging of, 130
  ethnic strife, 130
  French Canadian Catholic Bishops, 133
  Front de liberation du Quebec, 134
  Hydro-Quebec, 134
  influence of French leaders in Canada, 129–132
  kidnapping of the British Trade Commissioner, 135
  Meech Lake Accord, 137

Index   211

names of prime ministers, 129
nations equal in status, 130
Newfoundland, 131
Nobel Peace Prize, 131
NORAD agreement, 132
October Crisis of 1980, 133
Parliament of Canada, 137
Parti Quebecois, 135
Quebec separatism and the Quiet Revolution, 132–139
"sovereignty-association" plan, 136
Suez Canal crisis, 131
Mexico in the 20th century (growth, corruption, and U.S. interventions), 139–144
coalition of peasants, 140
Cristero Rebellion in Central Mexico, 139
fraudulent elections, 142
GATT consortium, 144
hacendados, 140
implementing the new constitution of 1917 with interference from the United States, 139–140
land expropriations, 140
Mexican Communist Party, 141
National Action Party, 142
National Revolutionary Party, 140
Obregon administration, 139
oil leasing policy, 139
oppression and change (transitioning to globalization), 142–144
revolutionary changes finally enacted, 140–141
"revolutionary family," 141
Summer Olympics, 143
Tripartite Convention, 143
U.S. Cold War interventions, 141–142
Monroe Doctrine, extension of in the 20th century (hemispheric exploitation and Cold War fears), 117–129
fascism, concerns leading to big business's form of, 118
hemp conspiracy, 128
House Un-American Activities Committee, 119
justice issues (role of de facto discrimination), 121–129
La Raza Unida Party, 127
Nazi propaganda activities, investigation of, 119
Panama Canal Department, 120
Vietnam conflict, 126
War on Drugs, 129
Watts riot, 126
yellow journalism, 128
United States and its "Indian problem," 101–117
allotment (dismantling Indian country), 101–103
backlash to Termination and Relocation, 108
Chippewa Tribe of Turtle Mountain Reservation, 105
citizenship, Indians granted, 103
cultural genocide, 113
FBI harassment, 108
Five Civilized Tribes, effort to eliminate, 103
Ghost Dance movement, 108
Guardians of the Oglala Nation squad, 108
Indian religious freedom, 113–114
Indian self-determination and the new federalism for Indian country, 109–117
legal issues, 105
legislation, 104
Manifest Destiny, main tenet of, 113
Mormons, 107
New Deal relief programs, 104
new federalism and Indian child welfare, 114–117
Pan-Indianism, 106
Public Law 280, 106, 107
religious artifacts, 114
reorganization, 103–104
termination/relocation, 104–109
urban populations, 107
Wounded Knee II battle, 109
Zimmerman Plan, 106
21st century, from NAFTA to, 145–165
border perspective since 9/11, 146–147
"the Borderlands," 146
"Fast Track" system, 146
illegal immigrant count, 146
Middle Eastern Muslims, 146
Western Hemisphere Travel Initiative, 146
border security's impact on North American Indians, 150–154
Canadian–aboriginal relations, foundation of, 151

cross-border tribes, 150
post–9/11 border requirements and their impact on border tribes, 152–154
status of Canada's indigenous people, 151–152
Tribal Government Homeland Security, 152
impact of the militarization of the U.S. borders, 147–150
Borderland sites, 147
coyotes, 148
Mexico–U.S. Plenary Group on Law Enforcement, 149
National Guard, 147
Operation Hold the Line, 148
Operation Jump Start, 147
Posse Comitatus Act, 147
Royal Canadian Mounted Police, 148
Mexico's daunting role as a filter for drug and human trafficking, 154–165
Central America and the Cold War, 155–157
geopolitical context, 155
homicide rates in Mexico, 158f
major events in U.S.–Mexico efforts to fight the War on Drugs, 159t
Merida Initiative, 162
Mexican war on drugs, 157–165
percentage of people living in poverty, 161f
push–pull effect, 165
Sandinista National Liberation Front, 156
U.S. drug, security, and immigration concerns, 158–165
Tzotzil, 18

U

Ultramontanism, 47, 73
Underground Railroad, 76
Union Bill (Canada), 46
United Nations (UN)
National Security Council, 131
Protection Force, 138
United States (emerging) and its expansionist mandate, 39–99
American Indians, policing of, 88–99
aboriginal right of occupancy, 88
agent provocateurs, 89
Buffalo Soldiers, 91
Confederate prisoners of war, 91
Crow Dog decision, 97
"hanging judge," 95
Indian police and policing Indian country (military versus civilian jurisdictions), 92–99
peace policy, 88
seven index crimes, 97
U.S. Army and the Indian Wars of 1865–1891, 89–92
Manifest Destiny and white Protestant supremacy (boundary maintenance 1776–1865), 39–70
Adams-Onís Treaty of 1819, 47–48
Anglo–American emigrants, 50
Bustamante Decree, 51
Canadian challenges during the Monroe Doctrine era, 71–79
emerging Texas republic, 53–54
empresario land grants, 48–50
ethnic cleansing, 40
Fredonian Rebellion, 50
Free Soilers, 65
Guadalupe Hidalgo Treaty, 60
Indian land grab, 40
Indian removal (U.S. experiment with ethnic cleansing), 41–45
intrusions into Canada, 45–47
land contractors, 49
Lewis and Clark Expedition, 40
Louisiana Purchase, 40, 47
Mexican constitution and the slavery issue, 51–53
new frontier (acquiring Spanish/Mexican territory), 47–56
Ostend Manifesto and Gadsden Purchase, 65–70
political disorganization following the Mexican War, 63–65
Polk's war and a divided nation, 57–61
"pony clubs," 44
"Pork and Beans War," 46
prelude to the U.S. civil war (annexation of Texas), 56–57
Reconstruction, 44
slavery and the Texas constitution, 54–56
Trail of Tears, 44
trickery by treaty government policy, 40, 44

Index

ultramontanism, 47
unresolved slavery issue, 61–63
War of 1812, 45
Whigs exit, Republicans emerge, 63–65
Monroe Doctrine and imperial designs (1865–1917), 70–79
  Aroostook War, 72
  Canadian challenges during the Monroe Doctrine era, 71–79
  dominion of Canada, 75–76
  Fenian challenge, 73–75
  Freedmen's Bureau, 71
  Irish Republican Brotherhood, 73
  Ku Klux Klan, 71
  Liberal-Conservative Coalition, 75
  Louis Riel and the Indian/Métis rebellions, 76–78
  "Pork and Beans War," 72
  ultramontanism, 73
  Underground Railroad, 76
Texas Rangers's reign of terror (prelude to Pancho Villa's U.S. raid), 84–88
  Pancho Villa's raid on the United States, 86–87
  Villista prisoners, harsh treatment of, 87–88
turbulence in Mexico (road to revolution), 79–84
  Ayutla Revolution, 79
  caste-like system, 80
  government goon squads, 81
  Porfiriato setting the stage for the Mexican revolution, 79–83
  reign of Porfirio Díaz (America's favorite despot), 79–84
  Rough Riders, 82
  seeds of Mexican discontent, 83–84
  Teller Amendment, 83
United States and its "Indian problem," 101–117
  allotment (dismantling Indian country), 101–103
  backlash to Termination and Relocation, 108
  Chippewa Tribe of Turtle Mountain Reservation, 105
  citizenship, Indians granted, 103
  cultural genocide, 113
  FBI harassment, 108
  Five Civilized Tribes, effort to eliminate, 103
  Ghost Dance movement, 108
  Guardians of the Oglala Nation squad, 108
  Indian religious freedom, 113–114
  Indian self-determination and the new federalism for Indian country, 109–117
  legal issues, 105
  legislation, 104
  Manifest Destiny, main tenet of, 113
  Meeds minority report, 111
  Mormons, 107
  New Deal relief programs, 104
  new federalism and Indian child welfare, 114–117
  Pan-Indianism, 106
  Public Law 280, 106, 107
  religious artifacts, 114
  reorganization, 103–104
  termination/relocation, 104–109
  urban populations, 107
  Wounded Knee II battle, 109
  Zimmerman Plan, 106
United States v. Kagama, 97
United States v. Wheeler, 112
U.S. Army and the Indian Wars of 1865–1891, 89–92
U.S. Army School of the Americas (SOA), 120
U.S. borders, militarization of, 147–150
U.S. Central Intelligence Agency (CIA), 120
U.S. Civil War, prelude to, 56–57
U.S. Department of Justice Inspector General, 145
U.S. Drug Enforcement Administration (DEA), 149
U.S. Immigration and Customs Enforcement (ICE), 146
USS Maine, 82

V

Van Buren, Martin, 63
Veterans of Foreign Wars (VFW), 119
Vietnam conflict, 126, 133
Villista prisoners, harsh treatment of, 87–88
Virginia House of Burgesses, 24

W

Wabanaki (Algonquin) Confederacy, 22
War on Drugs, 158

War of 1812, 45
War of the Grand Alliance, 21, 36
"War Hawks," 45
War of Reform, 69, 79
Washington, George, 23
Watts riot, 126
Webster, Daniel, 63
Western Hemisphere Travel Initiative (WHTI), 146
Wheeler-Howard Act of 1934, 104
Whigs, 58–59, 63
White Anglo-Saxon Protestant (WASP) administrations, 65
White supremacy, concept of, 4
Wichita, 18, 150
Wilmot Proviso, 58
Wilson, Woodrow, 86, 122, 147
Works Projects Administration, 106
Wounded Knee II battle, 98, 109

Y

Yaqui, 150
Yellow journalism, 128
Young Ireland movement, 73
Yuma, 150

Z

Zapata, Emiliano, 84, 139
Zapotec, 18
Zimmerman Plan of 1947, 106